STAFF MANAGEMENT IN LIBRARY AND INFORMATION WORK

STAFF MANAGEMENT IN LIBRARY AND INFORMATION WORK

Fourth Edition

Peter Jordan and Caroline Lloyd

ASHGATE

First edition printed in 1982 by Gower Publishing Limited
Second edition printed in 1987 by Gower Publishing Limited
Third edition printed in 1995 by Gower Publishing Limited

Published by
Ashgate Publishing Limited
Gower House
Croft Road
Aldershot
Hampshire GU11 3HR
England

Gower
131 Main Street
Burlington
Vermont 05401–5600
USA

British Library Cataloguing-in-Publication Data
Jordan, Peter, 1936–
    Staff management in library and information work. – 4th ed.
    1. Library personnel management—Great Britain 2. Information services—Great Britain—Personnel management.
    I. Title II. Lloyd, Caroline III. Jones, Noragh.
    023'.0941

ISBN 0-7546-1651-7

Library of Congress Control Number: 2001099635

Typeset in 10 point Palatino by Manton Typesetters, Louth, Lincolnshire and printed in Great Britain by MPG Books Ltd, Bodmin, Cornwall.

Contents

List of figures   vii

List of tables   xi

Preface   xiii

1 The working environment   1

2 Motivation and job satisfaction   31

3 Human resource planning   79

4 Job descriptions and person specifications   99

5 Recruitment and selection of staff   127

6 Staff appraisal   157

7 Staff training and development   183

8 Staff supervision and interpersonal skills training   239

References   289

Index   305

List of figures

1.1   The management cycle   5
1.2   The library management cycle in the current context   13
2.1   An adaptation of Burns' and Stalker's framework for
      organizational analysis   35
2.2   Maslow's hierarchy of needs   41
2.3   Range of management styles   47
2.4   The managerial grid based on the Blake and Mouton research   50
3.1   Volunteer policy and code of practice – Borough of Richmond
      upon Thames   88
3.2   Stages in drawing up a human resources plan for an individual
      library system   93
3.3   Influential factors in job change   95
4.1   The main stages in staff management   99
4.2   Job description for Marketing Co-ordinator at Reading
      University Library   107
4.3   Person specification for Marketing Co-ordinator at Reading
      University Library   110
4.4   Job description for Branch Administrator at London Borough of
      Barnet   111
4.5   Job description for Assistant Librarian – Enquiry Services at the
      Royal Society of Medicine Library   114
4.6   Job description for Senior Librarian at Sheffield City Council   118
4.7   Person specification for Senior Librarian at Sheffield City Council 120
5.1   The main information sources used in selection   128
5.2   Advert for post at Coventry University Library   134
5.3   Interview assessment form from the Royal Society of Medicine
      Library   140

5.4   Topic and guidelines for presentation given by candidates for the post of Assistant Library Services Manager at the Central School of Speech and Drama Library   148
6.1   Appraisee preparation notes (extract) – Sheffield Hallam University   160
6.2   Personal preparation checklist – De Monfort University   162
6.3   Staff appraisal scheme summary – University of Northumbria   163
6.4   Staff appraisal form – British Library of Political and Economic Science at the LSE   174
6.5   Appraisal preparation questions – Wrexham County Borough   176
6.6   Appraisal Record Form – Birkbeck College   178
6.7   Typical questions used to evaluate an appraisal interview   179
6.8   Reviewer interviewing skills – Napier University   180
6.9   Appraisal analysis form   181
7.1   The training cycle   184
7.2   The main CPD methods   186
7.3   Extract from Staff Development Policy – University of Bath Library   188
7.4   A checklist of points to include in a training and development policy (derived from the Fielden Report)   190
7.5   Training and development policy – Bolton MBC Educational Arts Department   191
7.6   Checklist of training activities   193
7.7   Learning request/post-learning evaluation form used by Essex Libraries   196
7.8   Training needs analysis used by University College London Library Services   200
7.9   General induction checklist – Essex Libraries   206
7.10   Extract from post-specific induction checklist – Essex Libraries   208
7.11   Extract from skills checklist – British Library of Political and Economic Science at the LSE   214
7.12   Setting training objectives   216
7.13   Extract from 'Training Hour' programme – Reading University Library   217
7.14   Checklist of features of a good presentation   220
7.15   Personal development record – De Montfort University Library   231
7.16   Example of training evaluation   233
7.17   The Library Association's guidelines for employers   236
8.1   Interaction analysis   263
8.2   Depicting ego states in Transactional Analysis   273
8.3   Adult-to-adult transactions   273

8.4	Crossed transactions	274
8.5	The 'OK Corral'	274
8.6	Causes of stress in rank order	276
8.7	Stress assessment questionnaire	279
8.8	Workaholic checklist	281
8.9	Library time-wasters	283
8.10	Dealing with time-wasters	284

List of tables

2.1   What motivates librarians? Summary of satisfaction and
        dissatisfaction in library work   65
2.2   Staff needs and management action   66
4.1   Comparison of Rodger's and Fraser's person specification
        classifications   121
5.1   Selected personality factors from Cattell's 16 PF Inventory   151
6.1   Cues used in American Library Association standard rating form   177
8.1   Trainees' rating of their supervisors' effectiveness   244
8.2   Group interaction record (derived from Rackham and Morgan)   262
8.3   Managerial styles   287
8.4   Scorecard   288

Preface

I wrote the first two editions of this book with Noragh Jones, and I revised the third edition myself. I had continued to lecture part-time at Manchester Metropolitan University until 1998, but since I no longer have day-to-day involvement with library management, it was appropriate that a practising librarian should join with me in writing this edition. Caroline Lloyd, Reader Services Librarian at Birkbeck College and a prominent member of the Library Association Personnel Training and Education Group, has jointly edited this edition and brought to it her current experience and knowledge of library management.

The technological, social, economic and political changes that have taken place in the last seven years have necessitated a complete rewrite of Chapter 1. Information technology continues to both shape and underpin the developments of library and information services. The change of UK government in 1997 brought a change of emphasis in the delivery of public services, and matters such as social inclusion and lifelong learning are now firmly part of the political agenda. Quality issues preoccupy all sectors, with government-led initiatives on the one hand and increased competition on the other. A great deal of new legislation has been passed, with the influence of European employment law more apparent. The present environment brought with it problems of staff motivation with an increase in de-professionalization and the loss of control felt by some staff as electronic developments affect more of their working lives. It was still felt necessary in Chapter 2 to remind readers of the basic motivation theories, which are still relevant. They have been presented in what we believe to be a more logical sequence and with less repetition than in previous editions.

Workforce planning has been slightly discredited over recent years, and much of the material previously in Chapter 3, now re-titled, was no longer relevant. The chapter now takes into account the modes of staffing appropriate for a turbulent environment, with flexibility an increasing necessity. Effective workforce planning requires excellent selection and recruitment procedures. Good practice and developments in this area are explored in Chapters 4 and 5.

In the 1982 edition, staff appraisal was quite rare in libraries outside the private sector. Now it is a fact of working life everywhere. It is a time-consuming task, and there is therefore a need to cut down on unnecessary documentation as organizations become well used to the processes. On the other hand, there is a search for better instruments. More attention has therefore been given to 360° and subordinate appraisal.

The last decade has seen increased emphasis on training and development as organizations recognize the vital role these play in equipping staff to deliver high-quality services in a climate of constant change. Chapter 7 has been reordered and expanded in order to reflect the considerable developments in training and development, and the greater prominence which these are now given by library and information services in all sectors.

Much of the material in Chapter 8 is fundamentally similar to the previous edition, since interpersonal skills are even more important today. The recent emphasis on leadership skills and counselling skills is reflected in this chapter, as is the growing need to do more with less through enhanced time management and stress management techniques.

During the preparation of this edition, discussions in the UK about a single unified professional body for the sector were concluded and the formation of such an organization agreed. The new organization is named the Chartered Institute of Library and Information Professionals (CILIP) and came into existence on 1 April 2002. For the sake of simplicity, Library Association (LA) and Institute of Information Scientists have been used when referring to the two professional bodies and to denote works by them throughout the text.

Once again, the generosity of colleagues has enabled the inclusion of actual documents which are being used by information and library services. Throughout the book, these illustrate and demonstrate good practice. The response to the call for examples was lower than in previous years, but the quality of material which was supplied was excellent. In many cases, it was difficult to choose just one or two examples of documents, as all those that had been provided were exemplary. Thanks are due, then, to everyone who responded to the request for documents. Particular thanks go to those who allowed their examples to be used and their working practices to be cited:

> Birkbeck College Library, The British Library of Political and Economic Science at the LSE, Bolton Libraries, Arts and Archives, Central School of Speech and Drama, Coventry University Library, De Montfort University, Essex Libraries, London Borough of Barnet, London Borough of Richmond upon Thames, Napier University, Royal Society of Medicine, Sheffield City Council, Sheffield Hallam University, University College London (UCL) Library Services, University of Bath, University

of Hertfordshire, University of Reading, University of Northumbria and Wrexham County Borough.

I am also grateful to Stuart Hannabuss for use of his appraisal form, and to Terry Looker and Olga Gregson for allowing me to use questionnaires from *Managing Stress*.

Peter Jordan

1   The working environment

Libraries and information units have become increasingly involved in management practices as their parent bodies (local authorities, educational institutions, voluntary organizations, industrial and professional firms) have adopted more systematic approaches to management, and so, in turn have impelled the information services to justify their operations in relation to user needs. Expenditure on staffing has not diminished, and in the vast majority of organizations it continues to account for over half the overall budget. Further staff are the means by which organizations can ensure that they deliver what their customers require. For these reasons, it is necessary to get the most value from this key resource, and this can be achieved by giving careful and well-informed attention to each stage in staff management.

First, it is important to analyse and evaluate existing jobs and staffing structures, and to modify them in relation to changing priorities, such as the delivery and support of information technology (see Chapter 4), whilst taking account of the balance between supply and demand for library and information workers (Chapter 3). Second, it is vital to have a well-thought out recruitment strategy using staff who are skilled in drawing up person specifications and following them through, in interviewing, and in other selection methods (see Chapter 5). Staff appraisal, whether formal or informal, reveals the success or otherwise of recruitment policies and practices, but staff cannot perform well if training and development are neglected. Frequently, appraisal reveals further training needs which, if met, will help staff to increase their expertise and overcome weaknesses in knowledge, skills or attitudes. Staff appraisal schemes are covered in Chapter 6, and training and development in Chapter 7.

All these phases in staff management can only be put into practice successfully by people with a range of communication skills, and an understanding of motivation at work. Chapter 2 considers motivation and job satisfaction. Chapter 8 suggests strategies for developing personal and interpersonal skills, particularly through assertiveness training, analysis of personal management styles, the management of stress, time management, and the development of skills which increase effectiveness in group work. It gives guidance on how to supervise staff, which seems to cause many problems in library and information work, both for new professionals and for more senior staff when promotion moves them to a job where they spend more time managing other people. Chapter 8 also discusses the need for strong leadership – essential in the climate of rapid change which has come to characterize all working environments.

A basic definition of management is 'getting things done through people', and the following questions, which are of current concern to library managers, indicate how pervasive staff management is in translating an organization's goals into reality:

1. How can we improve our performance by making more effective use of available resources such as funding, materials, accommodation and staff?
2. How can we manage innovation and develop a positive approach to change?
3. How can we evaluate information services, in order to justify our work to those who pay our salaries?
4. How can we analyse work methods and procedures to develop cost-effectiveness?
5. How can we ensure that staff development and organizational development take place, thus minimizing stagnation among more established staff, and frustration at lack of opportunities among new staff?
6. How can we encourage staff at all levels to assume more responsibility, come up with ideas and initiate projects, rather than interpret their jobs as unchanging routines?

Anyone who is responsible for other staff, even one or two, is – or should be – engaged in staff management. The term 'management' is often misunderstood by librarians, who believe that only 'managers' manage, or that management is something that happens at the most senior levels. Management is in some minds seen as an undesirable activity which removes one from the 'real' professional practice of librarianship, and incarcerates one in an office, to work endlessly on new bureaucratic rules and procedures. The view taken in this book is that management skills are useful at all levels. They are just as important for a subject librarian planning an induction programme for new students, or a community librarian planning an information service for the unemployed or the housebound, as they are for senior staff planning a matrix management structure, or assessing priorities over the next five years for staff training and development. Staff also need to be able to analyse the way they are being managed, and to learn from the experience.

THE MANAGEMENT CYCLE

The management of staff does not take place in a vacuum. It requires a clear idea of what has to be done, and therefore an understanding of the cyclical nature of effective management. The starting point has to be the objectives of the library or information service, which will have been derived from an analysis of its role in relation to the objectives of the organization of which it is a part and an examination of the needs of the community it is serving. In today's changing environment, in which political and economic pressures dominate, there is bound to be a good deal of heart-searching about the objectives or purposes of libraries.

The turbulent environment identified by such management gurus as Tom Peters has meant that organizations have had to develop 'clear, agreed, definitions of corporate aims' and have needed 'to identify the implications of organizational objectives in terms of information needs and information activities to meet the objectives successfully'.[1]

The popularity of various management techniques has changed over the years, but there is an acceptance of the need to evolve processes which ensure that all managers aim for and achieve what the organization requires. Management By Objectives (MBO), which was commonplace in the 1970s, can be seen to have evolved into systems which are of use to many organizations. The Investors in People (IiP) standard in the UK can be viewed as a natural development of this approach, focusing as it does on the achievement of business objectives through the effective management of the workforce.

The Investors in People standard emerged in the early 1990s from the work of the National Training Task Force in collaboration with bodies such as the Confederation of British Industry (CBI), the Trades Union Congress (TUC) and the Institute of Personnel and Development (IPD). The original impetus for the work was concern over the reasons behind the UK's lack of competitiveness within Europe. Following extensive testing, IiP was implemented in 1991:

> The Standard provides a national framework for improving business performance and competitiveness, through a planned approach to setting and communicating business objectives and developing people to meet these objectives. The result is that what people can do and are motivated to do, matches what the organisation needs them to do. The process is cyclical and should engender the culture of continuous improvement.[2]

IiP provides a framework which enables managers to ensure that the performance of their service is focused, effective and responsive to the many changes which influence it. For example, in the public library sector, where managers must respond to requirements of Best Value – that is, deliver continuous

3

improvement to services through a combination of economy, efficiency and effectiveness – IiP is 'an opportunity to prove their business-like credentials'.[3]

The clear link within IiP between organizational objectives and the development of skills has led many to view the standard as being purely concerned with staff training. This is not the case: 'the IiP focus is not just concerned with training and development on its own, but with the integration of human resources to corporate planning via a strategic framework'.[4]

There is often a good deal of confusion about objectives terminology. We have found it helpful to distinguish three types of objective:

- **Aims** (also referred to as philosophy, mission, overall objectives) state the business the library and information service believes it is engaged in, for example to promote the spread of knowledge, information, education and culture.
- **Key tasks** are broad statements which sum up the main objectives of the service, such as to encourage and support individuals in developing and maintaining the skill of reading.
- **Specific objectives** (also referred to as targets or goals) are usually concerned with specific services, or with management and administration, such as organizing customer care courses for all staff during the next twelve months.

The specific objectives and the key tasks need to be compatible with the aims. In many library and information services, staff will be required to decide upon specific objectives annually. The management style will dictate how decisions are made and who makes them. Chapters 2 and 8 will help readers to analyse management styles in their own institutions, which may well differ among departments. In a turbulent environment, staff have to change their objectives and priorities quickly, and the management style should not only permit this to happen, but should reward enterprise.

In order to achieve objectives, *activities* are needed, which require resources such as time, equipment and money. There should also be some control mechanisms to monitor and evaluate how well the objectives have been achieved, and to enable staff to learn from the experience and to make changes where necessary.

The management cycle will therefore resemble that shown in Figure 1.1.

The relationship between objectives, approaches and the appraisal of individuals can be readily appreciated, and is discussed further in Chapter 6.

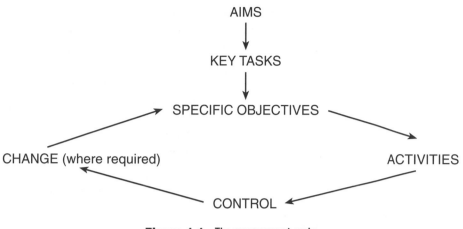

Figure 1.1 The management cycle

DRIVERS FOR CHANGE

Legislation, public opinion, government policy and social change all affect the library and information sector. In her 1998 presidential address to the Institute of Information Scientists, Ward identified the following as factors which 'are influencing and will continue to influence our development':

- intensifying competition
- accelerating change
- continuing information explosion
- communication and information technologies
- information for all
- information and knowledge-based differentiation
- knowledge management.[5]

Each of these points has been the focus of UK government attention at some point since the change in government in 1997, and prominence on the political agenda magnifies the effect that these factors have upon the library and information sector. In the Foreword to *Staff in the New Library: Skill Needs and Learning Choices*, Kempster states: 'Working in libraries will never be the same again.'[6] This statement encapsulates the sense of immense change which the library and information sector has been experiencing over the last few years. Kempster was introducing a report on the findings of a project which focused on the public library sector, but with a liberal interpretation of 'libraries', her words are equally applicable to every aspect of today's information profession. Continuous organizational change has become a feature in all sectors, and has been 'made necessary by the effects of the convergence of information technology (IT) and communications'.[7] This ongoing upheaval has led every part of the library and information sector to examine its role and function. Government, through its emphasis on issues such as competitiveness, lifelong learning and social inclusion, has provided impetus for this scrutiny and reappraisal of the role of the library/information professional. These factors, combined with the advent of a new millennium, have resulted in many projects, reports and articles in which the present and possible future roles of those working in the sector are explored and hypothesized.[8]

CHANGING ROLES

Libraries in higher education (HE) were prompted to reconsider their role ahead of other parts of the public sector when, in 1993, the Joint Funding Councils' Libraries Review Group published the Follett Report, which highlighted the expected changes for libraries in the sector.[9] The Fielden Report,[10] commissioned as a part of the review, to investigate the 'staffing aspects of library management',[11] made various predictions about the ways in which the work of library staff might change, and recommended steps to ensure that these changes were managed efficiently. Whilst not all the recommendations have been acted upon, the predictions have, by and large, proven to be correct. The Electronic Libraries Programme (eLib) was established by the Joint Information Systems Committee in response to the Follett Report, and represented an enormous investment in the applications of new technologies.

Whilst the HE sector was being encouraged to embrace the potential of new technologies in the 1990s, colleagues in the public library sector were the recipients of 'malign neglect'.[12] The election of a Labour government in 1997 represented a major shift in this approach to public services. This provided opportunities for the public library service, but these opportunities were accompanied by the sense that if public libraries did not grasp them successfully, someone else would, and that there would be no second chance.

A catalyst for the examination of roles and functions in the public library sector was provided when the Department of Culture, Media and Sport (DCMS) commissioned the Library and Information Commission (LIC) to consider how public libraries could respond to the challenge presented by the development of information and communication technologies. The result was *New Library: The People's Network*.[13] The subsequent LIC report, *Building the New Library Network*, describes *New Library: The People's Network* as:

> setting out a strategy for a radical transformation in the character and importance of our public libraries. It proposed that [public libraries] should be connected to a

national digital network, giving them a fundamentally new role as manager of electronic content and gateways to a vast wealth of online information.[14]

This latter report goes on to address exactly how this vision can be translated into reality, and recognizes the vital role which staff serve in the delivery of this vision:

> Library staff will play the central role in shaping the developing use of the public library service. They will need to manage the collections of materials – cataloguing, indexing and retrieving items on demand. They will provide access to the expanding range of digital information available through the New Library Network. They will also need to support people who use the service. They will be the key to the resource.[15]

Both *New Library: The People's Network* and *Building the New Library Network* go into some detail about the new roles which staff in public libraries will need to take on. The need for training was highlighted, and the latter report recommended ways in which the £20 million which had been made available through the New Opportunities Fund (NOF) could be used successfully to re-skill the workforce. The training and the necessary infrastructure continue to be rolled out, and throughout the public library sector managers are grappling with the reality of meeting the challenges of these reports and of ensuring that their staff and services can fulfil Chris Smith's (the then Secretary of State for Culture, Media and Sport) definition of public libraries as 'our street corner universities'.

Information professionals in the private sector have also been engaged in the analysis of their roles and positions. The concept of the knowledge economy started in the private sector and the move towards knowledge management (KM) as distinct from information management (IM) has been discussed and investigated by various people both within and outside the information profession. Abell and Chapman argue that the combination of the expectations held by information professionals and the perception of the information profession has resulted in a lack of participation by the profession. Information professionals have not, generally, been involved in setting 'the IM or KM strategy at business level or [determining] the resources to be allocated to building a robust information capacity'.[16] That there are opportunities for information professionals is not in doubt, and drawing on research undertaken by TFPL, Abell identified 'three levels of opportunity in the corporate sector':

1. **Senior Executive level** – for example, the Chief Knowledge Officer, Competitive Intelligence Executive, Change Manager
2. **Information and Knowledge middle management** – for example, Knowledge team members, Knowledge and Information Managers, Information analysts and researchers, Intranet content designers

3. **Tomorrow's information professionals** – for example, new recruits and front-line staff, Web Masters and knowledge hub members.[17]

A certain amount of risk-taking may be required for information professionals to fulfil the roles offered by the knowledge management approach. Abell and Chapman recommend retaining core information expertise whilst developing new skills, and combining this broader skills base with an attention to networking and developing a wider sphere of influence.[18]

The consideration and adoption of the knowledge management approach is becoming more widespread. The TFPL report *Skills for Knowledge Management: Building a Knowledge Economy* identified that 'for a few years knowledge management was the domain of early adopters but at the beginning of 1998 it became evident that many more organizations were exploring the potential of knowledge management principles'.[19] Statements from the Prime Minister such as 'The knowledge-driven economy is the economy of the future' and 'Government has put education, learning and the knowledge-driven economy at the heart of its ambition' encapsulate the government's endorsement of the concept of the knowledge economy, and have contributed to the increased interest in, and embracing of, this approach to organizational management. Initiatives such as the development of new library space 'designed to promote informal networking and knowledge sharing'[20] as the focus of the Countryside Agency's knowledge management programme demonstrate how KM is influencing the delivery of library services.

NEW MODES OF LEARNING

The statement by Tony Blair that 'Our three most important policies are Education, Education, Education' and the resulting emphasis of the 1997 election set the scene for the government's learning agenda and a plethora of initiatives. The 1998 Green Paper *The Learning Age*, and the subsequent government response,[21] demonstrated the government's commitment to lifelong learning. The importance of cross-sectoral co-operation in the successful support of lifelong learning was emphasized in *Empowering the Learning Community*, which recommended that public and education libraries should establish co-operative agreements and draw up access maps to 'enable users and learners to reach resources or assistance in other libraries on a managed basis'.[22] Learndirect and the National Grid for Learning (NGfL) are just two examples of ways in which lifelong learning is being supported. Learndirect is a service which was developed by the University for Industry (UfI). It aims to increase skills nationwide and to bring learning into people's lives. Courses are computer-based and can be accessed at home, work or via one of the many Learndirect centres.

The NGfL brings together Websites which support learning and provide educationally valuable content. The intention is that by 2002, all schools, colleges and libraries will be connected to the NGfL, and so the People's Network project can be seen to be part of a much wider national programme.

Within formal education networks, the increased potential of delivering education electronically is having an impact on library services. The rise in distance learning as a mode of study has led libraries to develop services which can be accessed remotely, and the move towards student-centred learning has resulted in libraries in the FE and HE sectors needing to support groups of students undertaking project-style assignments. In many cases, the challenge is to manage both print and electronic resources successfully. The hybrid library is now commonplace in the education sector, and staffing structures and responsibilities are changing to reflect this. The logical extension of delivering courses electronically is the 'e-university'. The United States has various virtual and corporate universities, and in the UK the first steps towards establishing an e-university have been taken. The proposal published by the Higher Education Funding Council for England (HEFCE) in October 2000 was described as combining 'an exciting vision of the potential of a UK electronic university with remarkably sensible suggestions for the technological platforms and pedagogical models that would be deployed'.[23] Professor Ron Cooke, Vice-Chancellor of York University and Chair of the HEFCE Steering Group for the e-university project, challenged SCONUL (Society of College, National and University Libraries) in April 2001 to draw up proposals as to how the e-university library should be managed. The resulting document can be accessed via the SCONUL Website.[24]

MEASURING QUALITY

Within the context of the changes which are affecting the library and information sector, there is a need – often a requirement – to continue to deliver high-quality services. The private sector needs to remain competitive, and the public sector is required to be accountable and to demonstrate that it provides excellent services which are value for money.

The *Modernising Government* White Paper set out the policies and principles which support the government's long-term programme of reform to modernize public service.[25] It placed great emphasis on the use of quality schemes as a means to improve performance. In March 2001, the UK Cabinet Office published *Getting it Together: A Guide to Quality Schemes and the Delivery of Public Services*.[26] This seeks to provide comprehensive guidance on quality schemes and public sector policies. It profiles four such schemes:

- Excellence Model
- Charter Mark
- Investors in People
- ISO 9000.

Each has a slightly different focus, and the emphases will affect the scheme, or schemes, which an organization considers most appropriate. With the exception of the Charter Mark, which is only available to public sector organizations, the quality schemes are open to organizations from both the public and private sectors. Various accounts of the processes have been written by librarians,[27] and *Getting it Together* aims to explain how the different schemes interact.

In addition to awards which organizations may choose to work towards, there are various quality programmes which public service organizations are obliged to participate in. For example, within the public library sector in England, planning must take place within the framework of Annual Library Plans, Best Value and the new standards for public libraries.

The requirement for libraries to produce Annual Library Plans was set out in *Reading the Future*.[28] Favret explains that 'it was not the Government's original intention to set performance targets for libraries', and that this was reiterated when the DCMS 'stated that the plans are intended as a management tool for each local authority library service'.[29] There is, however, a clear link between Annual Library Plans and Best Value, and Dolan, for example, has described how Best Value principles can be incorporated into library plans.[30]

The number of library services identified for review under Best Value has been small in comparison to other local authority services. In time, however, all library services will be reviewed as local authorities are required to Best Value-review all their departments over a five-year period. White has urged that Best Value be seen as an opportunity rather than a nightmare, a chance to 'start to restore some of our services to good health'.[31]

The DCMS, in consultation with the Library Association and Local Government Association, have produced standards for public library services in England.[32] Chris Smith describes the relationship between these standards, Annual Library Plans and Best Value in the Foreword:

> Annual Library Plans have been very successful but, while they have instilled useful management discipline into library authorities, they have not provided as much of a direct link to performance monitoring as I had hoped. It is right that they derive from the needs of an authority's citizens and link to its overall objectives. But, the service should also meet certain basic expectations across the country. The library standards which I now propose accordingly complement Annual Library Plans and will provide a link between planning and performance.
>
> [The standards] take account of the consultation which I launched in May 2000. The final standards have been fine-tuned, both in the light of what was said to us

and so that they better reflect service outcomes and the requirements of Best Value. This framework is a positive demonstration of the practical implementation of the Best Value concept. Library standards together with Best Value provisions are a powerful combination which should help authorities drive up library performance.[33]

The standards have obvious implications for staff and for staff management. For example, within the three-year planning cycle, 95 per cent of users must rank the knowledge of staff (standard 14) and staff helpfulness (standard 15) as 'good' or 'very good'.[34]

Within the current bidding culture, mandatory quality standards can provide managers with bargaining power when competing for appropriate resources. Goulding predicts that the new public library standards will be used in such a way, although, as she states, the success of this approach is likely to be affected by the fact that local government finance is provided by the Department of the Environment, Transport and the Regions, rather than by the DCMS.[35]

NATIONAL TRAINING ORGANIZATIONS

The facilitation of timely and appropriate training and staff development activities has been recognized as the key to enabling organizations to deliver the quality services that are demanded by both the Government and by the corporate sector. In the library and information sector, this delivery takes place within the context of needing to meet the demands posed by, on the one hand, the broad factors such as those identified by Ward, and on the other, specifics such as the implications for service provision of the Disability Discrimination Act (1995) and the Special Educational Needs and Disability Act (2001).

The establishment of a network of National Training Organisations (NTOs) in 1998 represented the government's response to the recognition of the vital place of training in the development of a competitive and skilled workforce. The NTOs brought together the work of the Industry Training Organisations, Lead Bodies and Occupations Standards Councils. NTOs can be seen to complement the government's agenda. Two White Papers, *Learning to Succeed*[36] and *Our Competitive Future: Building the Knowledge Driven Economy*,[37] are cited in the guidance issued for NTOs as being relevant to the developing agenda.[38] The *Modernising Government* White Paper[39] is also referred to elsewhere in the same report. Other developments which are cited as relevant include:

- University for Industry (UfI)
- the Qualifications and Curriculum Authority's major review of the National Framework of Qualifications

11

- Higher Still national courses and awards (in Scotland)
- the National Council for Education and Training for Wales (CETW)
- the formation of an overarching body for Sector Training Councils and NTOs in Northern Ireland.

The presence of an NTO in a sector enables employers to access information about the 'future learning and skill needs for their sectors' and provides a voice for employers to 'Government and all the key decision makers in education and training'.[40]

The NTO which represents the library and information sector, isNTO, was formally recognized in January 2000. The remit for isNTO is far wider than just the library and information sector, and includes archives services and record management services. The mission of the isNTO is 'to be the recognized focal point for strategic leadership and practical guidance in human resource development and skills provision, throughout the Information Services Sector'.[41] To this end, the isNTO has drawn up a work programme which includes such projects as:

- investigating the feasibility of national occupational standards for information/knowledge management
- an audit of training and education provision within the sector
- an analysis of the workforce
- work on reconciling the sector's professional qualifications with the spreading vocational qualifications.

The critical importance of these projects is obvious, and the isNTO provides employers and individuals in the sector with the opportunity to participate in, shape and drive developments in training and education relevant to information services.

SUMMARY

In Figure 1.2, the idea of the management cycle introduced earlier in this chapter can now be seen in the context of the present environment.

It can be seen that many of the management ideas currently in vogue fit quite well into the management cycle which is at the heart of effective management. What it requires to make it work is the sensitive application of the staff management techniques described and explained in the chapters that follow.

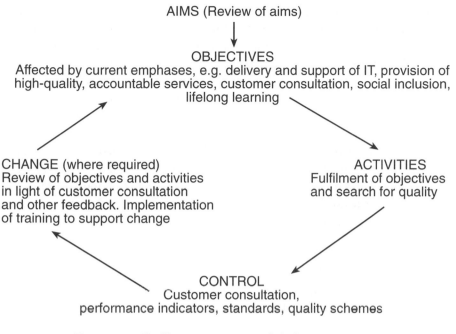

Figure 1.2 The library management cycle in the current context

LEGISLATION

It is very difficult for the non-lawyer to keep up to date with employment legislation and case law. Librarianship literature rarely gives it a mention, so it is necessary to consult personnel management and legal literature. We have found Lockton's *Employment Law*[42] and Chandler's *An A–Z of Employment Law*,[43] together with Clarke's *Women's Rights at Work*[44] and the regular 'Law at work' articles in *People Management* to be especially useful. It is important to note that only a summary is given in this section of those areas of employment law with which library managers should be familiar. The legislation itself contains more detail, and case law is continually interpreting the legislation.

It is incumbent on employers and employees to obey these laws, and most organizations, of which libraries are a part, will try to ensure staff are aware of their obligations. In large organizations such as universities, colleges, local authorities and large companies, the human resources department is likely to carry out this function.

When disputes between employers and employees arise which cannot be solved satisfactorily, recourse can be had to the legal system. Most proceedings involving employment rights are commenced at employment tribunals.

An employment tribunal is composed of a legally qualified chairperson and two lay members, one of whom is a nominee of an employer's organization and the other a nominee of a trade union, who are appointed by the Secretary of State for Employment. Proceedings are usually more informal, speedier and less expensive than claims brought in the courts. Before a case goes before an employment tribunal, a Conciliation Officer from the Advisory, Conciliation and Arbitration Service (ACAS) will try to promote a settlement without the matter going to a hearing.

Following a decision by an employment tribunal, either side can appeal. Appeals, which have to be made within 42 days of the tribunal decision, go to the Employment Appeal Tribunal, which consists of a President who is a High Court judge or a Lord Justice of Appeal, and two or four lay members. Appeals can only be made on points of law and errors of fact.

CONTRACT OF EMPLOYMENT

There is no legal formula for a contract of employment, and it can be in writing or oral. A contract of employment, like any other contract, leaves the parties free to negotiate terms and conditions that suit them. In practice, most librarians do not negotiate but are engaged on terms and conditions laid down in collective agreements. Although a written contract is not obligatory, there is a statutory obligation upon employers to supply a written statement not later than eight weeks after the beginning of the employment. The written statement must contain:

- the identity of the parties
- date the employment began, and when continuity with that employer began
- pay, methods of calculation and periods of payment
- hours of work
- holiday and sick pay entitlement
- pensions
- length of notice the employee is entitled to receive and obliged to give
- disciplinary rules and procedures
- title of job – there is no legal requirement to provide a job description (see Chapter 5) as part of the contract, and employers may regard it as prudent not to do so. It is advisable for employers to stipulate whether an employee is expected to work at more than one location. This is important if the sort of flexibility required of staff is to be achieved uncontentiously.

DISCIPLINARY PROCEDURES

Under the Employment Rights Act 1996, employers with more than 20 employees must give details of the disciplinary and grievance procedures to their employees at the start of their employment.

Guidance is provided by the ACAS Code of Practice on Disciplinary Practice and Procedures in Employment.[45] Most librarians work for organizations which have such procedures, and as managers, they should ensure they are familiar with them. Whilst very few librarians are likely to be involved with employment tribunals, many will have some involvement with internal disciplinary procedures.

Disciplinary procedures are one way in which employers can attempt to behave in a 'reasonable' way, which has been a legal requirement since 1974. Most procedures are likely to include the essential features outlined in paragraph 10 of the ACAS Code. They should:

(a) be in writing
(b) specify to whom they apply
(c) provide for matters to be dealt with quickly
(d) indicate the disciplinary actions which may be taken
(e) specify the levels of management which have the authority to take the various forms of disciplinary action, ensuring that immediate superiors do not normally have the power to dismiss without reference to senior management
(f) provide for individuals to be informed of the complaints against them and to be given an opportunity to state their case before decisions are reached
(g) give individuals the right to be accompanied by a trade union representative or by a fellow employee of their choice (now a right under section 10 of the Employment Relations Act 1999)
(h) ensure that, except for gross misconduct, no employees are dismissed for a first breach of discipline
(i) ensure that disciplinary action is not taken until the case has been carefully investigated
(j) ensure that individuals are given an explanation for any penalty imposed
(k) provide a right of appeal and specify the procedure to be followed.

Perusal of a number of procedures shows that it is normal to provide the person accused with a written statement on the nature of the accusation. The library manager therefore must be absolutely clear about the alleged offence(s), and must have evidence to support the case. Opportunity for individuals to present their cases is usually provided by means of a hearing in which witnesses can be called and documents produced in evidence.

A typical hearing opens with the management side presenting its case, followed by the accused presenting their case. All except the panel withdraw, and the panel considers the case and reaches a decision. The decision is

presented orally to the accused, appeal rights are explained, and written confirmation of the decision follows.

The disciplinary sanctions available are those allowed in the contract of
employment, and the principle usually followed is one of warnings of increasing severity leading finally to dismissal, the starting point being dependent on
the severity of the offence and the past disciplinary record of the individual.
For minor acts of misconduct, a written or oral warning can be issued, and if
further acts are committed then the result might be a final written warning.
Where gross misconduct is committed – that is misconduct so severe that the
employer cannot tolerate the continued presence of the employee on the
premises – dismissal without notice will be the appropriate sanction, with
suspension preceding the actual hearing.

Knowledge of internal disciplinary procedures is necessary as librarians are
likely to find themselves on panels or on either side of a case brought before a
panel. Even more important for everyday staff management, librarians must
ensure they are dealing with disciplinary problems correctly and that they are
shown to be good managers when evidence is produced in hearings, but more
especially so that problems can be solved without recourse to the necessarily
bureaucratic, time-consuming and unpleasant procedures that have been
described.

When problems do arise, it is sensible for library managers to record dates
and descriptions of events in case they are required later. This should be done
immediately after events have taken place, to ensure accuracy. It is also a good
idea to call in another member of staff not involved in the problem as a
witness. Choice of the person can be tricky, as it may not be desirable for the
problem to be widely known.

DISMISSAL OF STAFF

Employment legislation in Britain during the 1970s tended to favour employees, but with the change of government in 1979 there was a shift towards the
employer in the 1980 and 1982 Employment Acts. More protection was given
by the 1988 Act to trade union members who disagree with the union, including protection against dismissal of a union member who wishes to leave a
union where there is a 'closed shop' agreement. With the change of government in 1997, there was some shift towards unions with the 1999 Employment
Rights Act, which introduced a right where, if a majority of staff are in favour
of joining a union, then an employer must recognize that union in the
workplace. The Trade Union Reform and Employment Rights Act 1993 makes
it illegal to dismiss an employee on the grounds of union membership. The
legislation serves to emphasize the need for managers to be very careful

where dismissals are concerned, and this is as it should be, because dismissal is a serious matter.

Three different types of termination of employment fall within the definition of dismissal:

1. where a contract is terminated by the employer with or without notice
2. expiry and non-renewal of a fixed-term contract
3. where the contract is terminated with or without notice by the employee in such circumstances that the employee is entitled to terminate it without notice because of the employer's conduct – 'constructive dismissal'. For such dismissals to be judged as unfair, a serious breach of contract by the employer must be shown.

The law relating to unfair dismissal is to be found in the Employment Rights Act 1996, which provides that, subject to certain specified exceptions, every employee has the right not to be unfairly dismissed. The exceptions most relevant for library and information workers are employees who, at the effective date of termination of the contract, have been continuously employed for less than one year, and persons over retiring age. It should be noted that part-time workers must not be treated less favourably than comparable full-time workers (Part-Time Workers (Prevention of Less Favourable Treatment) Regulations 2000). These regulations implement an EC Directive of 1997 and a House of Lords ruling in 1994, and apply not only to dismissal, but to all matters of employment such as pay, sick pay, maternity leave, holiday entitlements, unpaid career breaks, access to occupational pension schemes, access to opportunities for training and promotion, redundancy selection criteria, and so on.

The list of 'legitimate' or permitted reasons for dismissal is to be found in the Employment Rights Act 1996:

1. **Incapability**, which includes lack of skill, attitude, physical or mental qualities. It is normal in many jobs for there to be an initial appraisal so that incapabilities of new staff can be quickly detected. With staffing cuts and lack of staff mobility, it has become even more important for libraries to avoid employing staff who are incapable of carrying out their duties in an adequate manner. Dismissal after a few months can be employed where inadequate staff have slipped through the selection net. Although such staff are not able to appeal through the legal system, organizations may still require normal disciplinary procedures to be followed. Where appeals are made, employment tribunals would have to be satisfied that employees dismissed for incapacity were given adequate training.

A member of staff may be considered incapable because of ill health. The law distinguishes between short-term illness and single long-term illness.

The procedure to be adopted with persistent absences through short-term illnesses is similar to that adopted for misconduct, with warnings as to the consequences of persistent absences. Some employers have a system whereby an investigation is automatically triggered after a certain number of days have been taken off and where there is a suspicious pattern such as absences for long weekends. It is often desirable to require a medical investigation to discover any underlying cause. In the case of long-term sickness the reason for dismissal would be incapability of doing the job. 'The employee's doctor cannot give information to an employer without the employee's consent … an employer does not have an implied right to require his employees to undergo a medical examination by a company doctor or a specialist.'[46] A refusal, however, may lead a tribunal to find any subsequent dismissal fair.

2. **Absence of appropriate qualifications** – Employers may require new qualifications to be attained, but must give time for existing employees to qualify before dismissal is possible.

3. **Misconduct**, such as dishonesty, disloyalty and refusal to obey a reasonable order. If, for example, an employee, makes a secret profit by stealing fines money or discloses confidential information to an unauthorized person these are grounds for dismissal. Behaviour is expected to be consistent with the standard expected: for example, excessive drinking would probably be considered unacceptable in many jobs. Dismissal for a single act of misconduct will usually only be considered fair in very serious cases.

4. **Contravention of statutory requirements**, such as loss of a permit or a licence such as a driving licence which make it impossible for the person to carry out the job.

5. **Redundancy** – The Employment Rights Act 1996 defines redundancy. It states that a redundancy has occurred if the dismissal is wholly or mainly attributable to:

    the fact that his employer has ceased or intends to cease, to carry on the business for the purposes of which the employee was employed; or has ceased, or intends to cease, to carry on that business in the place where the employee was so employed; or

    the fact that there is a reduced need for employees of the same category as that employee to carry out work of a particular kind in the place where that employee is employed.

    The Trade Union and Labour Relations (Consolidation) Act 1992 requires at least 90 days' consultation before dismissal takes effect where 100 or

18

more are to be made redundant, and 30 days if between 20 and 99 are to be made redundant. Consultations with appropriate representatives must include consultations about ways to (a) avoid dismissals, (b) reduce the number of employees to be dismissed, and (c) mitigate the consequences of the dismissals. The employer has to disclose in writing the following matters at the beginning of the consultation period:

(a) the reason for the proposals
(b) the number and description of employees whom it is proposed to dismiss
(c) the total number of employees of any such description employed by the employer at that establishment
(d) the proposed method of selecting the employees who may be dismissed (the most popular method has been 'last in first out' but case law has shown that employers are increasingly moving towards retaining those who have the necessary skills for the organization to remain viable)
(e) the proposed method of carrying out the dismissal, with due regard to any agreed procedure, including the period over which the dismissals are to take effect.

In many organizations which employ librarians, encouragement has been given for older staff to take early retirement, and in some cases there have been enhanced payments which are a considerable improvement on the minimum redundancy lump sum payments (shown below) available to those employed for two years or more before dismissal, who are under the normal retirement age and had not unreasonably refused an offer of suitable alternative employment:

1. half a week's pay for each complete year of service from 18 years to 21 years of age
2. one week's pay for years between 22 and 40
3. one-and-a-half weeks' pay for 41 onwards, reduced by one-twelfth for each month in the final year before reaching 64 years of age.

Older staff will wish to discuss their decisions; therefore, it is desirable for library managers to be aware of early retirement conditions. It may also be the case that early retirement posts are lost to the establishment, and can only be implemented with the agreement of the head of department or senior management equivalent. This is a difficult decision to make, but the librarian does have to consider carefully the effect on the library of the loss of posts in such a haphazard fashion. It may be possible to 'trade off' posts to enable the damage to be alleviated. Many organizations now provide support and advice to retirees, including courses on such matters as finance, leisure and social security.

DATA PROTECTION

With the coming into force in 2000 of the Data Protection Act (1998), 'the right of employees to be informed about (and to scrutinize) personal data kept on them by their employers is no longer restricted to information processed by computer'.[47] Employees may write asking an employer about the type of information held on their personal files, the sources of that information, the purposes for which it is being held, and the names and job titles of the people who routinely have access to that information. They also have a right to obtain copies of personal data held on their files. The Act also introduces special rules on the processing of 'sensitive data', including information about racial or ethnic origins, political opinions, religious or other beliefs, trade union membership, health or sexual life. Processing of such data is only permissible in certain circumstances, for example if required by law or for equal opportunities monitoring. It is important for managers to be aware that confidential references given by an employer are exempt from access, although confidential references supplied to and held by an employer are not, even though this may run counter to the express wishes of the reference writers.

DISCRIMINATION

A frequently prescribed management approach is one which treats individuals equally according to merit. Burns' and Stalker's theories,[48] discussed in Chapter 2, for example, are based on the belief that good ideas should be encouraged irrespective of their origin within the organization:

> If the aim of the organisation is to provide the best service or to produce a profit, then it needs effective staff. Any managers who restrict selection to, for example, men or whites or Protestants are simply not properly fulfilling their duty. The best staff are not obtained by ignoring large sections of the working population.[49]

This practical view of the position of sex, race and religion is enshrined in the legislation. In Britain, the Sex Discrimination Act (1975), the Sex Discrimination Act (1986), the Equal Pay Act (1970) and Equal Pay (Amendment) Regulations (1983) cover discrimination on grounds of sex, and the Race Relations Act (1976) prohibits discrimination on grounds of colour, race, nationality, ethnic or national origins.

The library manager is required to avoid *direct discrimination*, where a person is treated less favourably on grounds of race or sex than another person would be treated, and *indirect discrimination*, where a requirement is such that the proportion of one sex or racial group which can comply with it is considerably smaller than the proportion of the other sex or racial groups which can

20

comply. An employer must show that the requirement is justified if it is not to be judged discriminatory.

The effect of these laws is that library managers have to be extremely careful at all stages of human resources management discussed in this book. In particular, it is considered necessary for managers to be systematic: to be clear about what they are trying to do, to spell it out to all those involved, and to monitor the results. In practice, however, some managers may act in a quite different way, saying and writing down as little as possible to avoid it being misinterpreted and held against them. As might be expected the Equal Opportunities Commission's own Code of Practice advocates: 'the establishment and use of consistent criteria for selection, training, promotion, redundancy and dismissal which are made known to all employees. Without this consistency, decisions can be subjective and leave the way open for unlawful discrimination to occur.'[50]

In recruitment, it is unlawful to discriminate on arrangements made for the purpose of determining who should be offered employment, or the terms on which employment is offered, or to refuse or deliberately omit to offer employment. For example, advertising should be clear and unambiguous, and avoid anything, such as illustrations and wording, which is, or could be construed as, discriminatory. It is very easy to slip into discriminatory habits without being aware of it, but case law suggests that it is irrelevant what the advertisers subjectively intended the advertisement to mean. The test is whether the advertisement, when read as a whole and interpreted according to what a reasonable person would, without any special knowledge, find to be the natural and ordinary meaning of the words used, is considered discriminatory. Staff giving verbal information about jobs should be careful not to indicate any bias. Application forms should be as simple as possible, and should cater for minorities. It is usual to ask about race and gender in applications for jobs, but on separate forms (see Chapter 5).

The selection interview should be unbiased, and this is discussed in Chapter 5. During employment, discrimination can arise through the way an employer affords a person access to opportunities for promotion, transfer, training or any other benefit, facility or service, or by refusing or deliberately omitting to afford that person access to them.

The question of sexual harassment at work has received more attention in recent years, particularly by trade unions. The Trades Union Congress has defined it as 'repeated and unwanted verbal or sexual advances, sexually explicit derogatory statements or sexually discriminatory remarks'. The European Commission adopted a Code of Practice on Sexual Harassment in July 1991. Although not binding, its intent is to establish practical guidance to employers, unions and employees to ensure that sexual harassment does not occur, or where it has, to establish proceedings to respond to it.[51] Cases in the UK have confirmed that sexual and racial harassment are unlawful under the Sex Discrimination Act and the Race Relations Act. It has also been shown that the employer is liable for discrimination if the employees who cause the disadvantage to the individual were acting in the course of their employment. An employer may avoid liability where it can be shown that the claim has been investigated, but no subsequent action was taken because of lack of evidence. The Equal Opportunities Commission Code of Practice recommends that particular care be taken to deal effectively with all complaints of discrimination, victimization or harassment, and not to assume that allegations are made by those who are over-sensitive.

Disability

The Disability Discrimination Act (1995) makes all employers of 15 employees or more legally liable for discrimination against disabled people. Because an action only lies if persons are discriminated against because they are disabled, it does allow the employer to discriminate positively in favour of the disabled, unlike the Sex Discrimination Act and the Race Relations Act. Disability is described as physical or mental impairment which has a substantial and long-term adverse effect on the person's ability to carry out normal day-to-day activities. It is unlawful for an employer to discriminate against a disabled person in relation to:

- the arrangements for appointing employees
- the terms on which the employment is offered
- by refusing to offer the employment.

It is also unlawful to discriminate:

- in the terms of the employment
- in the opportunities offered for training, promotion, transfer or any other benefit
- by refusing to offer such opportunities
- by dismissing the employee, or subjecting the employee to any other detriment.

It is not unlawful to refuse to employ a disabled person. For example, a job may be unsuitable for a disabled person, or the means of access or work equipment may be incapable of being modified. Should a person with a disability be placed at a substantial disadvantage, an employer must take steps which are reasonable in the circumstances to prevent the disadvantageous effect. The Act lists examples of adjustments – adjustments to premises, allocating some of the employee's duties to another person, transferring the employee to an existing vacancy, altering the employee's working hours, assigning the employee to a different place of work, allowing time off for rehabilitation, assessment or treatment, arranging training, acquiring or modifying equipment, modifying instructions of reference manuals, modifying procedures for testing or assessment, providing a reader or interpreter, and providing supervision.

In deciding whether it is reasonable to expect the employer to take such steps, a number of factors should be taken into account, such as the extent of the steps, whether it is practicable, the cost and disruption, the financial resources of the employer, and availability of financial or other assistance.

Sexual orientation

As a result of a recent decision by the European Court of Human Rights, gays and lesbians now have some protection in the workplace: 'Because the Human Rights Act 1998 incorporates the convention [on Human Rights] and is directly enforceable against public bodies, this decision ... means that any policies by those bodies must not discriminate on grounds of sexual orientation.'[52] It is also 'hard to believe that a dismissal on grounds of sexual orientation by a private employer would not be considered unfair'.[53]

There are no limits to the amount of compensation which may be awarded by tribunals in discrimination cases. Limits in sex discrimination cases were removed in 1993, and in race discrimination cases in 1994.

Many organizations have written discrimination policies. Manchester Metropolitan University, for example, goes beyond the legislation in its Policy on Personal Harassment in the Workplace, which covers racial harassment, sexual harassment, harassment based on disability, harassment based on religious or political convictions, harassment based on age, and harassment based on sexuality or gender orientation. Its objectives are:

- to ensure that all staff understand their responsibilities to avoid conduct and behaviour that constitutes harassment of other staff
- to ensure that managers and supervisors understand their responsibilities to take measures to prevent harassment from taking place, and to take steps to deal with alleged harassment, including, where necessary, swift and effective disciplinary action
- to provide staff both with advice on how to deal with harassment and a procedure by which to seek resolution of the perceived harassment
- to ensure that all parties are treated fairly and equitably, and whenever possible, to seek a constructive resolution mutually acceptable to both parties.

MATERNITY RIGHTS

Under the Employment Rights Act (1996), an employee who is pregnant and who has, on the advice of a registered medical practitioner or registered midwife, made an appointment to attend at any place for the purpose of receiving ante-natal care, is entitled to take time off during working hours to keep the appointment, and must be paid her normal wage during her absence.

Under the Employment Rights Act (1999), every pregnant employee has the legal right to a minimum 18 weeks' ordinary maternity leave. If she has been continuously employed for one year or more at the beginning of the eleventh week before her expected week of confinement, she is entitled to 29 weeks' additional maternity leave. The employer must be informed at least 21 days before leave commences that she intends to exercise her rights, and of the date her absence will commence. The employer can write to the woman after 15 weeks of her maternity leave asking her to confirm the expected date of birth and whether she intends to return, and the employee must respond within 21 days of receipt of the letter. From a manager's point of view, the sooner such information is provided, the easier it is to provide maternity cover. It also has to be remembered that the woman will continue to accrue holiday leave during maternity leave.

A pregnant employee who has worked for her employer for 26 weeks or more by the end of the fifteenth week before her expected week of confinement is entitled to be paid up to 18 weeks' statutory maternity pay by her employer during her ordinary maternity leave period. It is possible for her to continue to take the holiday with pay entitled to her after her maternity pay has ceased, thus extending her period away from work.

A woman returning to work after her ordinary maternity leave period is entitled to take up the job in which she was employed before her absence began. This is also the case for a woman who takes additional maternity leave, but if this is not reasonably practicable, she can be given another job which is both suitable for her and appropriate for her in the circumstances.

An employee who is made genuinely redundant during her ordinary maternity leave must be offered suitable alternative employment before her employment under her old contract comes to an end. The job must be on terms and conditions not substantially less favourable than those which would have applied had she continued to be employed in her old job: 'An employer should be extremely cautious about dismissing an employee (for a reason other than redundancy) during her ordinary (or additional) maternity leave period ... to dismiss an employee *in absentia* will usually be held unfair.'[54] An employee who is dismissed during maternity leave must be provided by her employer with a written statement explaining the reasons for her dismissal within 14 days of the date on which her dismissal took place. Dismissal on maternity-related grounds will automatically be unfair.

Under the 1994 Management of Health and Safety at Work (Amendment) Regulations, every employer is obliged to carry out a risk assessment of the workplace. As part of this, risks to women in the workforce, whether pregnant or not, must be examined. If there is a risk to her health, then once the woman has given notice to her employer that she is pregnant, the employer has to alter her working conditions and/or her hours of work. If that is not possible, she must be offered alternative work, or be suspended on full pay.

A practical problem frequently arises when a temporary vacancy is filled, particularly where the appointment is an external one or when an internal candidate is given temporary promotion. In both cases, the temporary person may feel they are entitled to the post should the woman on maternity leave, for example, not return to work. It is therefore necessary to make it clear that the post will be advertised in the usual way, and that the person must compete against other applicants. If this is not done, there will be a feeling of resentment by staff who did not believe they had a fair chance. On the other hand, it increasingly seems to be the practice for temporary posts to be filled without public advertisement by appointing from within the staff or from a pool of temporary workers, often former employees, known to the librarian. The extent to which this practice is followed will be determined by the policies of the parent organization.

PARENTAL LEAVE

The Maternity and Parental Leave etc. Regulations 1999 entitle male and female workers to take unpaid parental leave to enable them to care for their child aged five or under for at least 13 weeks per child. No parent may take more than four weeks' leave in any particular twelve-month period. All employees who have been working for their employer for at least one year qualify, and they must be given their own job back on return if the leave was for four weeks or less. If the leave was longer and a return to their own jobs is not reasonably practicable, a similar job with the same terms, conditions and status must be found. A disputed provision in the legislation, which could be the subject of appeal to the European Court, is that leave is not permitted in respect of a child born before 15 December 1999.[55]

HEALTH AND SAFETY

According to the Health and Safety at Work Act (1974), employers have the duty of ensuring, so far as is reasonably practicable, the health, safety and welfare at work of all their employees. Every employee has a duty to take reasonable care of their own health and safety and that of others, including users of the library. The matters to which the duty extends include: the provision and maintenance of equipment; use, handling, storage and transport of articles and substances; provision of information, instruction, training and supervision; maintenance of buildings and the provision and maintenance of the working environment. In addition, EC directives require a number of health and safety measures to be taken. For example, the Management of Health and Safety at Work Regulations 1992 require all employers to carry out a risk assessment of their workers and others affected by what they do. Employers of five or more workers are required to record significant findings, including a list of hazards, the existing control measures in place, the extent to which they control the risks, and any group of employees at risk. A series of regulations issued in the 1990s cover a variety of health and safety matters, such as manual handling, personal protective equipment, provision and use of work equipment (which includes adequate training in its use), workplace regulations which cover such factors as ventilation, temperature, lighting, floors, sanitary and washing facilities and supply of drinking water, and display screen regulations which are designed to regulate the use of VDUs. The 1992 Regulations also impose a duty on employers to take such steps as are necessary to ensure that employees can retire to a room or area where they can take a rest break, drink or eat their sandwiches (or whatever) in relative comfort without experiencing discomfort from tobacco smoke.

Organizations are required to have an up-to-date health and safety at work policy, and this will probably be carried out by a Health and Safety Committee together with a Health and Safety Officer.

The library should be represented on the organization's committee, and many libraries will have their own Health and Safety Committee. This should meet regularly to ensure that attention is given to matters appertaining to the Act.

WORKING TIME

With the coming into force of the Working Time Regulations 1998, workers now enjoy the statutory right to paid annual holidays, in-work rest breaks, daily and weekly rest periods, and restrictions on the length of the working week. Under the '48 hour rule', workers have the right:

- not to work more than an average 48 hours a week (including overtime) calculated over a reference period of 17 weeks

- not to work at night for more than an average 8 hours in any 24-hour period, calculated over a reference period of 17 weeks
- to be offered free (and, where appropriate, repeat) health assessments when assigned or transferred to night work.

Workers may agree to work longer hours so long as the agreement is individual, voluntary and in writing. The upper limit on working hours does not apply to certain groups, including managing executives and other persons with autonomous decision-making powers; nor does it apply to people whose working time is not measured or predetermined by their employers, or who determine their own patterns of work.

Rest breaks and rest periods

The Working Time Regulations 1998, which apply to Great Britain only, entitle adult workers to a minimum in-work rest break of 20 minutes if their working day or shift exceeds 6 hours; a minimum daily rest period of 11 hours between the end of one working day or shift and the beginning of the next, and a minimum weekly rest period of 24 hours (or 48 hours averaged over a fortnight). Workers under the age of 18 are entitled to 30 minutes' rest if the shift exceeds 4½ hours, a minimum daily rest period of 12 hours between shifts and a minimum weekly rest period of 48 hours.

There are a number of workers excluded from these regulations, but most library and information workers are covered by them. Arrangements for meal and rest breaks will usually be incorporated into the contract of employment or a workforce agreement. The 1998 Regulations do not require employers to pay workers during meal and rest breaks, though it is normal to do so for short rest breaks.

Paid annual holidays

The Working Time Regulations 1998 also entitle every worker who has been continuously employed by the same or an associated employer for 13 or more weeks to a minimum of four weeks' paid holiday *pro rata* in every 'holiday year'.

Time off work

In addition to time off provisions for ante-natal appointments, the law creates other rights to:

- time off to carry out duties and undergo training as an official of a trade union recognized by the employer under the Trade Union and Labour

Relations (Consolidation) Act (1992). This right is with pay in working hours. Members of trade unions are entitled to reasonable time off in working hours, without pay, to take part in trade union activities.

- time off with pay to perform statutory duties and undergo training as a safety representative under the Health and Safety at Work Act (1974)

- time off, without pay, to perform specified public duties including magistracy, membership of a local authority, a statutory tribunal, a health authority, school governor, or membership of a water authority under the Employment Rights Act (1996)

- time off with pay if under notice of redundancy in order to look for work or make arrangements for training under the Employment Rights Act (1996). This right is only available to those who have been continuously employed for two years on the date the notice is due to expire.

- time off with pay to perform duties or undergo training as a trustee of an occupational pension scheme under the Employment Rights Act (1996)

- reasonable amount of time off to care for dependents under the Employment Relations Act (1999):
  - (a) to provide assistance on an occasion when a dependent falls ill, gives birth, or is injured or assaulted
  - (b) to make arrangements for the provision of care for a dependent who is ill or injured
  - (c) in consequence of the death of a dependent
  - (d) because of the unexpected disruption (or termination of existing arrangements) for the care of a dependent
  - (e) to deal with an incident which involves a child of the employee and which occurs unexpectedly.

With reductions in staffing levels, the granting of time off has become more difficult and puts a greater strain on libraries. At the same time, it is acknowledged that such activities have an important role to play in combating professional stagnation when opportunities for advancement are so limited.

STRESS

Library managers have to be careful under Health and Safety legislation not to cause undue stress to their employees. A landmark High Court ruling in 1994 against Northumberland County Council held that the Council had failed to foresee that John Walker was unable to cope with his workload after a breakdown – a workload which became heavier with no help or guidance from the Council. Employees who complain about being unable to cope should be listened to most sympathetically, otherwise their employer might well end up in court.

2 Motivation and job satisfaction

The study of job satisfaction is based on motivation theories. These are concerned with the factors that cause an individual to develop and sustain a particular mode of behaviour. They are also concerned with the subjective reactions of the individual during that behaviour. A distinction is usually made between *content* theories of motivation, and *process* theories.

Content theories try to identify needs that should be met or values that should be attained if a worker is to be motivated. Thus, it is generally accepted that people at work need security, reasonable working conditions and adequate pay. Beyond those basics, however, it becomes more complicated. People's higher-level needs – for recognition or responsibility, say – may be difficult to meet in routine work. Some staff may want more sociability from their work; others may want more sense of achievement than a traditional hierarchical structure gives.

Process theories suggest that the variables in a given work situation should all be considered, and that their relationship with each other or their mutual influence is very significant. The assumption is that 'satisfaction is a function of the correspondence between the reinforcer system of the work environment and the individual's needs'.[1] Whilst individual workers bring their own needs to the workplace, the nature of the tasks, the style of the supervisor and the overall management climate are equally significant in determining the degree of motivation that may be developed on the job. Thus, the inter-relationship between these variables (the process) must be considered, not just the content or worker's own needs.

Motivating staff is therefore a complex and delicate business. Individuals' sense of job satisfaction, or lack of it, does not depend only on their own motivation as, say, a professional librarian with a sense of service and trained expertise to support it. Nor does it depend only on the management styles and structures operating in the library. It is derived from the interaction between the individual's own attitudes, the nature of the task and of the work group, the management styles and the influence of the outer environment – financial constraints, political policies, technological innovation.

SYMPTOMS OF POOR MOTIVATION AND JOB DISSATISFACTION

The dangers of *not* applying some knowledge of motivation theories in staff development and supervision are that staff may suffer from endemic low morale. There will always be exceptions among the strongly self-motivated or 'self-starters' and the determined careerists, but among the rest of the staff the warning signs to look out for are a high turnover of junior staff (senior people may find it harder to move to other jobs because of low mobility at that level), more than average days off sick, persistent unpunctuality, and increasing complaints by users. As Levin and Kleiner advise, 'the primary function of the manager in the control of turnover and absenteeism is observation of the employee's behaviour and performance to detect any changes representing job dissatisfaction'.[2] There may also be a tendency for staff to identify with user complaints rather than to identify with the library and take responsibility for remedying the user's problem. A defeatist spiral develops in the worst cases, whereby staff and user expectations of the library decline mutually towards a nadir of apathy and inertia. Rules and regulations continue to be applied, but few staff know or care about the reasons that lie behind them, so readers are often fobbed off with bureaucratic excuses rather than explanations. If one tries to elicit from poorly motivated library staff what they are trying to achieve, they are likely to give an account of their routines and procedures, without any reference to purpose or justification. In the same way, our experience with staff who are persistently off sick and are not chronically ill is that they will often blame working conditions or bad luck. It is important that such staff are interviewed regularly to indicate that their record is unsatisfactory and that it handicaps the library in meeting its objectives. Staff who are persistently away sick can be referred for medical examination to the organization's medical officer so that an objective view can be obtained and further counselling given. Serious cases may be subject to disciplinary procedures.

These are some of the symptoms that develop when staff are required to operate a service about which they are never asked for their opinions, which they do not monitor for effectiveness to users, and where they cannot see beyond their own tasks to the overall service. The need for consultation, feedback on one's performance – positive as well as negative – and acknowledgement of one's contribution to the library's goals are expressed in all surveys of job satisfaction in library and information work. They match up quite closely with the findings in surveys of other professions and occupations, upon which the theories have been constructed.

We will now give a summary of the main schools of thought on motivating people at work, which have influenced managerial styles and affected the job satisfaction of staff for better or for worse. Job satisfaction is itself a complex individual matter – 'a perception or an emotional response on the part of individuals based on their own view of how well these expectations are fulfilled'.[3] The common assumption that job satisfaction leads to greater productivity is not borne out by recent studies that do show some positive correlation, but at a low level. Rather, they argue that satisfaction comes from the various rewards which follow from improved performance. This seems a more realistic assessment of the complex problems facing staff managers trying to help their staff get to 'lift-off', in terms of both performance and job satisfaction.

SCIENTIFIC MANAGEMENT AND ECONOMIC MAN

The scientific management school had its origin in the behavioural sciences at the turn of the century. Two of its main proponents were F.B. Gilbreth (1868–1924)[4] and F.W. Taylor (1856–1915).[5] They took the view that the average employee is motivated primarily by economic needs, so a pattern of status and financial rewards needs to be built into the career path to provide the main incentives. Employees are assumed to be inherently lazy, to lack any self-discipline, so they need to operate within a firm hierarchical structure, with clear lines of control and close supervision. The 'carrot and stick' approach of incentives and punishments is considered to be important, since it is assumed that workers have a natural inclination to 'slacking' and 'soldiering'. By 'soldiering', Taylor meant workers conspiring with each other to carry out an agreed minimum of work, just enough to keep their bosses off their backs, but not enough to stretch them. The concomitant argument about the role of managers was that they were generally incompetent. When they allocated work, they only guessed how long it took workers to do tasks. They knew little about workers' skills and abilities, and operated in a largely arbitrary and ill-informed way which encouraged workers to 'get away with it'.

The Taylorian response to inefficiency, of both employees and managers, was to introduce work study methods leading to job fragmentation. Tasks were broken up into clearly defined subtasks, and the time taken to perform them was worked out using a group of the 'best workers for the job'. Workers were not supposed to think about their work, since their supervisors were paid to do that for them. Nor were they supposed to take any initiative, for that was what the bosses were there for. They were to do 'a fair day's work for fair pay', and were to be given the necessary technical training to achieve this.

The implications of the scientific management school, which is by no means extinct in contemporary organizations, are that all decisions are taken by the manager, without any consultation with employees. Authority is concentrated at the top of a tall, narrow, hierarchical staffing structure, with little delegation. Figure 2.1 provides a checklist of characteristics by which scientific management may be recognized (see the left-hand column, headed 'Mechanistic'). The features are heavy centralization, closely defined job descriptions, and an emphasis on routines rather than the taking of initiatives. Communication tends to be largely one-way, from senior management downwards, and favours written memos and instructions rather than face-to-face discussion. Staff development is confined to technical training, for instance for new processes resulting from automation. The manager's job is seen as planning, controlling, inspecting and punishing. Staff are expected to be loyal to their section, and to obey instructions without looking to wider goals derived, for example, from their professional education or their social commitment.

The scientific approach to staff management may appear as the pervasive management style in a library, or it may co-exist alongside more people-centred styles. For example, it may be identified in some technical services sections of academic libraries, where the reader services are managed in a more participative or consultative style. The findings of the Sheffield Manpower Project indicated that in the mid-1970s it was more common in public libraries than in academic or special libraries. It may be that the problems of lack of consultation and emphasis on downwards communication were a result of the turbulence experienced in the public library sector as a result of local government reorganization in 1974, and then in the 1990s came further local government reorganization with the establishment of unitary authorities. In the late 1970s, it was the turn of academic libraries to experience turbulence as a result of mergers of colleges of education with other institutions (polytechnics or colleges of higher education) and the structural changes which continued into the 1990s with the incorporation of polytechnics and colleges and the changes in status resulting from the Education Reform Act along with convergence and de-convergence.

In both sectors, the inadequacies of scientific management approaches were highlighted. There was resistance to centralization among staff on sites with their own local loyalties and ways of doing things. They felt threatened by the loss of autonomy and the shift in decision-making from the local level to a seemingly remote senior management. Communication tended to be from the top down, and modes of consultation were experienced as unsatisfactory because they did not appear to feed back into the actual decision-making

Mechanistic/organismic paradigm

Mechanistic		Organismic
Authority concentrated at 'the top'; little delegation.	AUTHORITY	Dispersed; much delegation
Low and localized; bureaucracy tends to take its place.	PROFESSIONAL EXPERTISE	High and dispersed
Hierarchical. Favours centralization.	STRUCTURE	Network. Favours decentralization
Closely defined job description; sharp division of duties; fixed function of posts; emphasis on PROCESS (routine).	STAFF DEPLOYMENT	'Open-ended' job description; duties defined rather by purpose and staff interrelationships; team organization; emphasis on PROJECT
	COMMUNICATION	
Little	lines of	Much
One way, 'top' to 'bottom'	– content	Multi-directional
Mainly instructions, 'cut-and-dried' decisions		A Mainly information, advice, opinion-seeking
Emphasis on written communication	– format	Oral, 'face-to-face' is important
'Hygiene' factors important; reward and punishments.	JOB SATISFACTION	Herzberg's 'motivators' important. Opportunity for self-development and socially useful work
Obedience and loyalty to an individual leader and/or a part of the organization	COMMITMENT	To the organization as a whole, or, more likely, to professional goals, or, more likely, to a sense of social 'mission'
Claims a relatively small share of the organization's resources; confined to formal training in new skills and introduction of new knowledge	STAFF DEVELOPMENT	Claims a relatively large share of the organization's resources; employs a wide range of means to assist self-development; is concerned with attitude-change, as well as acquisition of knowledge and new skills
Works best in relatively static environments, meeting predictable demands: inflexible, and unreliable under stress	DEVELOPMENT CAPACITY OF THE ORGANIZATION	Adapts readily to rapidly changing and unpredictable situations; flexible, and reliable under stress

(*From:* Ross Shimmon (ed.), A Reader in Library Management, London: Bingley, 1976, p.126.)

Figure 2.1 An adaptation of Burns' and Stalker's framework for organizational analysis

process. Delegation appeared to be a hollow promise, since increasingly systems and procedures were 'rationalized' at the top of the hierarchical structure.

From the viewpoint of senior management, of course, a different picture emerges. To provide efficient and effective services in multi-site library systems, it was logical to centralize acquisitions and cataloguing, and to try to achieve consistent procedures and regulations (on lending, reservations, and so on) across all service points, even when this meant bringing previously autonomous libraries under centralized control, and leading to complaints that 'headquarters is slow to take decisions, unresponsive to suggestions, and out of touch with local needs'.[6] In a sense, autocratic management of the scientific school was forced on some senior management, because staff lower down the hierarchy at middle and junior management levels were reluctant to exercise authority and take decisions or initiate action. They preferred to sit it out, to wait and see what senior management would do. In short, they engaged in a considerable amount of 'buck-passing', when they were not positively clinging to their traditional ways of doing things as autonomous libraries. The situation was aggravated by what Ashworth calls 'motivation by self-preservation' on the part of some middle managers, who had reached 'the level of their own incompetence', a phenomenon known in management circles as the Peter Principle.

Special library staff were not immune to the pressures of change in the 1970s, though it took different forms from the organizational changes in the public and academic library sectors. Technological innovation was the main change agent in special libraries, and their reactions were early documented by Roberts:

> Staff resistance to change involving computers is less likely when systematic attention is paid to the need for consultation and keeping staff informed.[7]

By the mid-1980s, much more precise questions were being asked, and recommendations made on how to manage the new technology by, among others, the Industrial Society. These included an attention to staff and union participation which is quite alien to the scientific management approach. Participation considerations included:

- What are the systems of participation at present?
- Are people involved in issues that affect them?
- Are they being consulted specifically about the introduction of new technology?
- Is involvement early enough, and regular enough?[8]

These examples may indicate some of the shortcomings of scientific management in an era of rapid structural and technological change. However, there is still evidence of interest in some of the old-fashioned virtues associated with the scientific approach, with its emphasis on control and productivity. Partly, this is a result of financial pressures, leading to shortage of staff and the necessity for greater efficiency to get the most from diminishing resources. Research on the way libraries were affected during the local government changes of the 1990s highlighted the success achieved by managers who 'went to great lengths to keep staff informed and where possible included them in the decision processes' compared with those who were 'not good communicators – too much material was provided for the staff or too little, with no face-to-face discussion of the changes, no newsletters or bulletins and no counseling support'.[9]

There has been a certain amount of disillusion with early participative staff structures, where it was found that staff were not ready for, or skilled in, participative modes of behaviour. There are many routine and operational activities which library staff are engaged in which do not lend themselves to consultation. They are carried out most efficiently by providing clear written instructions and regular supervision. When any problems arise, they are best sorted out on the job, between staff member and immediate supervisor. There is little opportunity or need for meetings, decision-making working parties or other time-consuming group work.

Another point in favour of the scientific approach is that it provides a great deal of security for the many staff who are not particularly ambitious or seeking responsibility. There is a clear hierarchy of authority, in which the more senior staff take all the decisions, as their status and salary indicates they should. There are fixed function posts with clear job descriptions which, while being perhaps inflexible and unchallenging for more aspiring librarians, provide for many a comfort in 'knowing where I am, and what I have to do'. However, a 1984 research report indicated that younger professional librarians were becoming disillusioned and frustrated because they could not find interesting and responsible jobs to move to after their first professional post.[10] There is also a suggestion in many job satisfaction surveys that new library staff feel overqualified for the work they do, especially graduates, who become bored with routines. Is this because their managers and supervisors belong to the scientific school of thought, which leads to tight control and lack of delegation, or is it because they are given the expectation on library and information courses that they will be working in mainly participative structures, whereas in reality they find jobs in authoritarian structures? In one research report, only a third of the library staff responding named team membership as 'of interest to them in an ideal job, resulting in 23rd place [out of 31] for this factor'.[11] Is this because they prefer scientific to participative management structures, or is it because team systems have not evolved satisfactorily into genuinely participative vehicles for decision-making? Barlow, in a more recent study of team librarianship, has considerable doubts about its participative nature in Leicestershire, the pioneering authority, in which he detected a 'move away from organic, participative, or at least cooperative structures, towards more hierarchical forms'.[12]

Library managers who take a mechanistic approach argue that the majority of library tasks do not demand much creativity. What is wanted is efficiency rather than originality, skill rather than imagination, endurance and application rather than flair and insight. Most library staff for most of the time, it is argued, are engaged in predetermined procedures, whether in running acquisitions, streamlining inter-library loans, or cataloguing a special collection of eighteenth-century French literature. These are more typical of library jobs than designing and planning new services, which only happens from time to time – setting up a community information service, introducing on-line searching in a special library, or automating some of the housekeeping routines. Against this stance are those library managers who try to encourage creativity in their staff, or at least expect their graduate professionals to analyse their work critically and have some ideas from time to time about improving services, or increasing efficiency or effectiveness. They argue that the pace of innovation is now unprecedentedly high in library and information work, calling for a more creative response from staff.

In fact, it is negativist attitudes derived from mechanistic approaches that can frustrate creativity and change. Rooks gives helpful advice to managers faced with negative attitudes which can infect others and make progress difficult, especially when such attitudes are held by persons with influence.[13] Practical responses include:

1. demonstrating that positive rather than negative thinking will be rewarded
2. examining closely the worth of some of the negative points made, as they may have substance
3. arguing the consequences of not acting in a positive manner

Resistance to change is often based on fear of the unknown, and fear of failure. Therefore, adequate training should be given where necessary, and changes should be made gradually where they are difficult to implement. Sometimes, it is desirable to have an experimental period with monitoring and a review at the end of it. On a practical point, it is always very difficult to withdraw services to users once they have been implemented.

HUMAN RELATIONS SCHOOL OF MANAGEMENT

The human relations school of management had its origins in the United States in the 1920s. Since then, it has undergone a massive popularization. In particular since the 1950s, it has been widely used in organizations, and a vast body of literature embodies its approaches, from the theoretical academic tome to the staff management textbook studied by every student in business schools on both sides of the Atlantic. It has been just as massively attacked, by a wide range of critics across the left–right continuum. Right-wing economists consider human relations approaches to be 'soft' because they reject money as the main incentive to workers. Left-wing critics condemn it because it shows workers to have very complex and not necessarily rational needs at work, and this gets in the way of straight economic and power bargaining between bosses and workers. They may also consider human relations techniques to be manipulative, on the grounds that some staff managers may go too far in exploiting staff's complex needs for the benefit of the organization. It could be argued that the human relations approach encourages 'workaholics', and can turn people into willing slaves of the organization.

Any exposition of the human relations school must begin with Elton Mayo, who carried out a series of studies in the 1920s in the Hawthorne Works of the Western Electric Company in the United States.[14] One of his most significant discoveries was the importance of the 'informed organization' in any workplace. Alongside the formal staff structure or organization chart, there exists an informal social system which acts as an alternative communication channel, and may indeed in some cases subvert the official channel. A common manifestation of this is what people call 'the grapevine', a more or less accurate information network which can be highly influential in forming attitudes (for or against innovation, for example).

Mayo identified employees' need to have a stable social relationship at work, thus questioning the validity of the 'rabble hypothesis' of the scientific school, that individuals pursue their own self-interest irrespective of the work group. It follows that people at work need to be provided with a secure base for 'spontaneous co-operation'. This need can be met by deploying staff in a team or work group with which they can identify, and have a sense of belonging. Such an approach will, he argued, diminish conflict and disagreement, and enable individuals to commit themselves through the group to the aims of the organization. From the manager's point of view, leadership and counselling are indivisible, and it is through skilful communication between manager and workers that teams are built and sustained, because this is the way that supervisors can develop their staff's 'desire and capacity to work better with management'. His view that money means less to people than satisfying their non-logical need for being in a social group at work has led unkind critics to say that he substituted the 'tribal hypothesis' for the 'rabble hypothesis'. An important argument against the human relations school is that it elevated the importance of the work group and social collaboration to a point where other significant factors were ignored, such as the relationship between the nature of the tasks and the work group, or the basic differences between people in their individual or group orientation to work. Everyone was assumed to be primarily social-oriented, obsessed by the need for 'togetherness'.

There has been criticism of Mayo's methodology as well, since it appears that he was selective in writing up the results. It has been argued that some of his work groups were inevitably, in the end, good examples of co-operation and social belongingness, because:

> (1) members were deliberately selected for their co-operativeness; (2) two unco-operative members were soon replaced; (3) one of the replacements urged her associates to make high bonuses because she had unusual family responsibilities; and (4) the second relay assembly team responded to financial incentives.[15]

Bearing these criticisms in mind, one may now consider some of the results of actual experiments carried out by Mayo at the Hawthorne Works of the Western Electric Company in Chicago. He found that the work group was a major determinant of behaviour, and also that when supervisors and managers showed an interest in their workers and were prepared to consult them, there was improved productivity, whereas there did not appear to be improved productivity when material conditions only were improved. This was unexpected, since the scientific school of management had always argued for the 'carrot and stick' approach. By tinkering with material working conditions – like longer tea breaks, for example – it had been assumed you could create greater productivity. Now it seemed that a more significant incentive was the interest taken by managers, and their willingness to consult.

In another series of experiments, known as the Bank Wiring Room studies, Mayo also observed that employees have a way of controlling their own work activities, irrespective of the official management controls. The group of workers in this study was observed to have its own informal social structure and code of behaviour, which in fact clashed with that of management. They had a standard of output which no individual would exceed, and they were indifferent to the company's financial incentive scheme. Too much work was seen as 'rate-busting'; too little would be 'chiselling'. The company had assigned formal roles to the workers, but the really influential roles were the informal ones developed within the group by the employees themselves.

MASLOW'S HIERARCHY OF NEEDS

After the Second World War, the work of the humanist psychologist Abraham Maslow was influential in the development of the human relations school of management.[16] His approach continues to concentrate on the 'content' or 'substantive' theories of motivation, which try to arrive at a set of needs which must be fulfilled if workers are to be satisfied. It emphasizes the social rather than the technical factors present in the workplace, in contrast to the Tavistock School, which in Britain in the 1950s was studying the inter-relationship between technology and worker behaviour (a 'process' approach to motivation).[17]

Maslow's assumption is that it is necessary to understand the different levels of needs which people experience, because only then will it be possible to create a work environment which will satisfy staff needs and thus lead to high morale and, it is assumed, high output. Maslow drew up a hierarchy of needs (see Figure 2.2) which is intended to have wider application than the workplace. It has been used by psychologists in helping people draw up 'whole-life' programmes of self-development.

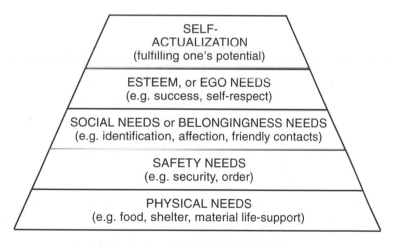

Figure 2.2   Maslow's hierarchy of needs

In Maslow's view, people are not able to progress to the satisfaction of their higher-level needs (such as social needs, esteem needs) until they have first satisfied their more humble needs (those which appear lower down the hierarchy, such as safety needs). In Western countries, most workers earn enough to take care of the basic material comforts of food, clothing and shelter. Once this level is met, people aspire to the next level, which is the need for safety and security. In this area is included not just security of income and tenure (though these are of increasing importance during times of high unemployment and in the present era of downsizing, rightsizing and outsourcing), but also the need for information, which can be an important source of security for employees. They need to know where their organization is going, what its future is likely to be, and how this may affect their jobs. This is why house magazines, bulletin boards and other such simple devices are so important. Equally important is the communication climate in an organization, the ease or difficulty with which important developments get passed on, formally and/or informally. Another source of security at work is adequate training for the job one has to do, and the support of backup written guidelines as well as verbal instruction. In periods of rapid technological and structural change in libraries, staff are made to feel insecure if they see their jobs under 'threat' of change, but they feel a great deal more insecure if inadequate provision is made – too little, too late – to retrain them. This applies not only to technical skills (needed in automation, for example), but also to interpersonal skills, such as learning to work effectively in a team structure, or training end-users in the use of relevant databases.

When the needs for material comforts and security are adequately met, Maslow argues that people then aspire to the next highest level, the social or 'belongingness' needs. Once staff have reasonable working conditions, reasonable salaries and a certain level of security, they will still not be positively motivated, because their needs are more complex than was assumed by classical or scientific management theorists. Of course, this is not to say that the lower-level needs are not important. It is to emphasize that by themselves they will not spur staff on to feelings of positive satisfaction and high achievement. There will always be employees whose expectations of work remain at a fairly basic level of need, and this applies to libraries as much as other organizations.

The implications of fulfilling staff needs for social contacts and belongingness lead to a consideration of group membership at work. We have already seen how Elton Mayo's experiments showed the value that employees attached to their work group, whether it is formally structured by management or informally arranged by the employees themselves. In libraries, team structures have been on the increase since the 1970s. In public libraries in particular, area teams have been formed to combat the isolation of branch librarians and draw them more fully into professional projects for the whole area, in some allocated specialism, so that within the team there is someone with responsibility for developing community information services, children's and schools' work, special services to the housebound or to institutions, and so on. In addition to these area teams, public library staff may belong to temporary *ad hoc* working parties where, for example, system migration projects are under way. In many public library structures, a matrix management system operates, cutting across the traditional hierarchy. Thus, an individual member of staff may take part in area team meetings, or in meetings of specialists, such as children's librarians or community information librarians, from across the whole system, and sometimes also in special interest meetings, for instance new technology applications.

In academic libraries, the basic 'team' has remained the group of professionals and assistants who serve subject communities, reflecting the primary need for the library to involve itself with the communities. Like public libraries, many have regular meetings of management groups and working parties set up to meet particular short-term needs, such as designing a system of charging for services, or standing groups concerned with continuing services such as staff training and user education. Sykes, for example, noted that 'a dramatic improvement in the climate of relations was achieved when working parties, involving members of staff from every level, were formed to create appropriate job descriptions for a converged environment'.[18] Bluck noted how motivation affects the work of a team, which can be capable of 'remarkable results', and also that the team itself can be a 'powerful motivating factor, providing both a communal desire to do well, and a certain peer group pressure not to let team colleagues down'.[19] However informal the structure, the number of library staff working as isolated individuals is decreasing, and the majority of academic librarians have some sense of belonging to a work group, if not a team.

The categories that appear to suffer most from isolation are school librarians and information workers in the smallest special libraries. It is often not possible for them even to get away on courses or conferences to meet kindred spirits, because of the practical problems of being a 'one-person unit'. Thus, they may suffer from a lack of professional self-identity, and in the early stages of their career, a lack of role models. They are dependent for their social and belongingness needs on users acknowledging their value, which may leave them relatively deprived, compared with the collegial support which many public and academic librarians experience.

The message which the Maslowian hierarchy has for managers about social or belongingness needs is important, because if the staffing structure does not allow for work groups and the encouragement of a sense of identity within the work group, staff are likely to form their own informal groups, which may end up pursuing different goals from senior management. There are many notorious examples of the flouting of this principle in the workplace. The open-plan office, for instance, diminishes the sense of identity and makes it more difficult to form work groups with a common purpose. Some aspects of library automation, such as buying in centralized cataloguing services, may similarly undermine an existing work group of cataloguers, by deskilling the activities and introducing more clerical workers rather than professionals.

As libraries have become larger and more complex in management structures – through mergers, in particular, the multi-site problem has grown and continues to grow – careful thought needs to be given to deploying staff in small work groups with which they can identify, and from which they can draw support. It is the 'primary' group, the people we meet face-to-face in our daily activities, with some common purpose, that matters to people, rather than the 'secondary' group which consists of the more formal official forums within the organization, usually named as management teams. Social psychologists argue that the best size for the primary group is between eight and twelve. The primary group is significant in moulding staff opinions, goals and ideals. If there is conflict between these and the secondary group (the larger organization) goals, the primary group is likely to prove stronger, and no amount of management 'propaganda' will change this. One solution in that case is to start with the primary group, 'where they are at', and see whether attitudes and entrenched ideas can be modified by involving them in planning their work in relation to the concerns of senior management, as well as their own concerns as a work group. It is important that all members of a senior management team are able to view matters from a system-wide perspective as well as through their own group interests. If this is not the case, then centrifugal tendencies can develop which are harmful when the wish is for the service to make progress as a whole.

The Maslowian hierarchy has at its highest levels people's needs for achievement, challenge, self-expression and 'self-actualization' or fulfilment of one's potential. In lean, twenty-first-century organizations, typically characterized by: 'lack of job security and promotion opportunities, the interplay between different levels of need may perhaps be seen in the continuing aspiration for promotion when there are few or no opportunities available. Promotion may be linked for many people with satisfying their higher-level needs.'[20] But many will find those needs unfulfilled.

The question is how to ensure that staff are encouraged to operate at the higher levels of their potential. The answer is not clear-cut, because there are so many variables. The nature of the tasks may not require much initiative or creativity, because library and information work contains a fair, or more than fair, share of routine rather than decision-making. The management structures may not be conducive to delegation or 'trusting' new professionals to carry out genuinely professional work. Some recruits to the profession may have been attracted by the safe nature of the job, and prefer routines to responsibility or innovative projects, or they may have had their expectations lowered by the contrast between their professional education and what they are permitted to do in their first posts. Financial constraints are a further factor, and in some libraries they have led to staff reverting to a larger proportion of purely housekeeping routines and day-to-day administration, after the brave new moves towards outreach, community analysis and expanded information services.

MCGREGOR'S THEORY X AND THEORY Y

Douglas McGregor took Maslow's ideas and developed them in the staff management context. In doing so, it has been argued, he oversimplified Maslow's sophisticated thinking about the 'role of association, habit and conditioning', and 'the relation between needs and cultural patterns', which may heavily influence individual needs.[21] His three major types of need are *physiological*, *social* and *self-fulfilment*. He considered that the scientific school of management, the 'hard approach', might satisfy staff needs for physiological or material security, but it frustrated their social needs and their need for self-fulfilment. He encapsulated the two extremes that managers could occupy, and called them Theory X (representing the scientific approach) and Theory Y (representing the human relations approach).[22]

According to Theory X, employees are, in general, indolent. They lack ambition and are resistant to change. They are inherently self-centred and indifferent to the organization's needs. Without the active intervention of management, people would be either passive or resistant to the organization's goals. It follows that management must impose firm direction and control on its staff, and attempt to modify their behaviour to fit in with the organization's goals.

There can be a hard or a soft interpretation of the Theory X approach by individual managers. The hard approach favours very tight inspection, checking and control. A certain amount of threat and coercion is usually implicit, though often concealed. There is little communication except downwards from seniors to juniors, and what there is tends to be rather formal, in writing rather than face-to-face communication. The experience of Theory X, hard-style managers in industry over the past fifty years suggests that workers respond in quite predictable ways. They restrict their output to the minimum demanded, undermine the objectives of senior management whenever possible, and form their own 'resistance' groups, which can take the form of informal groups of 'mates' playing the system, or of a more overtly political struggle between workers and bosses, in the form of militant trade unionism.

The soft approach to Theory X involves management speaking softly, but still using the 'carrot and stick' approach of rather crude incentives and punishments, derived from Theory X assumptions about workers' laziness and lack of commitment if not driven. In this case, workers' reactions are likely to be equally predictable, since few are deceived by the appearance of the velvet glove on the iron hand. The usual response is to take advantage by lowering

45

output or giving an inferior performance at work. There may be a kind of superficial harmony, because people are not anxious to rock the boat by bringing to the surface fundamental divisions, but there is a lack of real commitment to the organization, because there is little trust and expectations of workers' capabilities remain low.

McGregor argues that in many workplaces, observation might appear to confirm the assumptions of Theory X about workers' laziness, lack of commitment and passivity. However, he says that this is a consequence of management policies and practices, rather than the inevitable outcome of men's and women's natures. He is much indebted to Maslow for his views on needs at work, and he emphasizes that in many workplaces only the lower-level needs are satisfied. This leads to the frustration and anomie which is what causes people to behave in a lazy, uncommitted, irresponsible manner. Therefore, he says, we need an alternative theory based on more adequate assumptions about human nature. This is provided in the set of propositions called Theory Y.

Theory Y asserts that employees are capable of assuming responsibility and supporting the goals of the organization. It is the responsibility of management to provide the right conditions in which staff are able to fulfil their potential, and satisfy their higher-level needs for esteem, recognition and a sense of achievement. By being given more say in their work, people will not only achieve their own goals better, but will contribute more to the overall goal of the organization.

It sounds rather Utopian, and McGregor admits that there are problems putting it into practice. After people have been treated as passive and incapable of responsibility for some time, they are unlikely to be able to make the switch to being mature, self-activating beings just because there has been a change of management style. People who are used to being closely directed and strictly controlled at work are likely to turn to other spheres of their life for higher-level satisfactions, and offer only a minimal commitment to their jobs. Also, the fact must be faced that many jobs are not worth more than a minimal commitment, and this is a problem highlighted in the job satisfaction surveys in librarianship, which point out the problem of dull, routine procedural work in many areas of the profession. However, there are clearly areas for improvement, and Theory Y undoubtedly has an appeal in humanist terms, with its emphasis on individual responsibility, self-starters, and the dignity of men and women *vis-à-vis* their superiors. McGregor is anxious to point out that Theory Y approaches to staff management need not be 'soft', and that they can lead to high performance as well as a more satisfied staff. If they work, staff will to work is strengthened, and they commit themselves more sincerely to the service aims of their libraries. This may, unfortunately, be offset by a certain anarchy, and less willingness to plod through the duller work with competence and discipline, as they might be obliged to do under a Theory X régime.

It is important to note that real-life organizations rarely fall neatly into the Theory X or Theory Y category. Rather, there is a continuum from X to Y, with the majority of libraries, for example, grouped to left or right of the middle. Most libraries display a complex mixture of Theory X and Theory Y structures and styles. The head librarian may favour traditional hierarchical management (Theory X), but this may be offset by the deputy, who organizes participative (Theory Y) structures here and there in the organization, and encourages staff to work together and to take initiatives. Or the head may encourage (Theory Y) staff participation by restructuring the hierarchical pyramid so that staff have more meetings and work on projects with colleagues at their own level. But this may be subverted by Theory X long-serving staff lower down the hierarchy, who do not wish to consult their subordinates or to move beyond their own patch, or take an interest in the overall goals of the library.

RENSIS LIKERT AND PARTICIPATIVE MANAGEMENT

The human relations approach supposes that participative management structures and styles create conditions at work which enable staff to realize their potential, make greater use of their professional training, and thus improve the effectiveness of the service offered. Likert is one of the leading proponents of participative management, and holds the view that the majority of workers prefer this approach, and that it also results in better performance.[23] Figure 2.3 gives a summary of the range of management styles which are found in the workplace, in Likert's analysis.

Examples of all four management styles are to be found in libraries, and different styles may operate in different sections of the same library.

Stages 1 and 2 in Figure 2.3 show the two variations of authoritarian management styles. The more extreme is the exploitative. This assumes that 'buying a

1	2	3	4
← *Authoritative* →		← *Participative* →	
Exploitative authoritative	Benevolent authoritative	Consultative	Participative group

Figure 2.3 Range of management styles

47

man's time gives the employer control over the employee's behaviour', and that 'the organization must put direct hierarchical pressure upon its employees to produce at specified levels'. This is rare in libraries, perhaps because it is not common for libraries to measure their outputs and to impose clear-cut standards or levels of productivity on their staff, so that this approach would scarcely be feasible, even if it were considered desirable in human relations terms. Stage 2 is more common in libraries, and this 'benevolent authoritarian' style is marked by some show of representation of staff views, while retaining all the decision-making at the top of the hierarchy. Thus, authority remains concentrated among the few, with little delegation. The organization structure is likely to be tall and narrow, favouring centralized decision-making. The emphasis is on downward communication, rather than lateral or upward communication.

The consultative style, stage 3 in Figure 2.3, involves supervisors asking staff for their opinions and views, but not necessarily incorporating these into their decisions, which they still make on their own as 'the one in charge here'. Or they may take account of staff views in relation to their immediate day-to-day work, but not consult them on any wider issues, even though these may affect their work. This kind of consultation often goes with the *laissez-faire* management style which has been quite common in libraries. There are few considered management strategies, so people 'manage' without much conscious awareness of the effects on their subordinates.

The genuinely participative style, stage 4, means that individuals share in decision-making through their activity in the work group, and through meetings which have the power to arrive at decisions, rather than simply making recommendations to the people at the top. This is rare in libraries, where many meetings may be held, but the power to take decisions is quite limited, except at senior management team level.

The applications of participative approaches in libraries have not been entirely successful. In spite of expressed preferences for consultative and participative group approaches, as shown, for example, in Stewart's 1982 survey of job satisfaction,[24] Ritchie found that the obvious example of participation, working in teams, was not rated high as a source of satisfaction.[25] She suggests, however, that this may be because some teams are authoritarian rather than genuinely participative in the way they are run. So it appears that participative structures are not a guarantee of real participation. This is borne out by Barlow, who criticizes team-based structures in which it was thought that participation in the decision- and policy-making processes could not work because staff 'do not want to take responsibility for the decisions they are involved in making'.[26] Unfortunately, such an attitude seriously misinterprets the role of senior management in a participative system, as Likert defined it.

48

Likert's research techniques include asking staff some questions which may help to analyse just how genuinely participative work groups are:

1. To what extent does your supervisor try to understand your problems at work, and your personal and family difficulties?
2. Is he or she interested in helping you get the training which will help you in your present and future jobs?
3. How much confidence and trust do you have in your supervisor, and how much does he or she have in you, do you feel?
4. Does he or she ask your opinion when a problem comes up which involves your work? Following this, does he or she attach any value to your ideas, and try to use them?

Other significant findings in Likert's research (which was carried out in American industrial organizations, and may not necessarily be confirmed in public service organizations like libraries) were that the managers able to achieve high output are those who make more use of work groups in decision-making, and who involve their staff in work-related discussion. An important aspect of high performance also appears to be that high-performing people act as models for others, and provide an incentive, particularly in group working, or team working. The problem is that it can take a long time to develop co-operation rather than competitive individualism in a team, though if it can be achieved, it is rewarding both for the individuals and the organization. Some libraries recognize that training is needed in how to make teams more effective, and have devised practical exercises based on simulations of the team situation.[27] Training strategies are discussed in Chapter 8.

BLAKE AND MOUTON'S MANAGERIAL GRID

The managerial grid is a device which enables managers, or anyone who supervises staff, to plot, by means of self-scoring questionnaires, the extent to which their management style shows concern for output and concern for people, and in what proportions.[28] The grid is shown in Figure 2.4. Blake and Mouton's view is that the most satisfactory position on the grid, which staff managers should be aiming for, is the 9,9 position. This indicates both a high concern for output and a high concern for people. The practical value of the grid is as a starting point for training supervisors. Having found their present position on the grid, they can participate in in-service training or external courses which enable them to move closer to the 9,9 stance.

The 9,9 position of high participation, commitment to the workplace and concern for output is 'not for social purposes or to maintain morale as an end

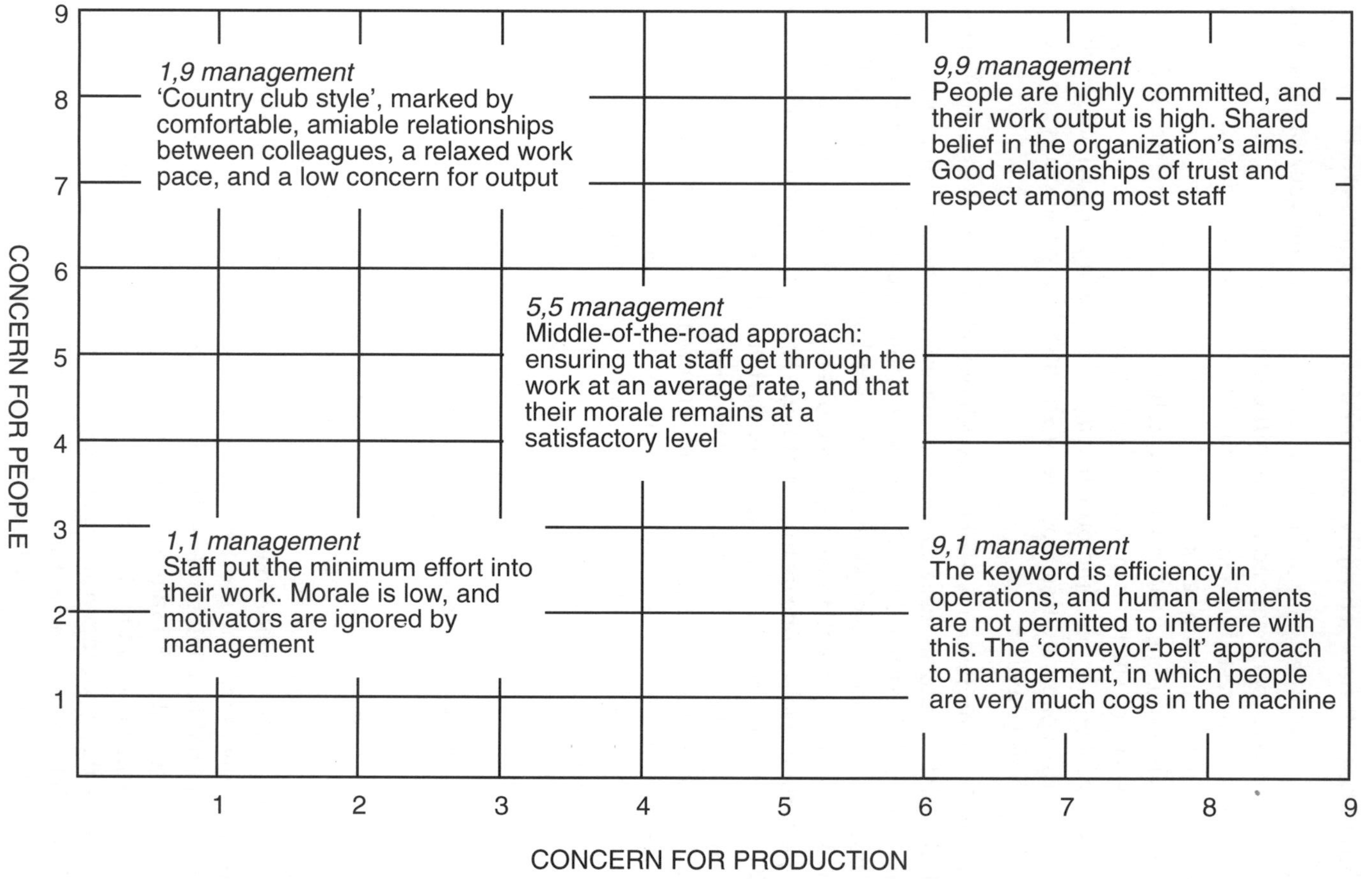

9
8
7
6
5
4
3
2
1
CONCERN FOR PEOPLE
1,9 management
'Country club style', marked by comfortable, amiable relationships between colleagues, a relaxed work pace, and a low concern for output
9,9 management
People are highly committed, and their work output is high. Shared belief in the organization's aims. Good relationships of trust and respect among most staff
5,5 management
Middle-of-the-road approach: ensuring that staff get through the work at an average rate, and that their morale remains at a satisfactory level
1,1 management
Staff put the minimum effort into their work. Morale is low, and motivators are ignored by management
9,1 management
The keyword is efficiency in operations, and human elements are not permitted to interfere with this. The 'conveyor-belt' approach to management, in which people are very much cogs in the machine
1
2
3
4
5
6
7
8
9
CONCERN FOR PRODUCTION

Figure 2.4 The managerial grid, based on the Blake and Mouton research

in itself, nor does the team concept provide a cloak of anonymity within which inadequate performance can be buried or hidden. Rather, sound interpersonal relations are seen as the *best* way to achieve or to maintain production at peak levels.'[29] Personal conflict can be worked through, rather than repressed or avoided (as in the 1,9 'country club style'), or punished from above (as in the 9,1 style).

Outside observers tend to see libraries as representing the 1,9 style – of low concern for output and high concern for people. There is seen to be a fairly relaxed work tempo and a friendly atmosphere (not competitive or aggressive) among staff work groups. However, the emphasis on quality and best value in recent years is forcing staff to change their attitudes, even if the perception outside has not changed. Generalizations can be rash, since there may be wide swings within a library from time to time: for example, academic libraries might seem to display 9,1 characteristics during their busiest periods in term time, but shift to 1,9 characteristics during vacations. Also, within the same library countervailing positions may be displayed by staff at different levels, for example 9,1 by line managers, 1,9 by a personnel officer, 9,9 by the head librarian, and 1,1 by stagnating time-servers.

There are also environmental and personality factors to be considered in discussing the feasibility of the 9,9 position. Limitations in resources may mean that staff do more routine operational work and get less satisfaction than if they were in a position to develop services. Personality may limit moves towards 'team socialization' and cause reluctance, if not actual subversion of management efforts to provide more participative structures. In recent years, there has been considerable emphasis on objectives, performance indicators based upon the objectives, and formalized staff appraisal systems. These are attempts to move towards a 9,9 position, and librarians are having to learn how to make the best use of these techniques.

HERZBERG'S SATISFIERS AND DISSATISFIERS

Herzberg is best known for the studies he carried out on groups of engineers and accountants to elicit their attitudes to work. Later studies applied his 'two-factor theory of job satisfaction' to other occupations, and Plate and Stone applied it to American librarians (1974).[30] Herzberg's theory may be summarized as follows:

> The factors involved in producing job satisfaction (and motivation) are separate and distinct from the factors that lead to job dissatisfaction. Since separate factors need to be considered … it follows that these two feelings are not opposites of each other. The opposite of job satisfaction is not job dissatisfaction, but rather, *no* job

51

satisfaction; and similarly the opposite of job dissatisfaction is not job satisfaction, but *no* job dissatisfaction.[31]

In other words, it is not enough to remove certain causes of dissatisfaction by raising pay or improving supervision or providing better working conditions. These will not in themselves increase satisfaction; they may merely remove sources of dissatisfaction. In order to provide positive satisfaction, Herzberg argues, it is necessary to bring into play 'motivators'. These are reminiscent of the higher needs in the Maslowian hierarchy. They include a sense of achievement, recognition, responsibility, advancement, and the nature of the work itself. The motivators must be present to create worker satisfaction; they relate more to the intrinsic nature of the job than to contextual factors. Contextual factors, external to the work itself, include pay, security, status, technical supervision, company policy and administration, and interpersonal relationships. These are Herzberg's 'hygiene factors', which may cause dissatisfaction if they are not acceptably worked out by management and employees. He uses the medical analogy of the hygiene factors to imply that by paying attention to these factors, an organization may *prevent* dissatisfaction, but without providing positive motivation. Nevertheless, the removal of dissatisfiers is important, just as hygiene factors in the medical context are important, since it clears the way for the benefits that may be obtained from the positive motivators.

It follows from Herzberg's studies that staff managers should be more concerned with job enrichment strategies and with job content changes rather than assuming that it is the low-motivated employees who are somehow at fault and that the job content is inviolate. He is sceptical of sacred words like 'achievement', 'challenge', 'growth' and 'responsibility' unless they are translated into practical strategies such as job enrichment and actual delegation.

Holbeche's researches into the effect on staff of flatter structures revealed how senior managers had talked of 'a sense of loss' brought about by the need to delegate areas of responsibility which they considered their own, whilst 'people in specialist posts are often under pressure to broaden their areas of work or move to a more useful specialism for the business.'[32] Shifts like these, for example on subject specialists in libraries, can be very demotivating as, in Herzberg's terms, strong motivators are being removed.

One problem with Herzberg's two-factor theory is that the choice of methodology determines the results. D'Elia warns that the two-factor theory 'is a consequence of its simplistic methodology', and more sophisticated attempts to replicate its results have been unsuccessful or inconclusive. It is therefore said to be a misleading theory on which to base practical strategies of staff motivation:

This method, by its very form, forces the employee to describe satisfying factors and dissatisfying factors separately, it permits the employee to accept responsibility for his good feelings and to ascribe to others the responsibility for his bad feelings, it is open to subjectivity on the part of the researcher who interprets and codes the employee's responses.[33]

This rather undermines studies like Plate and Stone's, which used the Herzberg methodology and replicated his results accordingly. However, it would be a pity if the 'critical incident' approach to exploring job satisfaction were to be thrown out because of its association with the two-factor theory. It is a useful device in a semi-structured questionnaire or interview to include questions like 'Please describe briefly an occasion at work when you felt particularly satisfied', and 'Please describe an occasion at work when you felt particularly dissatisfied.' In the authors' experience, the answers are illuminating, and do not divide neatly into Herzberg's motivators and hygiene factors, unless the researcher has set out with that particular methodology in mind. For example, library assistants' responses to automated circulation systems were collected during a student field study, and it was found that the decrease in sociability between staff and users was a source of dissatisfaction for some assistants, but a source of satisfaction for others, who liked to get their work done more quickly and efficiently. Thus, the same factor could be a source of satisfaction or dissatisfaction according to individuals' differing needs at work – as in the Maslowian hierarchy, where some staff may seek mainly social and belongingness needs, while others seek esteem or recognition for work well done.

PARTICIPATIVE MANAGEMENT AND THE HUMAN RELATIONS SCHOOL OF MOTIVATION

The human relations school places great emphasis on participative management as a method of satisfying a greater proportion of people's needs at work. It is considered conducive to high staff morale to provide more delegation, to push decision-making lower down the staff hierarchy, and to involve staff in setting their own objectives (projects, tasks to be completed by the end of a term/year) and in evaluating their achievements. The emphasis in organizational communication shifts from formal written memos and directives from the top down, to more informal face-to-face communication, through group and team and working party meetings. There is an increase in down/up and lateral communication. Emphasis is placed on 'self-starting' qualities, the capacity of staff to develop themselves in their own jobs, to grow professionally, and to reflect this in how they interpret their work.

It can be seen that these characteristics of participative management are derived from the thinking of Maslow, McGregor and others of their school. They follow from a conviction that people at work need to satisfy their higher-level needs for success, self-respect and self-actualization, as well as their basic needs for material support and security. As soon as people have achieved a secure job with reasonable pay and working conditions, they will escalate to higher-level needs for social and self-expression rewards at work. Some, at least, will express their higher-level needs, and expect work to provide them with opportunities for self-actualization.

An example of how participative management approaches were applied in an ICI information unit is described by Dutton.[34] The main features were that individual staff adopted their own individual targets; having defined these objectives, they were encouraged to attend relevant meetings and courses to get training, and to feed back their increased expertise to the unit. All jobs, including counter jobs, were subject to 'self-examination'. Everybody was expected to question the way they did things, and assess whether it could be improved. For example, a small study was conducted on the success rate for borrowing inter-library loans from various sources, and standard practice was reversed as a result of the findings. The general approach was to involve the staff at every level in dealing with problems and introducing and planning new systems. The more participative structure led to the elimination of excessive control and checking of minor matters. This meant economies in the use of time, besides encouraging staff at all times to differentiate between the essential and the trivial in their tasks.

Dutton sums up the value of motivation studies for the library managers as follows:

> These studies [Maslow and Herzberg] suggest that in developing staff we need to recognise two fundamentally different types of effect on motivation relating to hygiene factors and to motivation factors. Further, whilst the hygiene factors must be considered first, it is only necessary to ensure that these do not get out of line. The only practicable method for doing this is through comparison with similar units. It is not profitable to become continually preoccupied with improving these aspects ... Rather we must concentrate on trying to improve the motivation factors through the better organization of work, and experience points to staff participation as a highly effective means for doing this.[35]

In the academic library sector, Ashworth notes that with the development of multi-site polytechnic libraries from the late 1960s, the old hierarchical staffing structures with strong central control and little delegation proved inadequate:

> For example a local academic librarian can be faced with demands from a Board of Studies which conflict with the total library policy, and an embarrassing division

of loyalties ensues. If the secondary centres take independent action, the whole model fails.[36]

But if the site libraries are not able to take independent action, there are universal complaints from staff and users that the centre is out of touch with local needs, that it is slow to act, unreceptive to communications from periphery to centre. If these problems are to be resolved, Ashworth argues, library management must move away from the 'mechanistic' hierarchical model towards the 'organic' model (see Figure 2.1). The organic (or 'organismic', as the Americans call it) model derives from the human relations school of motivation. Behind its assumptions about human nature in the workplace lies the Maslowian hierarchy of needs, with its emphasis on social needs, needs for esteem and recognition, and the need to fulfil one's potential. The organic model represents McGregor's Theory Y, the optimistic image of employees, which sees them as capable of assuming responsibility, and of supporting the aims of the organization, provided they are given the supportive context of participative rather than mechanistic management.

Ashworth selects certain features of the organic structure which he sees as especially relevant to the problems of academic library management. First, the head librarian's role needs to change from omniscient being to pilot of a team, all of whom may be more professionally expert in their own specialisms than the head librarian can be. Second, staff are expected to take part in setting their own work goals, and evaluating their achievements as a matter of course. The emphasis should be on open-ended job descriptions, rather than very rigidly structured and detailed ones, so that staff are encouraged 'to stretch themselves and set their own reach for the stars standards'. Third, a good communications network is an essential characteristic of the organic model. This can begin, Ashworth suggests, with inter-branch working parties to make recommendations about standardizing as many routines as possible, to remove low-level causes of friction. These working parties should be drawn from all strata, and will form the basis for building up networks which can be used later for more important matters such as designing new services. To reduce the amount of time spent on round table discussions, the 'network' idea is to use, wherever possible, 'nodal' individuals who have emerged from group discussions as the people who will most efficiently facilitate specific developments and activities. This kind of communications network is more informal, *ad hoc* and decentralized than the traditional hierarchical communications system, which emphasizes one-way, top-to-bottom written communication, of mainly cut and dried decisions. In some areas, such as Manchester and London, consortia of academic libraries have been formed with staff involved in joint working parties on such matters as joint access arrangements, cooperative purchase, document delivery services and training.

Although he was writing about the 1960s and 1970s, Ashworth's views were still relevant in the 1990s as further expansion took place in the new universities and team working was given encouragement in the Fielden Report with the suggestion that 'new forms of team working are needed to help build commitment to the basic goals of each LIS'.[37] Bluck has examined the development of teams in university libraries and described in detail the structures at the University of Northumbria, where there has been 'a deliberate philosophy of delegated decision-making and team operation, together with measures to ensure consistently effective communication between all library staff'.[38] His survey of staff views at Northumbria showed that team working was perceived as genuinely participative, and 80 per cent believed they helped to motivate staff.

In the public library sector of the UK, the impetus towards more staff participation in management has come mainly through the spread of team structures, since local government reorganization in 1974. Typically, an area team consists of six to twelve professional librarians responsible for all the service points in their geographical area. In addition, each has a specialism to contribute to the development of the services in the area: information services, say, or publicity and promotion. Each librarian may also belong to a system-wide working party, for example to develop staff training or automation in the library as a whole. Responsibility is delegated from headquarters to the area teams. Individual professional librarians enjoy greater autonomy in shaping their work and developing their jobs, within the guidelines of overall aims and objectives, and with the collegial support of team members. There is more face-to-face communication through area team meetings and the attendance of the area team leader at senior management meetings to provide a bridge between centre and periphery. There are also meetings of specialists throughout the system – of children's librarians, say – so that as well as being a member of an area team, a professional librarian may develop particular interests with other enthusiasts. The role of non-professionals is enhanced, since they are in charge of the day-to-day operations in service points.

A further development of the team approach has been in large central libraries, where some public libraries have adopted a subject approach rather than the traditional division by function – lending, reference and so on. McClellan pioneered this deployment of staff in subject groups at Tottenham in the 1950s, to get away from the rigidity of 'reference' and 'lending' concepts, and to provide readers with 'service-in-depth'. The team of subject librarians at the central library would be engaged in selection of stock, stock editing, readers' advisory work, promotion (booklists and so on) and evaluation of their services.

56

A number of public libraries have tried setting up 'project groups', which in effect leads to a matrix management structure, where staff are drawn from different levels and sections of the library to take part in a project group working on particular problems or development areas. They thus retain affiliations with their line manager (their area team leader, for example), but at the same time have other loyalties to their project team leader, who may be appointed on grounds of expertise rather than seniority. Bryant notes that 'staff used to conventional organisations find it difficult to adjust to such a structure with its dual loyalties and temporary inversions of certain superior–subordinate relationships'.[39] This matrix approach is comparable to the 'networking' in academic libraries mentioned above. Both are intended to take participation to the point where the staff with the greatest expertise, rather than the most senior status, in a particular problem are drawn into a project group.

The team approach to public library staff management has provoked mixed reactions. At its best, 'the team provides a valuable training ground for newcomers. It meets their affiliative and support needs, helps them to discover their role, socializes them to the kind of professionalism which the team is endeavouring to practise, and offers safe space for individual venture'.[40] In service terms, teams can be high-performing, mission-oriented groups for moving a library onward towards its goals. But Jones notes two important reservations: 'They are inappropriate to the routine type of operations so important in librarianship', and they 'can flourish only where the human resources ideal is to some extent made flesh':

> They require numbers of mature and enthusiastic people who are able to acquire social skills and the necessary nose for management, and, above all, are keen to learn … when used appropriately, in the soft systems/human resources context, they are probably the most potent organizational phenomenon that there is. However, a third rate team system may be worse than useless.[41]

Where teams are imposed on a traditional hierarchy, without careful attention to developing group skills and without real delegation of decision-making power, staff may be unnerved rather than motivated. They may be made insecure by being removed from their fixed-function post in a branch library and given a wider roving commission. They may have been rendered incapable of initiative by many years of routine work in a Theory X mechanistic environment. They may see librarianship as basically routine clerical work, and therefore see no need for meetings to discuss it. They may even envy the para-professionals who are left to run the branches, and on their visits there, may try to take over their work rather than engage in professional project planning or implementation. Theory X people conditioned by their past experiences cannot be turned into Theory Y people with the wave of a wand and the production of a new staffing structure plan.

57

MORE COMPLEX MODELS OF MOTIVATION

Some theorists in motivation have evolved more complex models to explain people's behaviour and aspirations at work than the scientific or human relations schools provide. Vroom, for example, stresses the effect of individual differences among staff on their motivation.[42] Fiedler stresses both differences in the work situation and in the kind of supervisors or leaders which an organization has recruited.[43] It is accepted that staff motivation depends on a complicated interplay between the supervisor's management style, the organizational climate and the immediate work situation, where there may be significant differences in the management of technical services, say, compared with readers' services, in addition to the individual's needs of security, esteem and so on.

The 'complex systems' approach is usefully summarized by Schein.[44] He emphasizes in his research findings that any organization consists of a series of subsystems – in a library, these would include, for example, technical, social and environmental systems – and argues that the interplay of these subsystems is as important as, if not more important than, the individual's propensity to certain kinds of work behaviour. Staff can be motivated or demotivated as much by the work group to which they belong, and the roles and norms of their colleagues, as by their individual needs for self-identity, self-fulfilment and so on. Someone who is alienated in one library or section of a library may be motivated by moving to another post, or may find self-expression through union activities, while remaining inert and repressed on the job:

> Ultimate satisfaction and the ultimate effectiveness of the organization depends only in part on the nature of the motivation. The nature of the task to be performed, and the abilities and experience of the person on the job, and the nature of the other people in the organization all interact to produce a certain pattern of work and feelings. For example a highly skilled but poorly motivated worker may be as effective *and satisfied* as a very unskilled but highly motivated worker.[45]

Pirandello says that truth in a particular situation is a collection of what each person in the situation sees. If, in addition, everyone is wearing a *commedia del organizatione* mask (scapegoat, joker, token woman manager, Big Boss), whatever is the poor manager to do? Plate and Stone, as a result of their survey of job satisfaction among American librarians, say:

> Libraries, despite their homogeneity, differ considerably with regard to their organizational history, leadership climate, and even goals and objectives. Library procedures vary from library to library, and so must personnel practices and supervisory styles … library managers must therefore be skilled in the adaptation of existing principles of motivation to local requirements.[46]

58

A final approach to the 'process' school of motivation theories, in comparison to the 'content' approach of analysing categories of needs experienced by people at work, may be loosely summarized as the 'action approach'. This involves analysing the workplace as an arena in which workers take part in 'social processes', and their interactions – between bosses and subordinates, between peer groups, between professionals and clients – are explained in terms of the meanings they have for the 'actors', which are dependent on the different value systems and cultural backgrounds of the people involved. They are also, of course, subjective rather than objective meanings, and one criticism of this approach to analysing the workplace is that it ignores the realities of objective power. Some people have more power to impose their meanings on a situation than others, and ability to have one's definitions accepted, whether from a formal or informal power base, is part of the situation. For an organization to work at all, there has to be at least a working minimum of shared meanings among the people in it, and an acknowledgement, if not an acceptance, of objective structures and pressures within and without the organization. However, the contribution of the 'action school' of theorists is significant in that it draws our attention to the ways in which people at work attach their own meanings and values to their situation. There is no such thing as a purely objective view of the workplace, its technology, its staffing structure, its hierarchy of power. All these features are mediated by the subjectivity of those who experience them, and each person's subjectivity is a varied mix of individual aims and perceptions which are the result of that person's socially structured experiences and expectations. A useful derivative of the action approach is expectancy theory. This theory states that people act in ways that they think are likely to benefit them. Following the work of Vroom, Howard has developed an expectancy theory in which motivation is seen in terms of four primary process variables:

1. **E–P expectancy** – an individual's perception of the likelihood that their effort (E) will result in the successful performance (P) of specific behaviour(s)
2. **P–R expectancy** – the perception of the likelihood of being rewarded (R) for successful performance (P)
3. **R–N expectancy** – the perception of the likelihood that these rewards (R) will meet important personal needs (N)
4. **Valence** – the value the individual places on the object, such as performance, reward or need satisfaction, of any of the above expectancies.[47]

These concepts have been applied to *The Motivation to Train* by Crowder and Pupynin,[48] and can readily be seen as important contributions to our understanding of motivation in other areas of librarianship.

The action approach is a useful antidote to the scientific systems analysis of organizations, which assumes that logic and reason are all that is needed to understand and manage staff, and that central planning and more high technology will solve all problems. It is European rather than American – the seminal theorist was Touraine,[49] who carried out studies among industrial workers at Renault in France – and is an attempt to reinvest 'organization' man and woman with individual dignity and meaning, rather than being dependent on their status and function in the work machine (as seen by management) for their (assigned) meanings.

JOB SATISFACTION AND LIBRARIANS

The Minnesota University Industrial Relations Center produced a number of questionnaires in the late 1960s for collecting information on job characteristics and job satisfaction. D'Elia's study in 1979 of beginning librarians in the United States[50] and Russell's study in 1984 of non-professional library assistants in the United Kingdom[51] both used the Minnesota approach. Bundy also used the Minnesota Satisfaction questionnaire in evaluating the job satisfaction of subject librarians in British and Australian polytechnics,[52] as did Burgess, who employed the technique in surveying reference librarians and cataloguers.[53] It involves getting respondents to rate the degree of satisfaction they derive from a range of job characteristics. The 'job-related dimensions' which are measured include ability utilization, sense of achievement, nature of activity, opportunities for advancement, authority, company policies and practices, one's colleagues, independence, recognition, security, working conditions, and satisfaction at providing a service. It also covers the whole area of supervision, which is seen to have two aspects, the human relations dimension, and the technical competence dimension, both of which are important to staff supervised, but in different degrees depending on their particular needs at work.

D'Elia's findings were that the satisfaction needs among beginning librarians were quite similar, and that their job environments provided the characteristics which caused them satisfaction or dissatisfaction. The most important characteristics in providing job satisfaction were 'supervision–human relations' and 'ability utilization'. When these are translated into job dimensions, the former means library policy and practices and the supervisory climate. Ability utilization covers factors intrinsic to the job itself, such as use of one's training and expertise, which involves being allowed to exercise some responsibility and professional autonomy, and being given recognition for doing so. It would appear that there is an important relationship between the supervisory climate and opportunities for the beginning librarians to use their expertise creatively and autonomously. The climate may be deliberately participative, or it may be merely *laissez-faire*. It is suggested that the performance of library supervisors may be usefully diagnosed and evaluated by reviewing the job satisfaction of their staff.

Bundy found that the job satisfaction of subject librarians was significantly greater than that of reference librarians and cataloguers. He found that activity was the most satisfying dimension for subject librarians, but it did not rank in the first two for either reference librarians or cataloguers. Creativity, ability utilization and achievement were ranked 2, 3 and 5 by subject librarians, but were not ranked at all by cataloguers and reference librarians. Bundy concludes that it is likely that the additional elements in the role of subject librarians beyond basic information work contributes to the higher level of general job satisfaction. The factors that create the most dissatisfaction are those which are controlled by institutional and library management, such as security, recognition and authority. Burgess concludes: 'the dissatisfaction expressed by the respondents with library administration may be due to inept management, but it may also be due to lack of initiative on the part of librarians in not creating opportunities for participation and implementing decisions'

There has been a long tradition of job satisfaction studies of academic librarians in the United States. In a landmark study in the 1970s, Marchant identified participative management style as the strongest predictor of librarians' job satisfaction.[54] These findings were supported by Bengtson and Shields.[55] Mirfakhrai found higher overall levels of satisfaction in small-size university libraries compared with larger ones.[56] Horenstein surveyed a random sample of 300 universities and colleges in the United States with enrolments of 2000 or more students using a questionnaire designed by herself.[57] Her main focus was the relationship between faculty status/rank and job satisfaction. She found that librarians with faculty status and rank reported higher levels of overall satisfaction: 'Librarians who feel more involved, consulted, informed, and more in control are more satisfied. The key predictors of job satisfaction of academic librarians are perception of participation, salary, and possession of academic rank.'

An amended version of Horenstein's survey was used by Leckie and Brett in a study of Canadian university librarians.[58] The results, published in 1997, did not find significant differences in satisfaction levels between academic status librarians and other librarians, but in comparing the two studies, Leckie and Brett did discover great similarities with Horenstein in those aspects of librarians' work which brought most satisfaction:

> Intrinsic measures (such as relationship with users, opportunities for challenge, independence, judgment) were ranked in the top half, whereas extrinsic measures (such as management style, promotion opportunities, relationship with adminis-

61

tration) fell in the bottom half, with a few exceptions. This distribution is even more startling in Horenstein's data, where the midpoint item on working conditions marks a turning point; items ranked above it are intrinsic measures and those below it are extrinsic. This distribution suggests that academic librarians are most satisfied with the traditional elements of librarianship as a profession (such as service, working with users, independence of work, challenge) and less satisfied with the peculiarities of working in an academic environment.

In 1998, van Reenan compared the results of job satisfaction studies of librarians with those of other workers, and concluded that, although satisfaction rates were high for library workers, 'the average U.S. worker expressed a 10.6 percent higher overall job satisfaction rate than the highest rate for library workers from any of the studies.'[59] One reason he singled out was the stratification of library positions and the narrow scope of some jobs especially in technical and processing areas.

SUPPORT STAFF

The Russell survey of non-professional library staff, both part-time and full-time, in six British academic and public libraries received replies from 341 (or 60 per cent) of the library staff contacted.[60] The Minnesota Job Satisfaction Questionnaire was modified in two ways. The dimensions of social status and moral values as constituents of job satisfaction were omitted as 'not relevant to the context of this study', and eight other dimensions were added: career prospects, communication, comparison of self with professional librarians, education utilization, physical demands of job, supervision–participation, task completion and training. These, when added to the original Minnesota dimensions of job satisfaction – ability utilization, achievement, activity, authority, company policies, company practices, co-workers, creativity, independence, pay, promotion, recognition, responsibility, security, social service, supervision, variety and working conditions – provided a total of 26 dimensions. They were tested by asking the library assistants to tick on a Likert scale of 1 to 5 their degree of satisfaction with various aspects of their job representing the Minnesota dimensions.

Russell's findings were interesting both in relation to the methodological problems of investigating job satisfaction and in terms of the results. A direct question about job satisfaction revealed that 85 per cent of non-professionals were satisfied or very satisfied, but when these results were tested by asking direct questions, he found that 'the percentage dissatisfied may be somewhere between 30% and 40%'. The causes of their dissatisfaction were the nature of the supervision received, and lack of freedom of action in the performance of their duties. The most unsatisfactory aspects of their jobs were 'library policies', particularly their promotion and career prospects, their treatment by library management, and their relationship with professional staff. Sources of satisfaction centred on their actual duties and their co-workers. Thapisa's survey of full-time library assistants with at least two years' continuous experience in university libraries in England also found lack of promotional opportunities high on the list of causes of dissatisfaction.[61] The survey found that 68 per cent felt they were in dead-end jobs with no promotion prospects and 'nothing to work towards'. Very little was done to encourage library assistants to take up higher qualifications, leading to feelings of low esteem and unimportance. Similarly, Parmer and East, in a study of support staff in twelve Ohio academic libraries, found that the block to promotion for those without an MLS degree was a cause of resentment and dissatisfaction,[62] and Goulding's survey of public library support staff also found that limitations on promotion opportunities was a major gripe.[63] According to Russell, the greatest source of dissatisfaction was pay – 'the most prevalent feeling was that library assistants should be paid more since they were the ones that kept the library running', and it certainly was not considered adequate for young single people or people who were just married or setting up a new home. Banks, who carried out experiments with student assistants in academic libraries, supports the view that pay is the most important motivator for casual workers who generally do not work full-time, have only a partial psychological commitment to the organization and have no career notions.[64] She found that a pay increase across the board rather than pay tied to goals was the most effective motivator.

The alleviation of the problems experienced by para-professional staff in libraries – particularly those in academic libraries and those who work in technical services, for these are the most dissatisfied categories – would involve a multidimensional strategy. Recruitment policies are the starting point, and should begin with job analysis and job design, and the appointment of staff who can carry out those duties effectively. A particular problem has been the employment of overqualified people in library assistant posts. This is more likely at times when jobs are scarce and where applicants believe that contact with users will provide compensatory rewards. Goulding's interviews with graduate library assistants, who had chosen library work as a stopgap, found that the routine work was not stretching them, though it was work that had to be done.[65] Our own experience has been that success is possible for a period if the routine nature of the job and lack of promotion prospects are forcefully stated and the particular circumstances and personality of the applicant are taken into consideration. Once library assistants are in their jobs, it is of paramount importance that their contributions are appreciated: 'What I am trying to say is, although my job may be routine it is how I make my living and I need to be appreciated. All it needs is for someone to notice something I have done and the whole attitude to my work changes.'[66] This view is supported by Miletich, who speaks out on behalf of the non-professional – 'your front line of defense against time-robbers and energy-wasters' – compared with professionals, whom he considers as often transients on the look-out for better pay, more responsibility, always scanning the ads in various professional journals.[67]

Many libraries have been restructuring over the last decade, and this has often meant giving more of the clerical and administrative routines to non-professionals, and increasing the job satisfaction for professionals as well, by ensuring that a higher proportion of their work content is actually professional and therefore appropriate to the graduate profession that we have become. By 'actually professional', we mean a role in which:

> library needs are identified, problems are analysed, goals are set, and original and creative solutions are formulated for them, integrating theory into practice, and planning, organizing, communicating and administering successful programs of service to users of the library's materials and services.[68]

Often, the incentive for restructuring comes from outside financial considerations (one professional salary equals three non-professional salaries, and reducing the number of middle managers creates a cheaper, flatter structure) or for technological reasons, which not only alters non-professional jobs, but deskills, for example, cataloguing posts, which were once the preserve of graduate librarians but now only require trained non-professionals. It is an opportunity to reassess the tasks that make up jobs, and to analyse the responsibilities carried by jobs.

PRACTICAL APPLICATIONS OF MOTIVATION THEORIES IN LIBRARIES

With these findings in mind, Table 2.1 summarizes the most commonly stated sources of satisfaction and dissatisfaction when librarians are asked about their work. Note that the survey findings all identify 'intrinsic factors' (related to the content of the job) and 'extrinsic factors' (related to the context of the job) as important to people at work. The purpose of listing staff needs in this oversimplified way is to provide those involved in managing staff with a basic toolkit for taking action along the lines suggested in Table 2.2. Characteristics related to the job itself which are satisfying are variety, involvement with users, and the service ethic (thus, readers' services work is on the whole preferred to technical services work). 'Ability utilization' is very important, particularly at the beginning professional level, when many newly qualified

Table 2.1 What motivates librarians? Summary of satisfaction and dissatisfaction in library work

	Job content (intrinsic factors)	Job context (extrinsic factors)

S A T I S F Y I N G	Variety
	Involvement with users
	Satisfaction with books/
	    library materials
	Service orientation
	Personal/professional
	    growth
	Intellectual satisfaction/use
	    of professional expertise
	Ability utilization
	Empowerment
		Colleagues
		Atmosphere/work climate
		Supervision
		Participative management

D I S S A T I S F Y I N G	Routine
	Physical demands
		Management and
		    organization (staffing
		    structures, supervision)
		Working conditions (physical
		    aspects, unsocial hours
		    of work)
		Status
		Undermanning
		Pressure of work
		Salary
		Career prospects/security

Interaction needs of librarians at work

To give and receive recognition for work done
To feel a sense of achievement
To have opportunities for feedback about their work
To experience positive supervision ('affective' as well as task-oriented)
To identify with the system through a work group or team
To participate in decision-making about their own work and related areas

librarians are deployed, it seems, below their capabilities. The job content may also determine the sense of achievement, though that is a complex area where acknowledgement by one's supervisor may also be a factor, as may the overall management climate. Subject specialists, for example, have been under pressure as libraries try to introduce more flexibility. Walton et al. note how most participants at an IMPEL (IMpact on People of Electronic Libraries) seminar argued that subject specialists had a limited future.[69] Autonomy, a sense of responsibility and creativity or a chance to take initiatives are higher-level

Table 2.2 Staff needs and management action

	Staff needs	Action
Job content	Variety	Job rotation, job exchange, job enlargement
	Reducing routine	Systems analysis, organization and methods (O & M), automation
	Involvement with users	Job rotation (e.g. between technical and readers' services)
		Modify staffing structure, to give more staff contact with users
	Use of professional expertise/intellectual satisfaction	Increase delegation, job enrichment, assign projects to individuals/working parties
		Empower individuals to make decisions at lower levels
	Personal/professional growth	Involve staff in developing their own area of work (projects to be achieved in a term or year), and reporting on their progress
		Appraisal (formal or informal) and follow-up (e.g. training)
		Supportive staff structures, e.g. attention paid to teams, work groups, working parties, to improve their effectiveness, and quality of the group process
		Quality circles (informal groups of interested staff reading and running seminars on relevant issues/current problems)
		Networking (encouraging staff to develop contacts inside and outside the library with key people in their specialisms)
Job context	Quality of supervision	Coaching skills, positive and negative feedback, task-centred and people-centred approaches (See Chapter 8)
	Communication styles and structures	Up/down only, or two-way? Lateral communications, matrix approaches. Written or face-to-face. Diagnose failures of communication to pin-point bottlenecks/authoritarian supervisors
	Career prospects diminished for older staff	In periods of low mobility, match jobs to individuals in restructuring caused by fewer posts or automation. Include staff in task groups, and include senior staff in training

sources of job satisfaction, which are partly intrinsic to the job, but partly determined by the supervisory structures and styles.

Sources of satisfaction related to the work environment or job context are colleagues (more important in one's first professional post) and the supervisory climate, or general atmosphere or overall work climate. This may be analysed into a number of significant factors, which cannot be entirely separated from intrinsic factors of a job, especially for staff who are engaged in any supervisory work and are therefore themselves contributing to, as well as being on the receiving end of, the supervisory climate. It has been observed that librarians filling in questionnaires on job satisfaction have a tendency to attribute unsatisfactory aspects of their work to other people, and to give themselves credit for the satisfactory aspects. It is therefore important to see oneself as a contributory factor, at least, to the supervisory climate, and to ask whether one is a democratic manager who regularly seeks the views of one's staff, or only insists that one's own supervisor be democratic. This seemed to be widely wanted, according to the CLAIM survey of 1982, which found 80 per cent of the respondents expressing a preference for democratic managers.[70] It is noteworthy that staff could have confidence in and trust their managers while at the same time being dissatisfied by the quality and quantity of consultation and communication.

Intrinsic sources of dissatisfaction are the amount of dull routine work in librarianship and, for beginning librarians especially, lack of information to be able to carry out a job. This is related to extrinsic factors, since it connects with complaints that training and induction are poor, and that brings in management and the supervisory climate as a main area of dissatisfaction, highlighted in all the surveys. The connections between intrinsic and extrinsic factors are graphically shown by the CLAIM survey, which points out that staff's ability to derive intrinsic satisfaction from their job depends upon the resources and training available to them from management. It is significant, in a time of recession, that the 1988 cohort, surveyed in 1991, placed 'resources available' high on their list of least satisfactory aspects of their jobs.[71] Furthermore, ability to get satisfaction from achievement is restricted by 'predetermined work flows' in many lower-level jobs. Only as staff are promoted to higher levels do they begin to have any real flexibility in how they interpret their work, use their expertise, and set their own performance standards. Similar complaints were made in the USA by respondents in van Reenan's study, in which 40 per cent of library workers felt they were prevented from doing their best and using their full potential at work – a higher percentage than other workers, who scored 20 per cent.[72]

Communication between staff at different levels – senior, middle and junior, central or site – and between professionals and non-professionals leaves much to be desired, according to the job satisfaction surveys. Stewart makes some recommendations in this area:

> Professionally experienced staff should make others aware of the overall objectives of the library and should draw their attention to proposed changes and development, and better still involve them in discussing changes; they should praise and compliment employees as well as suggesting improvements in performance.[73]

Hirst, in his description of changes in the management of Shropshire Information and Community Services, provides a practical example of what can be done by highlighting the effort put into improving communication:

> An improved fortnightly staff newsletter, a series of roadshows across the county, giving staff an opportunity to question me about progress, and a more systematic approach to the circulation of routine information. Specifically on budget issues, our Chair has taken part in a series of staff briefings in recent years which have been especially welcomed.[74]

With the advent of electronic information a potential source of dissatisfaction has arisen – the IMPEL project reported on the frequency with which feelings of 'control' or 'loss of control' occurred:

> Library and information staff fear losing control to the computer center, to remote users, to expert academics, to skilled paraprofessionals. They fear loss of subject knowledge and expertise. They spend much time teaching but most have no teaching qualification. This sense of loss affects librarians most acutely, their profession having been based on concepts of organization and control.[75]

Although there is the fear of loss of control, library workers interviewed in the IMPEL project overwhelmingly agreed that the use of electronic information increased their job satisfaction. The work was felt to be more interesting, despite increased workloads: 'Electronic information was felt to give students a better learning experience; they were also quick to provide feedback. Many library staff enjoyed being at the forefront of information provision; one remarked that the sheer unpredictability of the electronic environment led to satisfaction.'[76]

STRATEGIES FOR INCREASING JOB SATISFACTION

Since there is a large proportion of routine work in libraries, both at professional and non-professional staff levels, it is important to build in variety, which all the surveys indicate is much appreciated by library workers. Job rotation may be used particularly to alleviate boredom in the humblest jobs – technical services routines or counter work. There are various patterns of rotation used in libraries, from daily to weekly, monthly or annually. In the USA, it is becoming fairly common for headships of libraries or library schools to rotate on an annual or three-year basis. This has seldom happened in the UK, in spite of models in the academic world. Indeed, there has been reluctance among professional librarians to become involved in job rotation when it is their own job that is under consideration. There are both sound and unsound reasons for this. Some argue that they have developed specialisms and knowledge of user communities, which would be wasted if they moved around at two-year or three-year intervals and that stability is important when other changes are being made. Others, it seems, are reluctant to reveal how they actually spend their time. In threatening circumstances of recession and change, staff may develop protective ploys to conceal rather than reveal what they do:

> We don't admit we have spare time on our hands in case something happens. You'd be a fool to admit you had spare time on your hands, but, on the other hand, you want something to do.[77]

As the writer of that research report indicates, such attitudes militate against the introduction of job rotation or exchange schemes within a library. Konn therefore goes on to recommend that when internal job exchange schemes are introduced, they 'need to include all members of staff without exception in order to avoid being regarded as a personal threat to particular individuals'. If this proves too difficult in practice, there is a more limited strategy which has been tried in Sheffield Public Libraries:

> In Sheffield we have developed the concept of training posts for professional staff. These are generally senior assistants' posts in specialist departments and are filled for a maximum of two years. This controlled turnover together with natural wastage is usually sufficient to allow anyone wishing to broaden their experience to transfer to a different kind of work within a reasonable period of time.[78]

The objective of job rotation is not only to increase job satisfaction for the staff, but also to give them a wider knowledge of the library system, or at least of what goes on elsewhere in their own section, which can improve the quality of the operation. At senior levels, it has been our experience that good-quality staff who have changed posts at the same level are better able to effect desirable changes than staff new to the system, because they are already aware of the library's aims and practices. However, job rotation which merely involves an increase in the variety of tasks undertaken is job 'enlargement' rather than 'enrichment', and at lower levels can be seen as inflicting a number of boring tasks instead of only one.

A more satisfying strategy which can be introduced is to add to people's jobs tasks which are of a more interesting or demanding kind, so that they have a mix of humdrum routines and a certain amount of responsibility, or at least the satisfaction of seeing a task through and getting recognition from colleagues or users for the end result. This is known as job enrichment. It has been introduced in libraries mainly through staff restructuring schemes, though it can also be introduced by concerned supervisors for their own sections, by sharing out the work to take account of job enrichment strategies. The most common examples of job enrichment are subject specialization structures in academic libraries, where staff are given responsibility for a particular area, and within that have the satisfaction of carrying out a variety of work, using their own initiative and specialist knowledge, and getting feedback from a known user group of academic staff and students. The problem is that as staff cuts take place, the job of the subject specialist may be impoverished rather than enriched, because it becomes necessary to spread the load of more procedural and administrative work, and they have to take their share, thus reducing the time they have for the more 'enriched' and rewarding side of subject specialization – user education, readers' advisory work, collection development.

In public libraries, team staffing structures are an indication of job enrichment strategies at work, though their degree of success has varied considerably. The intention is to give professional staff a higher proportion of challenging work, by taking them out of their solely branch library concerns, and putting them with other professionals for the purposes of developing projects to make the services more effective over the whole area covered by the team. When it works well, staff jobs are certainly enriched. They spend some time out in the community making contacts with other information providers and with community groups and opinion leaders. They use this 'community profile' insight to develop relevant community information services, or children's activities like story hours, or support services for identifiable disadvantaged groups. They get feedback on their efforts by monitoring the take-up of their services, and gauging the value of their projects to the community. This approach only seems to work well when staff are 'self-starting' and support the other members of the team. It requires a certain capacity for self-development, so that ideas are forthcoming and action taken as a result of team deliberations. As with subject specialization, the team approach can lead to job impoverishment rather than enrichment if it goes badly. Staff may miss the secure daily routines of branch librarianship, including the supervision of staff and the contacts with a known clientele of local users. Failure to work with others as a project-oriented team may be another source of dissatisfaction, giving the impression that team meetings are a waste of time, and that nothing significant ever comes out of them. These symptoms make a clear case for staff development in the form of team skills and self-appraisal techniques based on agreed targets.

The responsibility of individual supervisors to provide job enrichment for their own staff is also fraught with problems. Supervisors may be exclusively task-oriented rather than people-oriented, and they may have an underdeveloped understanding of staff management strategies. Proctor observes that the success of job enrichment depends on:

> supervisors being willing and able to delegate authority as well as responsibility. Many are over possessive or over prescriptive. Some lack the imagination to see how a job can be enriched and lose sight of the priorities in a surfeit of clerical routines.[79]

Techniques which may lead to job enrichment include more genuine delegation by supervisors, a project or 'mission-oriented' approach to work (agreed projects, and timetables for their achievement), and staff development strategies of an organic kind. Dutton provides a good example of the latter in his report on a staff development scheme at ICI which included the library staff in a company-wide application of Herzberg's motivators:

> To encourage the widest sharing of experience, in addition to homogeneous work groups, representative groups comprising staff of different grade levels and in different disciplines explored common problems. As anticipated, hygiene factors predominated initially, but a constructive approach to these moved attention to motivational factors. Thus individual staff from the most junior began to analyse and discuss their individual jobs, in the light of library operations; to single out and express the most important elements and existing shortcomings, and to suggest methods for improvement. A number of such operations, previously spread out over several individuals, were reconstituted and total responsibility allotted to one person.[80]

PROBLEMS IN THE APPLICATION OF MOTIVATION THEORIES AND STRATEGIES

CULTURAL BIAS

Much of the research into motivation originated in the USA, and the results may not be transferable to other countries. It may be that the 'achievement ethic' has not been as highly developed in Britain, for example, particularly as Britain declines in power, prestige and prosperity relative to other advanced industrial countries. In recent years, as some prosperity has returned, unemployment levels have fallen, the British work longer hours and stress levels increase, the 'achievement ethic' has enjoyed a revival. Certainly, increased demands for accountability reinforced by publicly available performance measurements have placed greater emphasis on achievement.

The 1960s and 1970s did witness the growth of an alternative stance in the professions. This may be defined as a socially committed viewpoint, which asks

71

the question, 'What can I do in my profession to help the disadvantaged and deprived?' rather than 'Where am I going in my professional career?' In public librarianship especially, this has been an important impetus behind the growth of the 'welfare librarianship' concept, which starts with a 'commitment to reducing inequalities in knowledge and information deriving from a realisation of the structural rather than the residual nature of these inequalities' in our society:

> Relevant services ... would include community information, basic education and services for the unemployed and ethnic minorities. In general terms the library would take an active stance on issues such as racism and sexism, with stock selection policies being adjusted accordingly.[81]

In recent years, there has been a renewal of interest in the potential of the public library for tackling social exclusion. In 1998, for example, a study financed by the Library and Information Commission aimed to make recommendations about the kinds of strategies that public libraries need to adopt if they are to serve successfully excluded communities and social groups.[82]

A further problem which the human relations approach to motivation seems to provoke among British librarians is that it invites self-analysis, and this may be anathema, agony or sheer bad form. It is all very well for Americans to be articulate and open about their motivation, by charting their needs at work using, say, the Maslowian hierarchy. The British shy away from such self-exposure, or condemn it as airy-fairy theory (the concept of self-actualization, for instance), which runs counter to their stolid pragmatism. This means that researchers must be most careful to speak the language of their respondents, rather than assuming any acceptance or even familiarity with motivation theory. When concepts like 'self-actualization' and 'identity needs' are translated into everyday terms like 'a sense of achievement at work', 'using one's intellectual or professional capacities to the full' or 'acknowledgement of what you do by your supervisor', it becomes possible for the gap between theory and practice to be bridged.

The situation may improve as more interest is taken in library education and training for interpersonal skills (see Chapter 8), which inevitably gets librarians into the habit of analysing group process and gives them toolkits for doing so. There is also growing interest in the UK in transatlantic approaches to self-growth through group work. The American encounter movement, and the work of the therapist Carl Rogers,[83] have had an impact in approaches to education and training, as well as in the original area of counselling and psychiatry. However, there are clearly problems in transferring self-development and group development strategies from one culture to another. Motivation theories which have been based on studies in one country may not be transferable to other cultures.

Some interesting research has been carried out by Hofstede on the impact of different national cultures on people's attitudes to work.[84] His thesis is that organizations and management are culture-bound, and he based his findings on an investigation into the problems that multinational companies experience in transferring management styles and structures from one country to another. He identified four measures for determining significant cultural differences between countries, which need to be taken into account when assessing people's behaviour at work, and in understanding their motivation.

First, there is the *Power Distance Index*. When this is high, employees are used to close supervision and display deference to superiors. They prefer (perhaps only because they are subject to it) paternalistic structures and styles of management, and staff managers need to provide clear-cut guidelines and close supervision to satisfy the needs of their workers.

Allied to the Power Distance Index is the *Uncertainty Avoidance Index*, which measures the degree to which staff are at home with definite rules and regulations, and prefer to avoid taking any decisions of their own. They prefer security, provided again by paternalistic managers, who make it absolutely clear what has to be done and leave little to the initiative of their staff.

Hofstede's third index is a *Masculinity* rating, which rates countries on a masculinity–femininity axis. He construed 'masculine' cultures as those where women were less likely to be employed in technical and professional work, where there was less concern for the physical environment, higher traffic speeds, and where there were more road deaths, and so on. The more strongly masculine countries display tendencies at work towards individual achievement rather than group or team achievements, and there is correspondingly more work-related stress and emphasis on career aspirations. Women in this kind of culture have to be more assertive to break into the male-dominated higher echelons at work. By contrast, in the more 'feminine' countries, typically Scandinavia, professional women can afford to be less assertive, a sense of achievement is more likely to stem from working co-operatively with a team or group than from individual success, and there is less career pressure and job-related stress.

Hofstede's fourth index measures the degree of *Individualism* to be found in different cultures. Where this is low, for example in Japan and Latin America, satisfaction at work is derived from loyalty, or indeed favouritism, within family firms or paternalistic organizations. Where it is high, for example in Britain and the USA, the emphasis is on satisfaction gained by individual achievement and recognition, rather than submersion of individual effort to the greater glory of the organization.

Ouchi's Theory Z is based upon these cultural differences, following his analysis of Japanese productivity.[85] He believes that the Japanese approach to management offers valuable lessons. For the Japanese, everything important in life happens as a result of team work or collective effort, which conflicts with the American concept of individualism. The Japanese organizations also hold a holistic view of people, involving a concern for employees at work and outside work which stems from a rapid move from a feudal to an industrial system and the provision by companies of accommodation and welfare for workers. Type Z organizations, on the Japanese model, tend to have long-term employment and non-specialized career paths, and decision-making is a participative process. Broad concern is also shown for the welfare of employees, and informal rather than hierarchical relationships are emphasized.

In Hofstede's analysis, Britain and the USA score high on Individualism and Masculinity, low on Power Distance and Uncertainty Avoidance. The implications for staff motivation are that these cultures produce people capable of Maslowian achievement up to the highest level of self-actualization, even if many of them do not realize this potential, or at least not at work. However, the Maslowian hierarchy cannot be used meaningfully in trying to understand motivation in countries where the rating is low on Individualism and high on Power Distance and Uncertainty Avoidance, such as Islamic countries and Latin America.

Hofstede provides a helpful starting point for understanding the problems of cultural bias in motivation theories. However, he seems to beg some questions. Do staff 'prefer' a paternalistic style, for example, because it is the only one they know, and would they in fact 'prefer' a more open participative style if they were offered it and trained to benefit from it? Librarians from developing countries attending courses in the UK have expressed the need for such a shift in their own library management back home, but that may be only because they are influenced by the Anglo-American motivation models presented to them in seminars. When they tackle case studies, they tend to produce solutions which are relatively more authoritarian or paternalistic than those produced by English students, perhaps supporting Hofstede's views about cultural bias in management.

A further problem with inter-cultural comparisons is that they perforce have to make generalizations about each country, which conceal a vast range of different stances which comprise a national trend. Job satisfaction surveys in librarianship, for instance, reveal differences between young less experienced managers, who are more human relations-oriented, and older managers, who are more disposed to the scientific school of management. They also suggest job satisfaction is influenced by the kind of work done – technical services or readers' services – because that generates sources of satisfaction (or fails to, in technical services) derived from user contact and recognition of services successfully delivered. Again, it is suggested that satisfaction of employees is to a greater or lesser degree dependent on their supervisors' management strategies and styles.[86] The variables are seemingly endless, and the truth of the matter highly complex, since it apparently lies not in any one set of criteria for job satisfaction – based on a hierarchy of needs, or one's cultural background, or the management climate in one's library, or the nature of the task assigned. Rather, it lies in the inter-relationships between all these variables, which takes us back to the point made at the beginning of this chapter. Theories of motivation which emphasize 'process' rather than 'content' are more helpful and realistic, because they give due weight to the inter-relationship between variables, rather than leaving it at identifying variables, such as Maslow's hierarchy of individual's needs, or Likert's continuum of management styles, or Blake and Mouton's grid. In making use of 'content' theories to understand a particular situation, it is essential to consider their interaction with such variables as cultural background, state of development of technology, staffing structure, supervisory styles, and the level of sophistication of education and training.

CLOSED-SYSTEM APPROACH IN MOTIVATION THEORIES

Work is only one facet of a person's life, and individuals' responses to it are affected to a greater or lesser degree by other aspects, such as personal relationships, domestic circumstances, individual interests and leisure pursuits. Yet when reading some of the human relations school of motivation theories, one sometimes forms the impression that the work situation is a world in itself, a closed system not affected by the varying situations and stances of all the people who operate within it. It must be recognized that for a large number of people, the various levels of need – for self-identity and social recognition, for esteem or sense of achievement – are met by situations and activities outside work, correspondingly reducing their needs at work: 'Even when people earn the same salary, their personal spending practices, lifestyles, second incomes, outside activities, age value systems, debt, health and so forth can affect where their need levels are.'[87] In some cases, people deliberately take jobs which include few responsibilities because they have responsibilities outside work, whilst others decide to 'downshift', preferring to opt out by adopting a less lucrative but more satisfying lifestyle with what they perceive to be a better balance between business and personal life. It could be argued that the human relations school of management has a tendency to idealize the satisfactions to be gained from work, and that for many people the expectations they have about work remain low, often justifiably in terms of their past experiences of work. In times of economic recession, when the funding of public services is low and when choice of jobs, promotion

75

prospects and job mobility are diminished, many people, whether beginning librarians or those in posts where they are likely to remain till they retire, find their expectations lowered even further.

CONSENSUS OR CONFLICT IN THE WORKPLACE

Both the scientific school and the human relations school of management seem to imply a greater degree of consensus in the workplace than experience suggests is justified. Theorists of the Marxian school make the important point that conflict must be recognized. Motivation looks very different from the point of view of senior management, lower levels of staff, or the trade unions. Trade unionists are naturally sceptical about job enrichment schemes, because from their standpoint it may mean that management is getting more higher-level work done 'on the cheap'. Participative schemes often look very different to different levels of staff. Senior staff may think they are good communicators and are consulting staff regularly, and engaging in delegation. Seen from the level below, it may not look like that at all. Stewart's findings were that in British libraries in the early 1980s, 'consultation and communication at all levels and in all types of library organization appeared to be unsatisfactory'.[88] And Konn, in her survey of continuing education needs in academic libraries, found that:

> there were glaring contradictions between the image which top librarians wished to project, indeed thought they were projecting, and that perceived by their staffs. Individuals from this top group expressed concern for the welfare of their staff ... Yet ... members of staff could complain at the lack of practical manifestations of such concern, or point to the neglect of human matters in favour of procedures and machines.[89]

Another example of different perspectives occurs when supervisors are put under pressure to delegate more, and to give their subordinates more participation in decision-making. The pressure most often comes from above, when there is a new head librarian with a less authoritarian attitude than the predecessor. The supervisors may resent these efforts to change their approaches, and may find ways to keep up a superficial appearance of participative management (meetings are held and bits of paper are circulated), while in the eyes of their juniors they are actually undermining participation. Typically, such supervisors retain for themselves all the decisions that really matter, they only attend to their staff's views when they happen to coincide with their own, and they tend to ignore suggestions or initiatives from their staff which have not been sought by the supervisor. There are more extreme ploys, such as when the supervisor 'accidentally' leaves some important matters off an agenda, or makes the excuse that there was not enough time for consultation, so that the supervisor can make the decision on their own.

The associated problem stems from the supervisor who is willing to delegate and be participative, but does not know how, because of long-term working experiences in very hierarchical mechanistic libraries. Chapter 8 suggests ways in which supervisors may learn, and encourage their staff, to be more responsive and to share in the organization of the work, through delegation, coaching, self-appraisal and positive as well as negative feedback on their performance. McGregor's categorization of staff as Theory X – lazy, indifferent workers, at best passive, at worst resistant to the organization's needs, only moved by material rewards or punishments, with no intrinsic motivation – or Theory Y – people ready to assume responsibility, take initiatives, identify with the organization, satisfy higher level needs for recognition and achievement in the workplace – has been criticized for its naive assumptions. Is it really feasible to transform Theory X workers into Theory Y workers? How can delegation and participation be introduced in a library where staff have been rendered fairly passive and inert during a long régime of more authoritarian management? The management literature offers only limited prescriptions, because the solution will be long-term and organic, rather than instant and mechanistic. A strategy adopted in industry (Sears Roebuck) forces authoritarian managers to delegate more by giving them more staff to supervise, until the wider span of control *compels* the managers to delegate. Thus, they are 'got off people's backs', leaving staff more space to plan and organize their own work within the company's objectives. The authoritarian manager may also be circumvented by adopting matrix management approaches, so that staff are engaged in projects which require them to report to others besides their immediate line manager.

The organic long-term approaches are summarized in the right-hand column of Burns and Stalker's checklist (Figure 2.1). It should be noted, however, that an all-out participative approach is by no means a universal panacea to increase staff satisfaction and performance. In recent years, a note of cynicism has crept into the literature, and the problems of participative management have been revealed by library managers' own experience. First, it is very time-consuming because of the increased number of meetings, so time-management courses are now becoming necessary to get people through their meetings effectively. Second, it has been found that team structures and similar participative frameworks can turn out to be as authoritarian as those they replaced, because of how they are practised by staff who either do not agree with participative stances or do not know how to practise them. Third, staff attitudes are influential, not just their rational responses. Attitudes are a complex set of responses, the product of cultural influences from home, education and society at large, as well as the more immediate outcome of organizational experiences. They are much more difficult to change than knowledge or skills, so training very often confines itself to the latter. This may not get to the root of the matter. It has been found, too, that in libraries many managers are over-optimistic about their communication skills. Communication only exists when the message has been understood by the recipients, not when it has been transmitted by the sender. Until more effective communication is established, participative structures will invariably work at less than their full potential.

The problem of socialization also needs to be taken into account. When staff join a library, they are under heavy pressure to adopt its norms and values, or at least the norms and values of one section where they will mainly be working. The problem is that although human relations management is:

> ... inherently or culturally appealing ... people are forced to depart from it in their working lives ... It is possible that the classical and pluralist models are so pervasive and strongly held in the workplace that people who enter the work force with different perspectives find themselves being socialised into adopting these approaches.[90]

Bowey, however, goes on to point out that the type of organizational structure affects the organization's capacity for adapting to change. In periods of rapid change, it is particularly important for libraries to move towards a more participative structure. In her study of attitudes to change in organizations, Bowey's findings were that change is more difficult and stressful where staff see the organization as 'essentially hierarchical, with rules and regulations to be conformed with, and with authority vested in senior positions', compared with staff who see the organization as an 'interdependent system of parts, all making their contribution to the development and survival of the organization in its environment (characterized by threats and opportunities)'.

3 Human resource planning

One of the characteristics of management is that its terminology changes frequently, and most of these changes are said to reflect new perspectives and attitudes among managers and management writers. 'Human resource planning' is a term that has replaced 'manpower' and 'workforce planning'. Bramham states that there is a big difference, the main one being that workforce planning is concerned with numerical elements of forecasting whereas human resource planning is concerned with motivating people which includes most of the material in this book.[1] We have chosen this title for the chapter in the same way as many others have replaced 'personnel' with 'human resource', although we find the term rather impersonal and sympathize with the person who wrote on a wall of Leeds University: 'People not Personnel'. We are still of the opinion that workforce planning has something to offer library and information work, though much of the criticism levelled at it is justified.

Workforce planning covers a range of activities designed to ensure a satisfactory balance between the supply and demand for library and information workers in both qualitative and quantitative terms. It is concerned with what kind of people, and how many, are needed now and in the future to run library and information services at all levels from junior assistants through para-professionals to professionals. It is about assessing the environment and bringing together the data required to plan the direction the service needs to take if it is to achieve its goals. Thus, for example, it has been very much concerned with government policies at national and local levels, since it is central government and local authorities who ultimately determine what funding is made available for staff, irrespective of the 'ideal' establishment in public and academic libraries. Central government also influences the numbers of students recruited by library and information studies schools although this influence has declined with reductions in student grants.

At the national level, the 1980s witnessed a spate of reports on workforce planning for library and information work. These emanated from professional associations, the Library and Information Services Council (LISC) and the Transbinary Group on Librarianship and Information Studies which was set up by the Department of Education and Science in 1985 to carry out an overall 'review of likely demand (both in terms of numbers and expertise) for library and information professionals'.[2] In 1981, the Library Association Council set up a Working Party on Manpower Forecasting to consider the qualitative and quantitative aspects of manpower. The Futures Working Party was formed, and produced its *Final Report* in late 1985.[3] Although informative basic data was published in the report, it was acknowledged that it was almost impossible to make recommendations on 'the scope and future manpower requirements of the library and information community' because:

> (a) public sector provision of library and information services is heavily dependent on government policies and perceptions about public spending,
> (b) traditional private sector provision is highly sensitive to the prevailing financial climate and ... libraries and information units are (like research departments) often among the first to be axed in unfavourable economic circumstances,
> (c) it is difficult quickly and accurately to 'fine tune' numbers of students to actual or perceived requirements.[4]

These conclusions illustrate well the current views of management writers about the limitations of workforce planning. As the environment becomes increasingly turbulent, it has become 'impossible to forecast the demand for and supply of labour with any accuracy – a classic case of a brilliant theory being undermined by insurmountable problems when put into practice'.[5] The main techniques involve the extrapolation of past trends and predictions based on assumptions about the way organizations interact with their environments. They thus tend to rely on past experience to predict future developments. Whilst the 1960s and 1970s experienced a relatively stable environment for organizations, the world has now become far more unpredictable. The statistical techniques employed in workforce planning have also been received with hostility, partly because of ignorance of mathematical methods and because managers prefer to trust their own judgement. The current dearth of national workforce plans for library and information work suggests that they are not considered important in the present climate, and that those produced in the 1980s were of limited value, though the Information Services National Training Organisation (isNTO) has stated that it has embarked on Workforce Analysis as part of a state-of-the-sector project.[6]

EDUCATION AND TRAINING

The purpose of an NTO is to take a strategic overview of education and training in its sector in order to ensure appropriate skills supply and development, and it is in this area that there has been a good deal of concern about whether the present education of library and information professionals is appropriate in the current environment. Naturally, those who recruit staff for library and information work are very much concerned with the supply of candidates for posts. Again, the 1980s saw activity in this area with the Transbinary Group of the University Grants Committee and the National Advisory Body reviewing education for librarianship and information studies and reporting in 1986. Following this report, the British Library Research and Development Department identified research into the size, structure and nature of the workforce as a key priority area, and two projects were funded. The greatest concern now, however, appears to be whether the present staff and those recruited can cope with the new demands. A central concern is the ability to use information technology. Many libraries, especially in the education and special library sectors, are now being described as 'hybrid', since digital elements exist alongside the traditional library: 'Arguably, so far, the digital library elements have served to augment, rather than replace, conventional libraries.'[7] Indeed, completely digital libraries might be envisaged for the future, consisting both of resources 'originally created in digital format, such as electronic journals and data sets, and those originally non-digital such as manuscripts and print, that are subsequently digitised.'[8] A view held by several of the eight persons with an interest, or involvement in the hybrid library, interviewed by Oppenheim and Smithson was that the individual professional might require hybrid skills, located between those of the traditional librarian and the computer service officer, whilst focus groups interviewed as part of the BUILDER (Birmingham University Integrated Library Development and Electronic Resource) project at the University of Birmingham, one of five eLib hybrid library projects, voiced 'concern that staff did not have the diverse range of skills necessary for new roles in the hybrid library; roles which they identified as intermediary, trainer, and in quality assurance'.[9]

SKILLS

In addition to information technology skills, other abilities are increasingly needed if librarians and information workers are to be effective. Pantry has provided a list with which we are in agreement: oral communication skills, meetings skills, interpersonal skills, writing skills, time management skills, management skills, project management skills, knowledge management skills, marketing and publicity skills, and the skill of being able to work alone or in a team.[10] Information technology has emphasized these skills and re-focused some of them. For example, writing skills include writing for Websites and knowledge management is concerned with 'knowing what is where and with whom! At the same time possessing information and technology skills to organise, manage, produce and maintain information systems.'[11] These skills can be closely matched with the essential qualities identified by library and information employers in research carried out for the British Library Research and Innovation Centre published in 1999.[12] The top five qualities were ability to accept pressure, flexibility and ability to respond to change, ability to deal with a range of users, written communication skills and inquisitiveness, whilst those found most lacking were commitment to organizational goals, friendliness, ability to accept pressure, reliability and energy. The conclusion of the research is that the 'typical' submissive, passive, self-abasing librarian is the very opposite of the personality required. In similar vein, Abell and Chapman note the 'unwelcome' findings from different research projects which perceive information workers as lacking business knowledge and an understanding of the interplay between information and organisational objectives, having poor team and leadership skills and lacking management skills.[13] Kinnell has also taken this view when devising a new MBA course for library and information professionals who are 'now facing more challenges than ever before both to anticipate and satisfy customer expectations, whilst balancing these against static or dwindling resources' so that they need to be 'managers, as well as information professionals.'[14]

Assessing the particular needs of public libraries, Pluse has voiced a number of human resource concerns:

- Are the most appropriate people being attracted into public library and information work?
- Is education and training for the sector what it should be?
- Are the more aspirant members of the public library community at a disadvantage in seeking higher posts within local authorities?[15]

Pluse's fears have been confirmed to a large extent by the finding of the Public Library Workforce Study, completed in 2000, which goes as far as to describe the present situation as 'a personnel timebomb that is slowly ticking away' since the quality of recruits and the ability of public libraries to retain quality staff are matters of real concern especially with the opportunities provided for them by the support of central government.[16]

FLEXIBILITY

A common theme among contemporary management writers is the need, in a rapidly changing environment, for flexibility in the workforce. In reporting their own research, Goulding and Kerslake highlight the fact that little had been written about its use in the library and information sector though it has been employed extensively.[17] In the past the word 'flexibility' has been used rather loosely, but Bramham has identified eight forms of flexibility which help us to explain what we mean: skills, job, location, work pattern, department, numbers, wage cost and the attitude of employees towards flexibility.[18] Skills flexibility emphasizes staff's competences rather than simply knowledge, and depends largely upon training, whilst job flexibility depends on the lack of demarcations which prevent staff from using their skills to the full. In industry, many of these barriers were due to trade union protectionism, which has not been so strong in library and information work, though professions like librarianship have practised their own sort of protectionism. Cataloguing, for example, has been an area in which older professionals have jealously guarded its secrets, perhaps because so much of their time at library school was spent practising the art. Our own experience has been that cataloguers have been reluctant to forgo this work, especially where difficult items were concerned. Shaughnessy, writing about restructuring at the University of Arizona Library, also experienced the way in which 'certain tasks which were once deemed to be of a professional nature are no longer so considered. Some librarians may perform them extremely well however, and may be reluctant to relinquish them to support staff or to paraprofessionals' but computerization and economic necessities have forced a change in attitudes in many libraries.[19] Professionals are assuming more important roles in planning and directing, whilst paraprofessionals take on tasks formerly assigned to professionals (see also Chapter 4, pp.102–3). A survey in the United States in the early 1990s found that 'fifty-one percent of all ARL [Association of Research Libraries] respondents regularly assign original descriptive cataloguing, and 36% assign both subject analysis and classification to paraprofessionals'.[20] This is a trend that is likely to continue as more bibliographic records become available through integrated library systems and vendor-supplied cataloguing services. Computerization has absorbed many routine tasks and caused previously non-routine tasks to become routine, as well as making it possible to combine tasks, necessitating a more flexible workforce:

> If book receipt and processing of payment to vendors as well as selection and review of the bibliographic record for the local catalog are merged as part of the same process, staff members will have more varied and flexible assignments if they are cross-trained to perform different tasks which also increase their knowledge and judgment in handling library materials.[21]

83

The changing roles of library assistants and paraprofessionals have necessitated a reassessment of their training and education requirements. The development of Scottish/National Vocational Qualifications (S/NVQs) in the Information and Library Sector from 1991, when the Lead Body was set up, and their introduction a few years later, has provided a nationally recognized route for paraprofessionals which is likely to follow the path of other sectors and become the standard non-professional qualification for librarians. A Level 4 qualification is now available, and could provide a route to professional status. Supporters of this path to professional recognition point out that although university graduates will have more theoretical knowledge, NVQ candidates will 'have practical experience and learning achieved by facing situations, making decisions and coping with the real results'.[22] The traditional view that library assistants should simply get on with their routine jobs and leave the thinking to the professionals has been challenged by those who 'recognise and accept that "support staff" might not just contribute to incremental improvements but actually inspire and drive radical change'.[23] Corrall relates how a new queuing system was inspired by an Aston University assistant's observation of retail outlets and how a special Quality Improvement Fund and Quality Team Meeting encouraged ideas from assistants.

LOCATION FLEXIBILITY

Most library and information services, such as educational institutions and public libraries, exist in locations closely tied to local communities. At senior management levels, the need for location flexibility is not an important consideration, but at levels just below, it is vital that staff accept relocations. Although they may not necessitate large geographical changes, staff often feel comfortable, sometimes too comfortable, in locations that they have occupied for long periods. It is our experience that staff often accept and appreciate a move once they have settled in. In the commercial world, with mergers and restructuring more prevalent, geographical mobility among staff at all levels is even more important.

WORK PATTERNS

Whereas a common perception of local government and Civil Service employees and those in education is that they try to concentrate work in as few days as possible and as few hours in the day, library and information services have tried to open during hours which can accommodate those who work during the day. With traditional working patterns changing, there is greater pressure on staff in many organizations to make themselves available for longer hours, especially with changes in trading laws. Whilst public libraries have found it difficult to respond, many academic libraries, particularly in higher education, have started to open at weekends, including Sundays, and later in the week-day evenings, including some twenty-four-hour opening. In order to do this, core staff have had to be flexible, at least initially, in setting it up and supervising, though many libraries will ultimately use special part-time staff employed specifically to provide services at weekends.

THE SHAMROCK ORGANIZATION

In order to achieve flexibility and reduce costs, many organizations have made considerable changes to their structures, either deliberately or by responding to pressures as they arose. Many now approximate to the pattern termed by Handy as a 'shamrock organization' with the first leaf representing core workers (the relatively small professional core), the second the contractual fringe of outside contractors and the third the part-time staff.[24] He also identified a fourth, the customer, who is now asked to perform some tasks such as self-service in a supermarket or drawing money from a cash machine. Most libraries offered self-service long before supermarkets. Self-issuing of materials and customer operated photocopying are now common features.

PROFESSIONAL CORE

As Handy points out, the professional core consists of essential people who 'own the organizational knowledge which distinguishes the organization from its counterparts. Lose them and you lose some of themselves.'[25] In the commercial world, these people are paid high salaries with fringe benefits, and are expected to work long hours. The latter is true of many librarians, but the salaries are rarely at premium rates.

FLEXIBLE WORKERS

Goulding and Kerslake have surveyed the use of staff employed on specified flexible working patterns in UK library and information services (permanent part-time, temporary part-time, job-share, homeworking, flexitime, temporary full-time, term-time only and annual hours contracts).[26] They found that there are flexible workers in all types of library at all levels of the organizational hierarchy, with the frequent exception of the most senior posts, in all departments. Only 13 per cent of the respondents said they employed only permanent full-time workers; 40 per cent of workers were in flexible posts – similar to the situation for the whole labour market.

The largest group of flexible workers were permanent part-timers (29 per cent of the whole workforce) followed by 4 per cent temporary part-timers, 3 per cent job share, and 2 per cent term-time only. All the organizations said that the use of flexible workers had increased over the last decade.

The most common reason given to Goulding and Kerslake for employing flexible workers was to manage variable workloads; the second most common was to ensure cover for weekend opening hours, and the third was to retain valued staff. In addition, they are used to cover for absences such as sickness and maternity leave and where there is uncertainty – for example, where organizational changes are taking place or where there are doubts about funding. The survey also found a very high level of satisfaction with flexible workers.

TEMPORARY WORKERS

Temporary part-time workers in the survey were considered less productive, less reliable, less committed, and had lower morale than full-time workers. Where possible, a casual staffing pool, often consisting of valued former staff whose domestic circumstances forced them to leave, is a useful source of good-quality temporary labour, though effort is needed to keep it up-to-date and, at the same time, to keep in touch with them. Handy, quite rightly, warns against treating temporary workers as casual labour, because if you do so, they are likely to respond casually. They should therefore be given training opportunities, rather than being denied them because there is no guarantee they would pay back the investment. Goulding and Kerslake's research into training flexible workers demonstrated that they did not have equal access to in-house and external training opportunities.[27] One manager interviewed in Goulding and Kerslake's initial survey of flexible working believed problems occurred because temporary workers probably wanted a full-time job and couldn't get one. Handy is likely to be more accurate when he says that:

> Organizations have to get used to the idea that not everyone wants to work for them all the time even if the jobs are available. The ways of the core cannot be and should not be the ways of the flexible labour force, for while some may hanker after fulltime lifetime jobs, many will not.[28]

STUDENT WORKERS

For academic libraries, students provide an easily accessible pool of potential workers, and many make use of them, especially to perform routine tasks such as shelving. In the United States, in places where there are severe personnel shortages:

> Student assistants are now being utilised to perform many high level functions and tasks that once were relegated only to staff or librarians. The use of student assistants to perform major public service jobs, such as reference and information assistance, and perform various jobs related to automation is becoming prevalent in academic libraries.[29]

Kenney and Painter give lots of valuable practical advice about orientation and training of student workers. Their experience is that this attention can help overcome problems of high turnover and the consequences of students' inevitable commitment to the demands of their courses, especially at times of assessment.

A source of temporary workers we have used over many years is that of graduate trainees. At one time, Manchester Metropolitan University Library employed as many as thirty on one-year contracts. The intention was to recruit students due to graduate who wished to study for postgraduate qualifications in library and information studies following the one year's work experience usually demanded by the Schools of Library and Information Studies. The quality of the recruits varied, with many good graduates eventually obtaining full-time posts in libraries, not infrequently in the library at which they had trained, and performing well. Apart from the amount of training required, the most time-consuming problem has been that of recruitment and selection. So far, only a handful of public libraries operate graduate trainee schemes. *The Public Library Workforce Study* favours a national system of studentships to attract the best graduates.[30]

VOLUNTEERS

Employment of volunteers has become fashionable. We are used to seeing them in charity shops, hospitals, organizing meals-on-wheels and so on. The government promised £120m for volunteers in public services to be spent in three years from April 2001. Research into the use of volunteers in public libraries completed in 2000 found that 85 English public libraries outside London were making use of volunteers, but few had a well-thought out policy.[31] The researchers, Cookman and Streatfield, believe that 'the policy

Volunteer Policy and Code of Practice

1. The purpose of this policy is to formally recognise the contribution that volunteers can make to the Library Service, and to provide a formal framework for their management.

2. The use of volunteers should be a mutually beneficial experience for all parties concerned. The benefits for the organisation include:
    ◊ Increased involvement with the community
    ◊ Access to new and different perspectives and a greater awareness of community views.
    ◊ Staff able to achieve better results for existing activities by having additional targeted support

3. The benefits for the volunteers include:
    ◊ An opportunity to be active and involved
    ◊ An opportunity to contribute ideas
    ◊ Develop and learn new skills
    ◊ Acquire and extend knowledge

4. A volunteer is an individual who chooses to undertake work, under supervision, on behalf of the Library Service, but for which they are not paid.

5. The Occupational Health and Safety Act 1991 requires the Council to take into consideration the safety, welfare and health of volunteers undertaking approved activities. The Council has a Duty of Care for its volunteers in accordance with this act, and are required to ensure that the guidelines of the OH & S Act are met for volunteers. Volunteers, once formally recruited, are covered by insurance for any accidental injury that may be incurred whilst carrying out duties on behalf of the Library Service.

6. Volunteers will be advertised for, recruited and managed in accordance with the Council's Equal Opportunities Policy. Volunteers must be over the age of 16.

7. The work volunteers undertake will extend and complement the work of paid staff. Voluntary personnel will not replace or decrease the work of paid staff.

8. All volunteers will be required to apply for a particular work area and will be required to fill in the standard application form and submit to an interview. References may be required. Successful candidates' details will be held confidentially, under the same principles as apply to the personal details of paid staff.

9. Rights and Responsibilities

    Volunteers have the right:
    ◊ To be clear about the extent of their remit, particularly in relation to paid staff.
    ◊ To information and details about the work they are undertaking, and the significance of that work

Figure 3.1   Volunteer policy and code of practice – Borough of Richmond upon Thames

88

◊ To regular one-to-one sessions with their supervisor to discuss their work
◊ To training which enables the volunteers to carry out the required tasks
◊ To claim out-of-pocket expenses in carrying out voluntary work (excluding fares to and from the Library).
◊ To say no if the volunteer is asked to undertake work outside the remit of their post
◊ To recognition and thanks, whether this be a verbal expression of appreciation, or a formal letter of reference for other work.
◊ To be entitled to respect, support and fair treatment from colleagues whether paid or unpaid.
◊ To participate in the decision making process relevant to their area of involvement.

10. Staff have the right to expect of the volunteer:
◊ A definite commitment in terms of time and attendance
◊ That all duties asked of volunteers will be undertaken in a responsible, punctual, dependable, conscientious and courteous manner
◊ To act as part of a team
◊ To observe the standards of discretion, ethics and customer care expected of paid employees.
◊ To observe the limitations on the activities permitted to volunteers (for example not having access to Galaxy 2000, the libraries' computer system)

11. Volunteers are expected to respect confidentiality at all times particularly with respect to personnel issues whether related to paid staff or other volunteers

12. Volunteers will be required to sign in and out of their workplace. The register will enable staff to keep a record of which volunteers have been present and when. As volunteers may be working away from public areas it is essential that staff know when they are on the premises.

13. Volunteers are covered by insurance for any accidental injury that may be incurred on Library premises whilst carrying out their voluntary work; Volunteers using their own car to deliver services for the housebound are required to inform their insurance company of this fact.

14. Volunteers are entitled to claim out-of-pocket expenses if incurred as a result of their volunteering activities. This does not include fares to and from the Library.

15. Staff are encouraged to inform their line manager of any problems experienced whilst working with volunteers. Volunteers experiencing problems should in the first instance speak to the Library Administrator of the Library at which they operate. If the situation remains unresolved they may refer to the Team manager for the relevant area.

16. Volunteers should give one weeks notice in writing that they wish to withdraw their services. Volunteers may be given one weeks notice that their services are no longer required. In the event of a breach of the Code of Practice the Library Service reserve the right, after appropriate investigation of the circumstances, to require a volunteer to give up their post immediately.

Figure 3.1 concluded

should say what the authority thinks about using volunteers, as a signal to staff about how they will be used and to provide recognition of their value'. There is bound to be some anxiety about volunteers who may seem to be depriving others of paid jobs, so it is necessary for staff to work through these problems through discussion of the policy. Volunteers need to be managed like other staff, and therefore should be given support and training, and should be integrated into teams of workers as far as possible. Their work should be appraised and evaluated, as they will have an impact on users and costs are involved. The worst scenario would be to employ volunteers who do their own thing with little supervision. Cookman and Streatfield ask that library managers look more proactively at volunteering: 'Options such as support for library users in exploiting ICT, leading and creating reading groups, and getting younger and older people involved with libraries offer possibilities for engaging with new types of volunteers or using existing volunteers in new ways.' Richmond upon Thames Libraries have a well-thought out policy on the use of volunteers (Figure 3.1).

JOB-SHARING

Although job-sharing has been around for some time, it has not been universally popular with managers. The increase in staff numbers can create communication and span of control problems, which can, of course, be the case for any part-time workers. Our experience has been that two job-sharers who are known to be valuable members of staff can contribute more than many full-time equivalents. They bring enthusiasm and commitment to the job, and are not worn out at the end of the week. For job-sharing to work, sharers have to trust each other and have the same overall level of professional commitment to the work.[32] Where this is so, they are likely to be reasonably flexible, filling in for each other where needs dictate, and organizing the handover of tasks professionally. Most job-sharing in libraries is undertaken by women. In the past, organizations had assumed 'that career-oriented employees will devote (sell) the majority of their time during their working years to the organization, while women's biological cycles demand major allocations of time during that same life-stage to child-bearing and child-rearing'.[33] Skills shortages are changing this view, as well as the desire of women to continue to keep working at least some of the time. Flexible measures are being taken by women to enable them to continue working, supported by changes in attitudes towards child-rearing and the age of child-bearing.

HOMEWORKING

Goulding and Kerslake found only four homeworkers in the 475 organizations responding to their survey,[34] although it is claimed that working partly at home and partly in an office will become much more popular as 'the growth of local computer power, falling costs and ever more sophisticated telecommunications networks have made the home, or remote office a feasible alternative for individuals and organizations'.[35] Lett sees the development, for example, of business information services and academic institutions' electronic campuses, providing teleworking jobs from home in the future.[36] Remote working will extend flexibility to space, offering organizations and workers more choice and control over location. Not everyone is suited to homeworking, so selection of the right people is essential. They need to be self-motivated, to possess good communication skills, and to be trustworthy, self-disciplined and able to cope with lack of social contact. Their performance record must be good, and they must be technically competent, as opportunities to learn from colleagues will be limited.

CONTRACT WORKERS

Searching for more flexibility and cost-effectiveness in their key resource – staff – many organizations are exploring new ways of getting work done. Many of these involve people working on contract, on or off site, as consultants or sub-contractors or on temporary assignments.[37] Outside contractors carry out work which could be done by someone else other than in-house staff, often specialists who should, in theory, be able to do it for less cost than it would be in-house. In local government, contracting out has become a normal feature. In many libraries, staff not employed by the library carry out much of the cataloguing and book preparation, whilst Brent has gone further, and may well be followed by other local authorities, in contracting out the provision of information technology in order to deliver the range of new services for the People's Network.[38]

Managing peripheral staff brings with it particular problems which Lawes has divided into three categories – finding the right people, communication and performance management, and development and training.[39] In some cases, the sub-contracted workforce will not be integrated with the existing workforce, though it is more usual for them to be integrated in some way. Lawes considers the most worrying problem to be organizational commitment, which, if accompanied by a different value set and attitude to service, may well cause a manager problems. Existing staff have to be prepared to work with contract workers. Time spent introducing contract workers to the organization and its aims will help to engender commitment. Opportunities should also be taken to involve them in organizational events and meetings. Once employed, there needs to be a monitoring system to assess performance using performance indicators, report mechanisms and an appraisal scheme. This book is based on the view that such features are a necessity for all staff, but especially so for contract workers, as their previous performance may be unknown. The library manager will become familiar with agencies that provide contract workers, and will be able to assess their abilities to supply effective staff.

HUMAN RESOURCE PLANNING FOR THE INDIVIDUAL LIBRARY

As the earlier part of this chapter indicated, there is a good deal of controversy about the importance of human resource planning/workforce planning as practised in the 1970s and 1980s. Our view is that it can be a useful tool for the manager so long as its limitations in a more turbulent environment are appreciated. Figure 3.2 summarizes the stages necessary in drawing up a human resources plan for an individual library. It will be seen that the basic aim is to create a balance between supply and demand in both quantitative and qualitative terms. The supply side of the formula involves collecting accurate information on the existing jobs and expertise of the people doing them, then calculating likely wastage rates over the period under review, say over five years, though the longer the period the more inaccurate the forecast is likely to be. The demand side of the formula concerns making a realistic assessment of staffing needs, taking account of existing services, new projects and necessary cuts. The final plan brings together supply and demand factors, and is often incorporated into proposals for restructuring and/or services, which take account of ways to improve performance and provide staff with greater job satisfaction. The main stages of workforce planning are shown below.

ANALYSIS OF EXISTING STAFF AND THEIR JOBS

All libraries keep personnel records, though the nature and extent of their contents differ markedly from one organization to another. Sometimes, application forms, references and other material from the selection interview make up the entire record. Increasingly, however, schemes of staff appraisal or 'performance review' are being introduced (see Chapter 6 for details). Appraisal may be carried out on a regular basis, usually once a year, and a record kept of the appraisal interview, sometimes with input from both the supervisor and the member of staff being appraised. Staff appraisal systems, when linked

STAGE ONE

Analysis of existing staff → The people – skills inventory
The jobs:
1 job analysis and evaluation leading to job descriptions
2 organization chart (showing staffing structure)

STAGE TWO

Analysis of wastage rates → Retirements
Resignations (through promotion, appointment with other employers, illness, domestic commitments)
Recruitment problems
Redundacnies (NB: employer's policy)

STAGE THREE

Analysis of staffing needs → To maintain existing services
To improve existing services
To develop new services
To respond to change

STAGE FOUR

The human resources plan → Covers: recruiting policies
monitoring staff structure
staff flexibility
succession planning
staff appraisal
staff development and training
redeployment

SUPPLY

DEMAND

BALANCING SUPPLY AND DEMAND

NB: *Overall environment of staff planning: library aims and objectives* – based on continuing and/or changing needs of users
New technologies – application of IT
Trends in staffing structures – subject specialists in academic libraries, team structures in public libraries, systems analysts and research and development staff in all kinds of libraries
Trends in education and training for librarianship – Library Association structure for post-qualification approval, SNVQs
Demographic Trends

Figure 3.2 Stages in drawing up a human resources plan for an individual library system

with job analysis and description (see Chapter 4), enable a manager to make more regular and systematic links between allocation of staff and effectiveness of services. This is a necessity whether a complete staff restructuring is in the offing, or simply to achieve a closer match between staff expertise and the jobs that have to be done. It is particularly important in periods of rapid change when a library is introducing new services – Internet access or community information services, for example – or undergoing new ways of carrying out existing services – such as inter-library loans, serials control or acquisitions. In these circumstances, existing job descriptions may become redundant, but staff may go on pretending their job is not changing, because of security needs or fear that any admission of spare time will only attract a new heap of work which they may not feel like taking on. Managers should handle such situations sympathetically, and provide support in the form of retraining.

Analysis of staff in existing posts may also be used to spot 'high fliers', such as those with management potential. The use of 'potential reviews' in making this analysis is described in Chapter 6, but some organizations also plan at a system-wide level, particularly in the private sector. Promotion blockages can be detected, and remedial action taken where necessary. In private companies, there is frequently a policy of recruiting internally for posts at the top, though this may result in a lack of new ideas. Andrew Mayo of ICL describes a model that visualizes the organization as broadly pyramidal and divides it into a number of hierarchical levels. At each level, it is calculated that 40 per cent or so will need to be people with some potential. The exercise started at ICL with an 'organizational audit', assessing the ratio of people with upwards versus people with lateral potential. As a result of the analysis, ICL increased its numbers of young entrants substantially. It also discovered that it was not accelerating high-potential people quickly enough: 'Frustrated ones left for greener pastures. So we have brought the average age of entry to "senior" management grades steadily downwards.'[40] *The Public Library Workforce Study* contrasts the situation in public libraries with that in other high-profile public and private sector organizations in which recruitment, identification and development of high-calibre graduates is regarded as an intrinsic part of the framework for succession planning and a crucial investment for the future.[41]

ANALYSIS OF STAFF WASTAGE RATES

It was noted earlier in this chapter, in the introductory section on national workforce planning for library and information work, that social, economic and technological trends have a significant impact on the reality of library staffing levels, irrespective of what might be considered an ideal establishment by senior library managers. Local variations in unemployment figures, in local authority expenditure on libraries, and in policies on early retirement and redundancy agreements between employers and unions all affect the wastage rates which can be predicted over a five-year period. National social trends, such as women staying on in their professional jobs and postponing having children until they are in their thirties, so as to get a better foothold in their chosen careers, may also vary regionally. It is therefore rash to generalize, but it is probably safe to assert that in staff wastage in the last decade or so, the push–pull ratio is changing significantly. Figure 3.3 identifies the most common 'push' and 'pull' factors which are influential when staff leave jobs.

Push factors	Pull factors
Induction crisis, or adjustment problems in a new situation	Higher earnings
Interpersonal conflicts	Promotion to further one's career
Redundancy or early retirement schemes offered by employers	Alternative job opportunities
Pressures from changed working requirements, e.g. impact of automation, staff restructuring, or loss of contact with users	Alternative roles, e.g. motherhood, self-employment, voluntary work, or a combination of alternative roles, including:
	Emerging work structures, e.g. job sharing

Figure 3.3 Influential factors in job change

Because of the changing age structure of the profession, a greater number of young professionals sought promotion, or at least a change of job opportunity, after their first post, but a blockage was caused because not enough people were of the age to retire. This has led to low mobility and job stagnation, which has been partially alleviated by early retirement schemes, though not where staff taking advantage of these were not replaced by the parent organization. Thus, pressure of work has increased for those left, without any corresponding reward in the way of increased salary or a rise in status. A changing 'push' factor has been that people were more inclined to put up with not very satisfactory or motivating situations at work, because the possibilities of moving to another job were diminished by cuts in public expenditure. Security has become more significant, so staff have tended to be more tolerant of traditional push factors such as interpersonal conflicts or unwillingness to be socialized into an apathetic, time-serving work group, when previously they would have been driven to look for other jobs as soon as possible.

With property values, particularly in the south-east of England, falling dramatically, then more recently rising again, mobility has been seriously affected as people are uncertain of the future. Our experience has been that strong shortlists for senior staff have been difficult to compile.

Here are a number of quantitative formulae for calculating wastage rates, in order to establish yearly trends and work out likely needs in the years ahead. The simplest of these is:

$$\frac{\text{Number of staff leaving in a year}}{\text{Average number of employees}} \times 100 = \text{percentage wastage}$$

However, this may conceal a high turnover in one area of the library, or at one level of staff, such as junior non-professionals on the counter. So it is more representative of the true wastage rate to calculate:

$$\frac{\text{Number of staff with over one year's service}}{\text{Number of staff employed one year ago}} \times 100$$

The result is a 'labour stability index', which can be used to keep a check on staff trends in a specific library. This kind of information may be politically useful in drawing up arguments to safeguard a library from staffing cuts, but should be allied to other common formulae, such as number of library users per staff member (full-time equivalents – student numbers in education – FTEs; population served in public libraries; number of researchers who need SDI in a special library).

FORECASTING THE DEMAND FOR STAFF IN AN INDIVIDUAL LIBRARY

An accurate forecast is almost impossible, as so much depends on changing social, economic and political factors affecting funding. Clearly, there are dangers in making comparisons between apparently comparable libraries. The outcome may be that the better staffed may be cut, rather than the worse off improved. It is noteworthy that there are wide variations, for example in staffing ratios in university libraries (excluding the School of Advanced Study, London University and the Open University) SCONUL (Society of College, National and University Libraries) statistics for 1998–99 show that the number of FTE (full-time equivalent) students per FTE library staff member ranged from 48 to 259, with the mean at 148.[42] Similar figures for professional staff were 123 to 829, with a mean of 406. Staff and operating expenditure per FTE student ranged from £87 to £567. Significant factors which affect such statistics are the number of site libraries, and degrees of centralization of, for instance, technical services. Beyond this, professional judgements are involved, on the priorities attached to certain services or to the book fund, or to information technology projects. For the latter, it may be easier to get capital funding than for other projects, though the subsequent costs of upkeep may prove crippling to the materials fund.

STANDARDS

Comparisons can also be made with published standards and guidelines. In the past, standards issued by professional and other bodies frequently contained numerical guidance on staffing matters. Many of the recommended standards today provide broader guidelines, recognizing that the situations in individual libraries differ so much that numerical standards are inappropriate. For example, the current *Guidelines for Learning Resource Services in Further and Higher Education*, published by the Library Association, no longer deal in quantities, but instead list the factors involved – the size of the institution, the number of sites, the style of curriculum delivery, the range of services provided, the requirement of access at times that are convenient to users, the need to maintain managerial, support and developmental activities, as well as front-line service delivery, the need to ensure the safety of staff and students, and to maintain the quality of learning environments, and the need to maintain agreed levels of service.[43] The Department for Culture, Media and Sport's draft national standards for English public libraries did contain a much disputed figure of 29 per cent of the total number of staff to be professional, but this was deleted.[44] Remaining staffing standards refer to the knowledge and helpfulness of staff, as demonstrated by Cipfa Plus surveys, and to 'appropriate numbers' of staff with information/ICT qualifications.[45] Because there is such a wide variation among special libraries, it would be extremely difficult to provide anything in the way of numerical standards, and many of them employ few staff. Bray and Turner calculated the average staffing as five in 1991,[46] and Nankivell's survey in the same year found that 16.7 per cent of the cohort were working in isolation.[47]

4   Job descriptions and person specifications

Recruitment, selection, staff appraisal and training are activities of staff management which are all connected, as can be seen in Figure 4.1. A lack of effective recruitment procedures may not show up until appraisal systems, formal or informal, reveal that a member of staff needs considerable development to fulfil the requirements of the post to which they were appointed. Accurate job descriptions underpin recruitment, selection, appraisal and training, and we are of the opinion that they help to ensure that these processes are conducted in a thorough and systematic way.

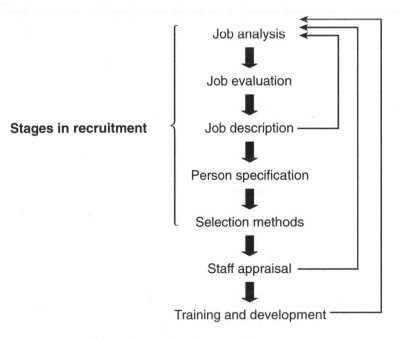

Figure 4.1   The main stages in staff management

The first step in writing job descriptions is job analysis. This may be followed by job evaluation. Once devised, job descriptions can be used to formulate person specifications. Unlike job descriptions, the use of person specifications is restricted to recruitment and selection. The library will need to work with the parent organization when drawing up job descriptions and person specifications, as there are likely to be internal polices regarding hours of work and tasks which may or may not be carried out by staff at certain grades, or appropriate qualifications and salary grades which are applicable to a particular post. Professional bodies and trade unions may also lay down guidelines relating to these issues.

JOB ANALYSIS

Casteleyn describes job analysis as 'the systematic reviewing and recording of the activities of a job'.[1] Job analysis can reveal that, perhaps as a result of introducing information technology (IT) or through other changes in the working environment, jobs have become diminished, or in some cases have disappeared entirely, although they remain within the established posts.

The two classic examples invariably quoted in the literature are the extra man in the artillery team, whose job originally was to hold the horses, and whose post continued even after horses had been replaced by mechanization, and the Civil Service post (in its later stages an office job) still listed on the permanent staff listing in the 1950s, the purpose of which was to patrol the cliffs of Dover to give early warning of Napoleon's invasion of our shores. In the library and information context, vigilance is just as necessary to ensure that posts are modified or created to make sense in terms of the organization's current and future, rather than past, commitments and priorities. This is especially difficult, but even more necessary, when posts are frozen. At such times, there can be concern from individuals and trade unions that employers are aiming to maintain work levels with a diminishing number of employees. Nonetheless, in the present climate of change, it is vital that posts are described in such a way as to be sufficiently adaptable to future demands.

METHODS OF JOB ANALYSIS

The usual methods used are chosen from the following:

- Post holders are asked to write their own description of their job, either freely or within a framework of given headings similar to those used in job evaluation or the job description (decision-making, supervisory duties, and so on).

- The immediate supervisor writes the description, with or without the participation of the post holder.
- The supervisor or an outside job analyst carries out a detailed 'observation' of the work being done.
- Post holders are asked to keep work diaries over a period.

Casteleyn and Webb suggest that exit interviews can be used as a means to gather information that will assist with job analysis: 'Although the replies may sometimes be subjective, they may lead you to consider redesigning the post or redistributing the workload.'[2] Exit interviews are discussed further in Chapter 7. Often, a combination of methods is used as a check on the reliability of any one method.

PRACTICAL USES OF JOB ANALYSIS

Job analysis is useful as a preliminary step to the following activities:

- filling a vacancy
- reviewing the content of a number of posts
- designing new jobs
- conducting job evaluation.

Filling a vacancy

When someone leaves an organization, there is often a sense that the post must be filled as quickly as possible. However, this reflex should be resisted. A vacancy presents an opportunity to analyse the role the post holder held, and how it fits in with the organization's purposes, which may be taking new directions or adapting to new developments. Furthermore, job analysis may suggest that internal promotion or transfer of existing staff may be more appropriate than an external advertisement for the particular job that has fallen vacant. There may be staff in other jobs who would be ideal in terms of their qualifications and skills, and who may not be fulfilling their potential in their present post. The parent body may have particular policies relating to internal appointments, and the library will need to adhere to these. Where internal promotion is viable, either on a permanent or temporary basis, it can provide excellent motivation for staff.

Whatever decision is made about a new appointment or a 'reshuffle' of existing staff, it should be done from a well-informed basis, through careful analysis of the job vacancy.

Reviewing the content of a number of posts

Job analysis has uses beyond the consideration of a single post. Indeed, changing the remit of one job usually has an impact on others within the library. Whilst the duties and responsibilities of a particular post should be considered each time it becomes vacant, there are also times when organizations will need to engage in a review of the allocation of work across a number of posts, or even throughout the entire department. This may be necessary as a response to budget cuts, or to enable the department to meet new demands. Job analysis can be used as an aid when considering staff structuring and allocation of work, but it may also appear as a predatory activity carried out by parent bodies such as a local authority, company or educational institution, with a view to cutting staff. It is therefore crucial that relevant trade unions are consulted at an early stage, in order to reach agreement on restructuring. When more than a single post is under review, it is likely that the Human Resources department will also need to be involved. In such times of upheaval, it is vital that staff are kept informed, and are involved as much as possible. This will help to prevent rumours spreading, and avoid adverse effects on morale.

Restructuring is an opportunity for job enlargement and job enrichment. As mentioned in the previous chapter, the balance of work carried out by paraprofessional and professional staff has shifted. This has been necessary in order to enable libraries to meet the new demands that they face within relatively static staffing budgets. The use of IT and the move towards prioritizing customer care have had an impact on libraries in all sectors.

The Fielden Report stated: 'The main burden of change is expected to fall on three groups of LIS staff: the senior managers, the subject or information librarians and the library assistants'.[3] Rapid change was predicted for the role of the library assistant, 'as this grade takes on more functions formerly associated with the "professional" staff grades'.[4] One example of this is the move towards using para-professional staff to answer and filter queries. In this approach, front-line services are designed so that readers initially consult para-professional staff. These staff will deal with straightforward queries. More complex queries can be referred to a member of professional staff, either immediately, if the member of professional staff is on call, or via an appointment system.

At the University of Hertfordshire, a new department of Learning and Information Services was set up in 1997 to deliver integrated computing, library and media services. One of the features of the new arrangements is an integrated helpdesk staffed by para-professionals. Prior to the reorganization, analysis of the usage of the previously separate library enquiry desk and the computing helpdesk had indicated that approximately 60–70 per cent of enquiries at both service points were routine, did not require the expertise of professionally qualified staff and could be resolved on the spot within two or three minutes. Similar patterns of usage have continued subsequently for the integrated helpdesk.

The integrated helpdesk forms the second of three steps to help available. For the most routine and repetitive enquiries, self-help guides have been published to remove the need for users to go to the helpdesk at all (Step 1). If a query is too complex to be dealt with by the helpdesk staff, an appointment will be arranged with the appropriate information, computing or media specialists, who also run programmes of skills sessions for students to promote expert user self-sufficiency (Step 3). These arrangements allow for the time of the information professionals to be focused at a relevant level of expertise to support the high emphasis Hertfordshire places on working in partnership with academic faculties. It is worth noting that the University of Hertfordshire is intending to continue with this approach when it opens its next new Learning Resources Centre in 2003.

Reducing the time which professional staff spend on helpdesks provides the opportunity for them to focus on supporting readers in other ways. As the Fielden Report anticipated, these activities can include:

- Providing tuition (and setting and marking the relevant tests/examinations) on study skills programmes ...
- Helping academic staff either informally or formally ... to understand the resources which are available ...
- Providing technical support for staff and students through advice on how to get to, and through, the electronic texts and databases ...
- Assisting students with any technical or access problems when they are in the Library or Resource Centre ...[5]

The classification and cataloguing of material is another area in which para-professional staff are carrying out tasks which were previously considered to be the responsibility of professional staff. The downloading of catalogue records is now commonplace throughout all sectors of library and information work. In many cases, the record will be downloaded at the order stage, and the material will arrive at the library in a shelf-ready form with the classmark and security devices having been added by the supplier. Professional staff will only be involved when advice is required, for example in relation to foreign-language material.

In special libraries and information units, it has been important for information officers to develop in-depth information services to confirm their worth. Using job analysis to enrich their jobs and rewriting job descriptions to include more dynamic duties and responsibilities can help to re-educate senior management and clarify the tasks and responsibilities that are appropriate for information officers.

Designing new jobs

Job analysis should be used when designing new jobs. New posts may come about through the reorganization of workloads, or a library may be able to use income which it generates to fund a post. Since the early 1990s, libraries and information units have increasingly become involved in externally funded projects. These present an opportunity to investigate new services or new means of delivery. Such projects have a finite length, and any associated posts are likely to be temporary. Successful projects may lead to libraries bidding for establishment funding in order to incorporate the new service as a mainstream activity.

In designing a new job, the manager must have knowledge and understanding of what makes a satisfying job, in addition to listing tasks which have to be carried out. Motivation theories are highly relevant here, because it is important to build into jobs some positive motivators such as responsibility, sense of achievement and opportunity to use expertise, as well as providing for the aspects which Herzberg termed hygiene factors, such as pay, working conditions and status.

Motivation theories suggest that periods of backroom work should be alternated with periods of sociable work, in contact with users or with other members of staff. Most people at work want to have a sense of belonging, and this is satisfied by designing jobs so that everyone is a member of an identifiable work group, whether or not it is a formal team. In very small or one-person libraries this is not possible, and the sociability factor must be built up in the larger environment of the parent company or firm. This can have useful spin-offs in getting to know the user community better, as well as keeping isolation at bay. Motivation theories are explained fully in Chapter 2.

Redesigning existing jobs is closely allied to designing new jobs, and both activities often occur when staff restructuring is taking place.

Conducting job evaluation

Job evaluation is the technique used to compare the relative worth of jobs in an organization in order to create equitable grading and reward systems. The process should evaluate the job, not the job holder. It may also be used as a means to demonstrate that a post should be regraded. For example, changes in the working environment, perhaps through the impact of IT or the increased use of a service, can result in a post being extended far beyond the clerical tasks which it originally covered, so that the job carries higher levels of decision-making, communication outside the unit, and advanced use of IT. In these circumstances, job evaluation should be welcomed, in order to have the job regraded from clerical upwards.

Methods of job evaluation The methods used are usually divided into non-analytical and analytical, though all systems are analytical in a sense. The non-analytical systems compare whole jobs, resulting in a ranking which can be translated into grades. Jobs are analysed, descriptions written, and grades assigned after comparison with other jobs.

Non-analytical methods make no attempt to assign values, and often the evaluation is made in a fairly unsophisticated manner, although it can usually be said to work reasonably well. If recruitment and performance are satisfactory, there may be no strong reason to change the system. It is good practice to include the opportunity for review by an objective panel, so that post holders have a means to appeal if the results are perceived to be unfair.

Analytical methods have developed because the non-analytical methods appeared to be insufficiently scientific and objective. In order to be recognized under the Equal Pay Act of 1970, a job evaluation scheme must be analytical. The analytical methods all involve the analysis of jobs by factors, and the assignment of values to those factors. In some systems, the factors are weighted according to importance. The factors which are to be taken into account must be selected very carefully, as these have greatest impact on the final ranking of posts.

Factors which could be considered include:

- expertise and experience
- service delivery
- planning and organising resources
- advisory responsibility
- communication and contacts
- judgement and decision-making
- work complexity, adaptability, pressure
- teaching and training
- working environment.

The job description should be used as the primary document for job evaluation. It may also be relevant to compare the post to similar posts elsewhere.

The right of equal pay for equal work necessitates that job evaluation schemes must be free of sex bias. The Equal Opportunities Commission has published a good practice guide which contains excellent advice on how to avoid such discrimination in job evaluation schemes.[6]

Job evaluation leading to job grading and salary structures is mainly the concern of employing bodies. Specific libraries are more likely to use job evaluation to produce job descriptions for use in the selection, appraisal and training of staff.

JOB DESCRIPTIONS

A job description is a statement of the objectives, main tasks, supervisory duties and place in the staff structure which the post holder is expected to accept. It should be the outcome of careful job analysis, rather than an automatic retention of previous duties. Examples of informative, well-designed job descriptions are shown in Figures 4.2, 4.4, 4.5 and 4.6.

Employers are not required by law to provide job descriptions. In the UK prior to 1993, it was only necessary to provide a job title. The European Directive on Written Information 1991 stated that the place or places of work must be specified. The Trade Union Reform and Employment Rights Act (1993) brought this into effect in the UK. This Act and the European Directive also made provision to give a brief description of the work for which the employee is employed, as an alternative to a job title. Whilst job descriptions are not a legal requirement, employers are obliged to provide a written statement of a 'defined list of terms and conditions of employment within two months of the commencement of employment'.[7] This is discussed further in Chapter 1.

Although job descriptions are not a legal requirement they are vital to staff management, and it is good practice to produce them and to use them as a means to support various activities. The uses of job descriptions include:

- recruitment and selection
- induction
- assessing training needs
- appraisal
- job evaluation and workforce planning.

During the recruitment process, the job description is sent to potential applicants and used as the basis of the advertisement. The job description will inform the person specification, and both documents should be used as the basis for designing the selection methods which will be used.

Following the recruitment process, the job description should be used to plan the induction programme for a new member of staff. The successful candidate will have been selected because they demonstrated a close match to the job description and the person specification. Nonetheless, initial training will be required, and should relate to tasks specified in the job description.

Job description

The Marketing Co-ordinator is a new post, based at the Bulmershe Library, but with a Library-wide remit requiring some travelling between sites.

Purpose and role

- To plan, manage, co-ordinate and support market research, service promotion and public relations activities on a Library-wide basis;
- To deliver and develop services and to manage collections to meet the particular needs of staff and students of designated academic units within the Faculty, in line with the strategic priorities of the Library and the University;
- To contribute to planning and policy-making for Library services generally and participate in service development projects.

Management relationships

Reports to	Deputy Librarian (Head of Services and Resources) = Line Manager
Supervised by	Faculty Team Manager, Education and Community Studies = Manager/Co-ordinator for liaison role
Line manager of	Library Assistant (part-time) in Faculty Team
Supervisor of	Other Library Assistants doing Faculty Team work or carrying out timetabled evening/weekend duties
Guidance to	Other Library Staff in relation to marketing activities
Liaison with	Support Services Manager *re* house style, design and production of publications
	Library Web Manager *re* promotion and publicity via the Library web-site
	Faculty Team Manager, Science (as info skills co-ordinator) *re* content and format of information resource guides
	EDC Librarian (as co-ordinator of Library displays) *re* design, timing and location of on-site displays
	Registrar's Division *re* staff and student data for user surveys promotion and publicity via the University Bulletin
	Library Representatives and Heads of academic units *re* information needs and priorities of academic groups
	SCONUL Newsletter Editor *re* submission of news and articles for publication

Figure 4.2   Job description for Marketing Co-ordinator at Reading University Library

Budget provision

Marketing activities are currently funded mainly from the Stationery/consumables budget (annual allocation c£35K) and the Projects budget (annual allocation c£10K). The postholder will be expected to prepare costed estimates to support a case for an earmarked recurrent allocation for future years.

Responsibilities and main duties

Specialist responsibilities *(initially about 40% of the postholder's time)*
1. *User surveys*: to manage an ongoing programme of surveys, including a comprehensive survey every four years and other surveys of particular groups or services as required; to provide a focus of expertise on survey methods, acting as the primary contact for Priority Search and training other staff in the methodology.

2. *Promotional literature*: to act as editor and quality controller for the Library's series of printed and electronic guides to collections and services, including subject guides to information resources: to provide guidelines and templates for colleagues in order to ensure consistency and compliance with the Library's house style.

3. *Public relations*: to commission, draft and edit copy for the Library's termly newsletter, *The Library News*; to co-ordinate the submission of Library news and information to *The University of Reading Bulletin*; to assist with the design and drafting of the Library's annual review; to act as the official contact for the *SCONUL Newsletter* and co-ordinate the submission of news and articles on the Library's behalf; to oversee entries publicising RUL in external printed or electronic resource directories; to manage *ad hoc* service and product launches and other events.

4. *Professional visits*: to organise *ad hoc* programmes for individual and group visitors to the Library in response to requests, liaising with colleagues on content, timing, locations, handouts and practical arrangements.

Liaison responsibilities *(initially about 50% of the postholder's time)*

5. *Departmental communication*: to provide the principal channel of communication between the Library and the academic units served; to have regular meetings with the Library Representative(s) and *ad hoc* meetings with the Head of the unit(s) and teaching/research staff, in order to establish information needs and priorities and to exchange views on matters of mutual interest; to attend relevant Faculty/ School/Departmental Library and Staff-Student Committees.

6. *Information resource management*: to ensure that the Library's collections meet the needs of the academic groups and that stock in general is up-to-date and reflects current academic priorities; to select new material and weed existing stock, in consultation with teaching and research staff; to identify and obtain reading list material; to monitor the resources budgets of the academic units and ensure throughput of orders; to catalogue books and other media selected and to contribute descriptions of networked resources to subject information gateways.

Figure 4.2   continued

7. *Information skills*: to design, develop and deliver user education programmes for undergraduate and postgraduate students and staff, including talks, tours, seminars and workshops, with particular emphasis on the use of electronic sources of information; to produce subject guides to information sources, instructions for use of electronic systems and promotional materials for print and electronic distribution; and to ensure that teaching and research staff are kept up-to-date with new sources.

8. *Information services*: to provide reference services to Library users, by staffing enquiry points and providing subject-specific support.

General responsibilities (about 10% of the postholder's time)

9. To contribute to policy and planning activities in the Faculty Team and for the Library as a whole, including involvement in discussions on strategic and operational issues and participation in projects designed to review, improve or develop resources and services; to represent the Team at meetings, on task forces and in special interest groups within the Library.

10. To keep abreast of trends and developments in service marketing, library/information services and higher education by scanning literature, establishing external contacts and attending professional meetings, with particular reference to developments in electronic communication, scholarly publishing and information provision in relevant disciplines.

11. To undertake such other Library duties as may reasonably be assigned, including participation in rotas for evening and weekend duties.

Figure 4.2 concluded

A further use for job descriptions is in diagnosing and responding to training needs. A job description provides a basis for a training officer when drawing up relevant programmes of staff development or when selecting courses. It can also be used as a checklist for trainers in the design of training. Job descriptions are key documents in the appraisal process, providing a yardstick against which to assess the strengths and weaknesses of staff when carrying out the various aspects of their jobs. As a result of such appraisal on a regular basis, it is possible to plan training and staff development activities with greater attention to established need. Training needs identified during appraisal should be linked to the job description. Appraisal, as discussed in Chapter 6, also provides a means to ensure that job descriptions are kept up to date.

Finally, as demonstrated earlier, job analysis, job evaluation and human resource planning all draw on existing job descriptions, as well as producing new ones which are relevant to the current and future direction of the service.

Qualifications and experience required

Essential
- A first degree in an academic discipline and a postgraduate degree or diploma in library/information science or equivalent subject area;
- A minimum of three years professional experience in an academic or special library;
- Experience of reference and information work, and a demonstrable commitment to the effective application of Information Technology to information services;
- Knowledge of UK MARC, AACR2, LCSH and DDC for cataloguing procedures;
- Good communication and interpersonal skills, an energetic and flexible approach, and the ability to exercise initiative and work without close supervision.

Desirable
- Experience in supervising and training staff;
- Knowledge of survey methods (particularly the Priority Search methodology) and statistical techniques;
- Experience in training information users in searching and retrieval techniques, especially in relation to electronic information sources;
- Familiarity with information resources in relevant academic disciplines;
- Chartered or corporate membership of an appropriate professional body (eg the Library Association or the Institute of Information Scientists).

Figure 4.3   Person specification for Marketing Co-ordinator at Reading University Library

CONTENT OF JOB DESCRIPTIONS

Job title

Every job needs a title. As has already been stated, the provision of a job title is no longer a legal requirement, and employers may provide a short summary of the job rather than a title. However, assigning a title will simplify the recruitment process, and will provide the post holder with a sense of place within the staffing structure. Job titles should be descriptive, and should convey the level and the nature of the post.

Statement of purpose, objectives of the job

The examples of job descriptions in Figures 4.2, 4.4, 4.5 and 4.6 show clearly how a particular post is related to the overall activities of the library, and also give specific objectives for the particular job.

It might be argued that such statements of purpose merely state the obvious, but they very often set the scene for a more detailed description of what the job is about, by placing it in the wider context of the library and its

LONDON BOROUGH OF BARNET
JOB DESCRIPTION

SERVICE: **CULTURAL SERVICES**

SECTION: **OPERATIONS AND DEVELOPMENT**

SERVICE AREA: **LIBRARIES**

JOB TITLE: **BRANCH ADMINISTRATOR**

POST NO:

GRADE: **BARNET BAND I : Scp. 18-21**

REPORTING ARRANGEMENTS

Reports to the Library Manager on a day to day basis; is a member of the team working in all libraries across the area; managed overall by the Area Manager.

CONTEXT AND PURPOSE OF JOB

To assist the Library Manager in the efficient operation of service to the public ensuring that agreed standards of service are met.

To be responsible for all aspects of administrative work in a level 2 library.

MAIN DUTIES AND RESPONSIBILITIES

1. Customer Care / Service Delivery

- Support the Library Manager with the efficient operation of a level 2 library to ensure that effective service delivery to the public and agreed standards of service are met.

- Undertake required periods of duty on the counters and enquiry desk. Take enquiries from the public and initiate action, referring to senior staff as appropriate.

- Under the direction of senior staff, organise all aspects of stock maintenance including processing, repairs, binding, withdrawals and preparation of stock for sale.

- Assist the senior staff with the promotion of the library service to the community.

- Assist the Library Manager with income generation projects.

- Organise the administration of hall and room lettings and booking of display space.

Figure 4.4   Job description for Branch Administrator at London Borough of Barnet

111

- Be responsible for the day to day supervision of all counter routines and report any faults to the IT section promptly.

- Be responsible for the stationery control, stock control on merchandise and the completion of weekly returns and statistics as required.

- In the absence of senior staff, take responsibility for the efficient day to day running of any library in the area.

- Be aware of the codes of practice for health and safety of staff within public libraries

- Ensure that customer services policies are implemented efficiently.

- Attend meetings and training sessions as required.

2. Staff Management/Supervision

- Be responsible for the efficient utilisation of staff including preparation of timetables and organisation of reliefs across the Area as required.

- Assist the Library Manager with the recruitment and selection of Senior Library Assistants and Library Assistants ensuring that targets and standards are met and reviewed on a regular basis.

- Be responsible for the training, motivation and supervision of Senior Library Assistants, Library Assistants and Saturday/Evening staff as required, and co-ordinate their timetable of daily duties.

3. Financial Responsibility

- Be responsible for the financial administration in a level 2 library, including the daily and weekly cash and income procedures, banking and petty cash.

- Be responsible for the collection, security and delivery to the Director of Finance's representative for all monies received in the library.

4. Premises Management

- Liaise with the Library Buildings Supervisor on all aspects of cleaning monitoring and routine building maintenance.

- In the absence of senior staff, be responsible for the security of libraries, ensuring that premises are locked and alarm systems set correctly.

5. Promotion of Corporate Values

- Comply with all council policies on equal opportunities to ensure that they are carried through into all aspects of service delivery and staff management

Figure 4.4 continued

6. Flexibility

- In order to deliver services effectively a degree of flexibility is needed, and the post holder may be required to perform work not specifically referred to above. Such duties, however, will fall within the scope of the post at the appropriate grade.

- The post holder will be based in a level 2 library and will work in all libraries across the Group as directed by the Area Manager and at the exigencies of the service.

- The post holder will work at least one evening until 8 p.m. and on alternate Saturdays until 5 p.m.

7. Staff Supervised

Senior Library Assistants
Library Assistants
Saturday/Evening staff

Figure 4.4 concluded

community of users. The most useful ones make strong links between the job and the library's overall aims, so that the post holder, if prepared to take the job objectives seriously, could develop a firm sense of playing a purposeful part in the library's complex network of activities and services to its public.

Main tasks and duties

This section of the job description is often a straightforward list of the activities which the post holder will be expected to perform. In the example from Reading University Library (Figure 4.2), the main duties are divided into three areas of responsibility: *Specialist*, *Liaison* and *General*. Weighting is given to each of these three areas in terms of the proportion of time to be spent on tasks. The example from Barnet (Figure 4.4) groups the duties under headings such as: 'Customer Care/Service Delivery' and 'Financial Responsibility'.

There is an argument for not being too specific, since this may straitjacket the post holder, thus preventing or discouraging creative or new approaches, and reducing the flexibility of the post. Guidelines rather than complete specifications are more supportive of staff development, besides leaving room for flexibility of staff, a factor which is essential in the current climate of change. The job description from the London Borough of Barnet includes a section titled 'Flexibility', which explains that post holders may be required to perform tasks, which have not been explicitly specified. The need for flexibility in the workforce is discussed in Chapter 3.

THE ROYAL SOCIETY OF MEDICINE

Position: Assistant Librarian – Enquiry Services
Department: Information Services
Grade:
Accountable To: Librarian – Enquiry and Document Delivery Services
Responsible Far: Senior Library Assistant – Document Delivery

Job Purpose:

To deliver customer focused enquiry, issue and document delivery services to agreed quality standards.

Key Results:

Effective enquiry, issue and document delivery services, demonstrated by:

- Providing a responsive service – striving to meet users' expectations within available resources

- Ensuring agreed service standards and deadlines are met

Responsibilities:

1. Day to day management of enquiry and issue services, including co-ordinating staffing and timetabling, responsibility for staff training and development, enquiry desk duties (including Saturday and evening duties on a rota basis), and the collection of statistics.

2. Day to day supervision of document delivery services (covering article delivery; loans; ILLs), including line management of Senior Library Assistant-Document Delivery.

3. Management of Library Assistants in the delivery of these services, including delegation of tasks as appropriate.

4. Maintain effective communication and liaison with IS teams (e.g. covering stock, information resources and equipment), RSM Departments, Committees, user groups and external suppliers.

5. Management and promotion of the sale of RSM Publications.

6. Develop services, reviewing and documenting procedures on a regular basis.

7. Responsibility for quality and providing management information.

8. Complying with the Society's policies and procedures, in particular with regard to Health & Safety – ensuring that all equipment is working and maintaining a safe working environment, and other legal requirements.

9. Deputise for Librarian – Enquiry and Document Delivery Services.

10. Other reasonable duties as agreed with the Librarian – Enquiry and Document Delivery Services.

Figure 4.5   Job description for Assistant Librarian – Enquiry Services at the Royal Society of Medicine Library

Place of the post in the library's staffing structure

The job description needs to convey clearly to whom the member of staff is responsible, and whom they are required to supervise in turn. In the example from Sheffield City Council (Figure 4.6), this information is given in two brief statements about reporting arrangements.

The place within the staffing structure can also be demonstrated by including an organization chart within the job description. It is important to make clear the range and level of decision-making involved in the job, in addition to a bald statement about position in the staff hierarchy. This involves some indication of the amount of guidance which will be given by the post holder's superiors, the existence or lack of clearly outlined policies and procedures and precedents, the gravity of the problems likely to arise, the degree of innovation likely to be required in the work, and the effect on other staff (how widespread and significant) of decisions taken by the holder of this job. The use of terms such as 'responsible for …' and 'assist with …' will convey to the post holder the extent to which they are required to take responsibility for an activity. The sample job descriptions indicate the dimensions of the posts and the support which is available. For example the Branch Administrator at Barnet (Figure 4.4) will:

- *Assist* the Library Manager with income generation projects.
- *Organize* the administration of hall and room lettings and booking of display space.

Contacts within and beyond the library

It is useful to indicate the range and level of people with whom the post holder will be required to develop and maintain contacts. The 'Management relationships' section of the Reading example (Figure 4.2) includes a statement about the staff for whom the post holder will be expected to provide guidance, and a list of those staff with whom the post holder will liaise. At the Royal Society of Medicine (RSM) the Assistant Librarian – Enquiry Services (Figure 4.5) is expected to:

> Maintain effective communication and liaison with IS [Information Services] teams … RSM Departments, Committees, user groups and external suppliers.

Salary scales and working conditions

These are part of the *context*, rather than the content, of the job, and are essential, particularly when used in the recruitment process. Some organizations choose to include them in the body of the job description, whilst others provide the details separately. Working conditions include details of hours,

115

holidays, opportunities for staff development such as time and expenses for attending professional workshops and conferences, and prospects for promotion. When job descriptions are being used for recruitment purposes, it is important to remember that some applicants may not understand the terms which are used, for example in the case of salary grades. A reference to a particular grade should be supported by an explanation of the salary range to which the grade relates.

Organizational factors

In some job descriptions, libraries take a lot of trouble to convey the philosophy and structure of the service as they operate it. When the job description is being written for recruitment, this can help to ensure that it will attract the most suitable staff for the organization. In the examples given, the philosophy of the service comes through in the descriptions. The example from Barnet (Figure 4.4) stresses that the post holder will contribute to the efficient operation of the service, in the description of the purpose of the post and at various points throughout the 'Main Duties and Responsibilities' section. This part of the job description also contains a section entitled 'Promotion of Corporate Values'. The role of the Assistant Librarian – Enquiry Services at the Royal Society of Medicine in the provision of a high-quality service is summarized in the sections headed 'Job Purpose' and 'Key Results' (Figure 4.5). Further detail is provided in the particular responsibility statements.

When job descriptions are being used for recruitment purposes, it is good practice to supply additional material which can provide background to the post and help potential candidates to make a decision about submitting an application. Job descriptions used in this context may also contain an invitation to contact a named individual, usually the line manager for the post, for an informal discussion about the job.

AVOIDING THE PROBLEMS ASSOCIATED WITH JOB DESCRIPTIONS

The job description is an important management tool, and failure to pay sufficient attention to design and currency can lead to difficulties. Bearing in mind the following points will help to ensure that job descriptions are as effective as possible.

- They must be updated regularly, otherwise they become irrelevant and ignored. In many libraries, job descriptions seem only to be used when jobs become vacant and have to be filled. Between vacancies, they remain in the files, becoming increasingly obsolete. Failing to update job descriptions to encompass changing duties can lead to inflexibility and a reluctance on the part of the post holder to develop in accordance with the demands of the job.

- The value of job descriptions depends very much on how they are used in a library, and extends beyond the recruiting phase. In order to fulfil their potential, job descriptions should be referred to when staff appraisal and staff development are taking place, and when policy decisions are being taken on workforce planning.

- They must leave some scope for initiative and innovation on the part of the post holder. If they are too specific and detailed, they can encourage the post holder to continue merely to do what their predecessor did, rather than motivating them to be creative and introduce improvements.

- When job descriptions are introduced, or modified, as part of a restructuring process, it is vital that the post holders are consulted or personally involved in compiling the new job descriptions. Failure to do so may lead to reluctance on the part of the post holders in following the job descriptions, and can result in them being ignored as far as possible.

PERSON SPECIFICATION

The job description describes the *job*; the person specification describes the *person capable of doing the job*. The job description should be sufficiently informative to enable the identification of the attributes which will need to be demonstrated by the post holder. Thus, within the recruitment context, the person specification can be developed from the job description, and will state the qualifications, experience and personal qualities, the skills, knowledge and abilities which are required to carry out a particular job. Unlike the job description, the person specification is relevant only to the process of recruitment and selection.

The job description and the person specification are often combined in one document for recruitment purposes. Job applicants who request further details receive information on the duties and responsibilities of the job, and also on the qualifications, experience and qualities required in the person who will be appointed. The person specifications for the post of Marketing Co-ordinator at Reading University Library and Senior Librarian at Sheffield City Council are shown in Figures 4.3 and 4.7.

It is sometimes useful to have an intermediate stage after the compilation of the job description and before the person specification is written. This is the job specification, in which the characteristics of the job are listed in terms of

117

City of Sheffield
JOB DESCRIPTION

DEPARTMENT	DEL, LEISURE
DIVISION/SECTION	LIBRARIES, ARCHIVES AND INFORMATION
POST TITLE	SENIOR LIBRARIAN
GRADE	SUG 6/7
RESPONSIBLE TO	GROUP MANAGER
RESPONSIBLE FOR	COMMUNITY LIBRARIANS, LIBRARY INFORMATION ASSISTANTS AND MANUAL STAFF
HOLIDAY AND SICKNESS RELIEF	STAFF WITHIN THE GROUP AS APPROPRIATE

PURPOSE OF JOB

TO ENSURE THE DELIVERY OF QUALITY SERVICES BASED ON COMMUNITY NEED. TO CREATE STRATEGIC ALLIANCES AND PARTNERSHIPS THAT ASSIST IN THE DELIVERY OF QUALITY SERVICES.

TO TAKE FORWARD THE VISION LAID OUT FOR LIBRARY & INFORMATION SERVICES IN 'NEW LIBRARY, THE PEOPLE'S NETWORK' INTO THE NEXT CENTURY

SPECIFIC DUTIES AND RESPONSIBILITIES

SENIOR LIBRARIAN

The postholder must at all times carry out his/her responsibilities in compliance with City Council policies and procedures

1   To contribute to the corporate delivery of the Council's vision, goal and core values, providing a clear sense of direction and purpose within the service.

2   To contribute to the designated service within Libraries having due regard to the Council's fundamental policy commitments to effective service provision and promotion of equal opportunities, a health and safety culture and good employee relations.

3   To provide effective Library Archive and Information Services appropriate to the needs of the Community.

4   To ensure the operational effectiveness of the Service Group.

5 · To meet the objectives and targets set for the post along with effective and efficient resource management, workforce deployment, premises and equipment.

6   To contribute to the effective management of the groups workforce, including active participation within the Employee Appraisal scheme.

Figure 4.6   Job description for Senior Librarian at Sheffield City Council

7　To assist the Group Manager in the preparation and monitoring of budgets, including liaison with finance officers.

8　To undertake Project work as required by the Group Manager. Including managing and active involvement in project based working and preparing bids and applications for funding.

9　To assume specific areas of responsibility as agreed with the Group Manager, some examples are: Collection Management; ICT; Statistics; Workforce deployment and development; User consultation.

10　To prepare and present reports and presentations to Members and other bodies as appropriate.

11　To assist in the development and provision of Service Standards and benchmarking Performance Indicators.

12　To deputise for the Group Manager.

13　To work effectively with appropriate staff in the Service/Directorate/Council/Outside agencies/local, regional and national organisations/Community and voluntary groups in order to deliver quality services that offer best value.

14　To sustain a commitment to Professional Personal Development.

15　To undertake any other duties and responsibilities which do not change the character and purpose of the post as may be determined after negotiations between management, the postholder and the appropriate trade union.

Figure 4.6　concluded

complexity, responsibility and supervising load. These are then used to determine the characteristics of the person needed to do the job. In library practice, the job specification is usually merged with the job description.

HOW TO COMPILE A PERSON SPECIFICATION

As long as the job description gives a clear and accurate account of the content and context of a post, and the levels of performance required in terms of decision-making, policy and planning are clearly defined, it is relatively straightforward to decide on the skills, experience and qualities required for the job.

Given that the person specification is a selection tool, it is vital that it only contains those requirements which are directly related to the duties. Inclusion of irrelevant requirements may lead to self-deselection by potential applicants, and can result in discrimination. If essential requirements are not listed, the selectors' task will become much more onerous. The number of applications from candidates who are not suitable will increase, and demonstrating why the final shortlist has been selected for further consideration will be difficult. Selectors need to be clear about how the presence, or absence, of each require-

rt

PERSON SPECIFICATION

Post Title:- SENIOR LIBRARIAN
Method of Assessment – KEY: P = Presentation   A = Application Form
                                  R = References   I = Interview

MINIMUM ESSENTIAL REQUIREMENTS	METHOD OF ASSESSMENT
Skills/Knowledge	
- management and supervisory skills at an appropriate level for the grade and responsibility. Including a commitment to the development of others.	A/R/I
- ability to work effectively and creatively in a corporate and partnership environment	A/R/I
- ability to lead and motivate the workforce as individuals and within teams	A/R/I
- have the vision and capability to contribute to the development and implementation of identified policies and priorities	P/I
- effective communicator both written and verbal	A/P/R/I
- project management skills	A/I
- ICT awareness and transferable skills	A/R/I
- financial skills including the ability to build, control and monitor budgets	R/A
- problem solving skills including an ability to be creative when approaching projects and tasks	I/P/R
- a clear understanding of current National and Local Government issues: Public Library, current and future developments: and how the two interact in affecting service delivery	A/I/P
- a clear understanding of ICT issues as they affect the delivery of Library and Information services	A/I/P
- a clear understanding of equal opportunities issues	A/I/P
ExperienceIQualifications/Training etc (if any)	
- a professional library/information qualification or its appropriate equivalent is desirable	A
- a full driving licence is desirable	A
- at least 3 years appropriate library experience, demonstrating a high level of success in staff and resources management	A/R
- experience of working with and developing ICT solutions: Collection Management and Lifelong Learning	A/I
- experience of working with and a clear understanding of the needs of a wide range of users including Voluntary Statutory and Community Groups.	A/I/P
Work Related Circumstances (including working conditions)	
- confidence in self and ability to present oneself positively to others	P/I
- enthusiasm for change and challenge	A/P/1
- ability to work with multiple tasks and deadlines	A/I
- willingness to work flexibly	I/R
- self motivated who can also work within a team	I/R
- commitment to personal development and the development of others including users.	A/R/I

Figure 4.7   Person specification for Senior Librarian at Sheffield City Council

ment will be ascertained. Person specifications which list requirements that cannot be judged are not helpful to the recruitment and selection process. The sample person specification from Sheffield (Figure 4.7) states which selection method will be used to assess each requirement.

It is helpful to both potential applicants and selectors to categorize the requirements under relevant headings. These headings vary from organization to organization, and are often derived from those identified by Alec Rodger and J. Munro Fraser. Both Rodger's Seven-point Plan[8] and Fraser's Five-point Plan[9] list attributes which are still relevant when drawing up person specifications, and which can be measured by standard selection methods.

Table 4.1 Comparison of Rodger's and Fraser's person specification classifications

Rodger's Seven-point Plan	Fraser's Five-point Plan
Physical make-up	Impact on other people
Attainments	Qualifications
General intelligence	Innate abilities
Specialized aptitudes	Motivation
Interest	Adjustment
Disposition	
Circumstances	

The two classifications overlap almost completely, so they are not to be seen as alternative guidelines in drawing up a person specification, but rather as suggesting common categories to be considered.

The requirements may then be further divided into 'essential' and 'desirable', as in the example from Reading (Figure 4.3). Jago advises that 'identifying desirable as well as essential characteristics at this stage will help you to select the best candidate later in the process – especially if you have a strong field to choose from'.[10]

Physical make-up and impact on others

In Fraser's and Rodger's plans, these attributes include appearance, bearing and speech, and the reaction they elicit in other people, both colleagues and users. Aspects of health and physique necessary for library work are also covered. Very closely related is Rodger's 'disposition', the set of attitudes and personality traits which to a large extent determine the impact made on the public and on other staff in the work group.

Many organizations use informal interviews as part of the selection process. These can take the form of a tour or an informal meeting. The use of such methods enables other members of staff to meet candidates and form opinions about their general disposition and impact. They can give their views on how well they think candidates may fit in, or alternatively, whether the candidates could act as a lively stimulus. The matter of 'fit' needs to be given careful consideration. Recruiting staff who are similar to the existing workforce can rule out a vital means of introducing new ideas and approaches into an organization. Nonetheless, the vast majority of posts require an element of team work, and recruiting staff who may disrupt existing working patterns can have a negative effect on staff morale. Discrimination must be avoided, and selectors need to ensure that they are not forming opinions about the future performance of candidates based on preconceived ideas that gender, race, religion or other factors will result in certain traits of behaviour. A well-designed person specification can help to avoid such pre-judgements, as it will direct selectors to consider specific requirements, rather than encouraging them to reach conclusions based on subjective observations.

Ability to express oneself reasonably fluently can be said to fall within this category. This may be more effectively assessed outside the awesome atmosphere of the interviewing room. Selectors will want to look for qualities which include articulacy on matters where knowledge might be expected (previous work experience, professional issues, higher education courses, studies), an ability to be clear in communicating, and a degree of amiability in responding to other people. When public speaking or presentation skills are particularly important, this requirement is best judged by asking candidates to give a presentation on a specified topic.

In terms of physical stamina, some library jobs (counter work, for example) make quite high demands, perhaps surprisingly so in the light of the public image of librarians. The physical requirements of a post need to be conveyed clearly in order to enable potential applicants to make a decision about whether to apply or not. The Disability Discrimination Act 1995 (which applies to all firms with 15 or more employees) places a duty on employers to make reasonable adjustments to ensure that disabled persons are not put at a substantial disadvantage in comparison to a non-disabled person. This includes people with physical disabilities, and employers need to be confident that potential candidates with physical disabilities are not discriminated against. The Disability Rights Commission publishes a variety of guides which offer valuable advice to employers on how to ensure the requirements of the Disability Discrimination Act 1995 are met.

Qualifications and attainments

Fraser distinguishes between general education, specialist training, and work experience. Rodger likewise includes under 'Attainments' all those educational and professional experiences which the applicant has had, from school through higher education to the previous job.

This is an area in which the standards that are set can result in indirect discrimination. The Equal Opportunities Commission warns: 'Requirements with age barriers or minimum periods of relevant experience will often be unfairly discriminatory because many women have career breaks for child bearing.'[11] In terms of qualifications, suitable applicants may be ruled out if their education has been unconventional. Once again, standards must be related to the requirements of the post. When designing a person specification, it is necessary to ask whether a qualification is required, or whether experience of an activity is more appropriate. For example, a Senior Library Assistant post may involve taking responsibility for balancing the cash and cheques received in a library. In such a case, experience of cash handling would be more relevant than a qualification in mathematics. The equivalency of different types of qualification, overseas or vocational for example, should also be recognized, and asking for 'a good general level of education, GCSEs or equivalent' will ensure that indirect discrimination is avoided.

The relevance of a professional qualification in library and information work should be considered, rather than assumed. In the past, it was expected that posts at certain grades, for example academic-related posts in university libraries, would necessitate that the post holder had a professional qualification in library and information studies. The need to recruit a flexible workforce, and in particular the incorporation of IT into every aspect of librarianship, has led employers to question the validity of such an approach. Many library services now employ dedicated IT staff, and in such cases the requirements of the post are more likely to be met through a qualification, or experience, in IT than a professional qualification in library and information work.

Where a professional qualification in library and information work is identified as being relevant to the post, thought should be given to the statement in the person specification. The example from Sheffield (Figure 4.7) states that 'a professional library/information qualification or its appropriate equivalent is desirable'. This covers the range of qualifications which are available in the library and information field, both in the UK and beyond. For certain posts, employers may opt to consider experience in a relevant field as a viable alternative to an undergraduate or postgraduate degree.

For more senior appointments, the whole area of continuing education is relevant, and there are many opportunities open to practising librarians by which they may develop professionally and achieve formal qualifications. Employers are now less likely to require applicants to have achieved Chartered Membership of the Library Association or Corporate Membership of the

Institute of Information Science, and where this is included in a person specification, it will probably be listed as desirable rather than essential. When a commitment to professional development is considered important to a post, the person specification may state that Chartered Membership of the Library Association or Corporate Membership of the Institute of Information Science will be accepted as a demonstration of such commitment.

In the appointment of new professionals to their first post, selectors should also be aware of the difficulties faced by entrants to the profession in gaining work experience. The number of pre-qualification or Graduate Trainee schemes, which were once so common, has diminished. The only work experience the applicant may have had could be the few weeks spent on placement during their library and information studies course. Work experience prior to undertaking the course should not be dismissed, as it may be relevant to the organization. For example, time spent working in retail will have enabled the applicant to develop their customer care skills.

General intelligence/innate abilities/specialized aptitudes

Fraser and Rodger diverge a little in what they recommend selectors to value. Rodger emphasizes the ability to apply intelligence. Fraser's interpretation of 'innate abilities' seems to be those rather indefinable qualities which stem from a person's education and experience, but go beyond these to give 'a general quickness in the uptake' and 'special aptitudes'. Rodger's category of 'special aptitudes' includes mechanical aptitude, manual dexterity, facility in written or verbal expression, facility with figures, and creative talent in, say, designing or graphics.

Rodger's and Fraser's terms for these requirements are not now generally used in person specifications, and have been replaced by 'skills/knowledge' or a similar category. The skills and knowledge which are required will vary according to the post, but may include such areas as:

- organizational ability
- IT literacy (either general, or in specified processes such as word processing)
- supervisory and/or management skills
- knowledge of technical skills such as MARC and AACR2
- language skills.

The presence of certain skills or knowledge is most effectively ascertained through practical tests or exercises. For example, several of the requirements listed under 'Skills/Knowledge' in the Sheffield person specification (Figure 4.7) are assessed through a presentation.

Clearly, there is overlap between the requirements in this category and those that may be specified under 'Qualifications/attainments'. Some person specifications will include the requirements from both sections under a general heading such as 'Experience/qualifications'. This approach is shown in the example from Reading. The grouping will depend on many factors, and there is no single recommended template. What is crucial is clarity and relevance to the post.

Motivation

Fraser defines this as the way in which the individual applies their abilities in practical situations, and to what extent they achieve effective results. This is a complex area, and it will be helpful to refer back to Chapter 2 on the relevance of motivation theories to library staffing. The importance of assessing applicants' motivation is inestimable, since staff frustration and ineffective results are likely when there is a mismatch between the post and the person. For instance, the person who would be effective answering routine queries, or doing issue-desk work in contact with users, might well be someone whose motivation to work stems mainly from social needs, rather than what Maslow calls identity needs or self-actualization needs. If the person appointed to this job was motivated by self-actualization needs (they wanted to be stretched to the limit of their potential, to be faced with challenge, and to take on responsibility), the results could be disappointing.

Another example might be the person who is motivated mainly by security needs. Difficulties may arise when innovations take place, say in staffing structures, and the individual becomes a member of an area team rather than working as a fairly isolated professional in a branch library where there was a secure niche and familiar routines. For those motivated by identity needs and social needs, the change would be a source of positive satisfaction, but for the staff member who is mainly concerned with security at work, the change might lead to unease and withdrawal symptoms.

Adjustment

Fraser describes 'adjustment' as emotional stability, and is concerned with the amount of stress a person at work is capable of withstanding, particularly in interacting with other people (public or colleagues). As with motivation, it is important to achieve a match between the individual's needs and the job requirements. Changes in staff structure, particularly those which occur in response to budget cuts, can result in a more pressurized work environment. For many people, this is a source of satisfaction, and will provide motivation. Such changes have also led to more team-based structures, and again, for some, this can be the preferred way of working, but for others the lack of opportunity to work alone may be a drawback. Stating the extent to which the post holder will interact with others and the level of pressure within the post will enable the selectors to choose the candidate who demonstrates the ability to adjust to the organization's working environment, and thus avert future difficulties.

Interests

It is now rare for selectors to ask about personal interests. As has been demonstrated, person specifications must relate to the job description and the tasks which the post holder will perform. Ascertaining that an applicant has an interest in a particular area is not likely to assist with the selection process. Rather, interests which may be relevant to the post, such as language skills, should be referred to elsewhere in the person specification.

Circumstances

The person specification provides an opportunity to mention practical job requirements, such as irregular hours of work. All the details must be provided so that potential applicants can make an informed decision about how suitable the post is for them. Parry advises:

> It is not acceptable for the selectors to make assumptions about the individual's ability in these areas. For example, it must not be assumed that a person with children might find it difficult to work in the evenings or at weekends.[12]

The place of job descriptions and person specifications in the recruitment and selection processes is investigated further in Chapter 5.

5 ■ Recruitment and selection of staff

The ability to recruit staff successfully is one of the essential skills that a manager needs. Usually, the process will require liaison with the Human Resources section of the parent organization, although in some organizations managers may be expected to take full responsibility for the process. The selection process presents an opportunity to involve staff in a development activity. This provides a means of maintaining morale, and also helps to ensure that those who know most about the job and with whom the person appointed would be working closely make an appropriate choice.

The starting point for successful recruitment and selection is a relevant and up-to-date job description and person specification. These documents should inform each stage of the process. The person specification should list the attributes required of a person for a particular post, and the task of any selector is to discover to what extent these attributes are present in applicants. This needs to be conducted with due regard for the appropriate legislation. Particular knowledge and skills are required to enable recruitment and selection to be carried out competently, and we are in agreement with Jago's opinion that staff responsible for this process should attend a short course on interviewing and selection.[1]

SOURCES OF INFORMATION

It is useful to have an overview of the information sources available, because there is a tendency to concentrate so much on one source, such as the formal interview, as to make insufficient use of others. Figure 5.1 indicates the main sources used in selection.

The diagram illustrates a number of ideas that are central to a discussion of selection. As important as any is the fact that information is obtained throughout the process by both selectors and applicants. Too often, selectors will

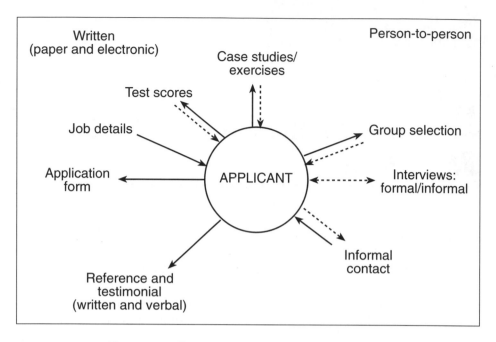

Figure 5.1 The main information sources used in selection

perceive the exercise as one-way only, and forget that the applicant is all the time finding out about the post and the library. A study of succession at senior management level demonstrated that librarians applying for posts at senior levels used a variety of sources prior to interview in order to prepare themselves.[2] These included published sources, such as directories, yearbooks, statistical publications, prospectuses, surveys, council reports, local newspapers, professional literature and annual reports. They also contacted individuals known to them who worked in the library advertising the post or who were knowledgeable about it. Visits, usually made on the applicant's own initiative, looking round the library like a user, were also popular. Increasingly, this approach is not confined to those applying for senior management positions, and similar research is carried out by applicants for posts at a wide variety of levels. Many libraries now have a Website which, in addition to providing information for the users of the service, may also provide potential applicants with another means to gather information on the organization. For example, the Birkbeck Library Website provides links to the library's annual report and strategic plan.

Some librarians provide only brief information about a job and its context, and leave the rest to the initiative of the applicants. The amount of preparation carried out by applicants can be a useful guide to their general approach to tasks, but there is a danger that applicants may pick up quite erroneous ideas about the job, and also that significant information may be missed. As success--ful recruitment is dependent upon attracting applicants of sufficiently high calibre, the information which a potential applicant receives needs to convey a positive impression. As libraries have become more aware of the impact that poorly presented supporting information can have, the quality of supplementary packs supplied to potential applicants has improved.

Effective management demands systematic planning, and from the beginning thought should be given to the information provided for the applicants throughout the selection process, as well as how to obtain information about the applicants. Gould emphasizes:

> The organization has to attract them to apply, and throughout the process, particularly when ready to offer a job, has to present itself in such a way that the preferred candidate will be disposed to accept.[3]

The trend of offering the opportunity to contact someone within the organization for an informal discussion prior to submitting an application provides potential candidates with another means of gaining information about the post. It is usual for the named contact to be the line manager for the advertised post, who is in a position to give accurate information about the post which is to be filled. The willingness of a potential applicant to follow up this offer may give some indication of their commitment and interest in the post. Care should be taken not to attach too much importance to this move on the part of an applicant. Other applicants who have not made informal contact may be equally, or more, suitable for the post. We are of the opinion that making contact prior to the application or interview is primarily a means for the applicant to gain information about the place of work, rather than a useful way for the recruiters to gain an insight into the applicant's suitability.

Figure 5.1 also suggests that information is communicated in two main forms: written (including both paper and electronic formats), and person-to-person. The written information can be read and re-read at leisure, and compared. On the one hand, the applicant can compare job details for several libraries, while the selectors can compare the written applications, references, test scores and so on. Case studies and exercises may be completed in written form, or can be carried out orally. Group selection methods and the interview are oral exercises, and although written summaries and assessments might be made, the applicants and selectors acquire their information by listening and observing.

In selection, two sorts of information are obtained. The most obvious is that which is obtained directly from the applicant, for example in response to a question in an interview or on an application form; from the selectors' side, it is the information provided in the job details. The other sort of information is that which is provided indirectly through the process itself, for example the presentation of the information on the application form or at the interview; from the selectors' side, it is the way they conduct the interview or the quality of the information provided to potential applicants. Both 'sides' have to be aware whether or not the message they think they have presented is the one received by the intended audience. This is why opportunities should be taken to discover the message that is being received. At the very least, applicants who fail to be successful at interviews, and libraries which do not attract quality recruits, ought to become interested in such knowledge. This is likely to be a difficult process, but is one which must be undertaken if the situation is to improve.

Both 'sides' in the selection process will be involved in a matching exercise. The selectors will be trying to match the person specification to the applicants, and the applicants will be matching the job to their requirements. This may or may not be carried out systematically, but it is certain that both sides will have built up a rich, 'holistic' picture of their own situation. The selectors, for example, will be aware of the history of the library's achievements, the management style of the library, and the various individuals with whom the successful applicant will be working. The applicants will be aware of their own domestic situations, their career aspirations, and their likes and dislikes concerning jobs and people. The richer pictures may contain elements which neither side particularly wants to present to the other.

The selectors and applicants should also avoid treating the present situation as an unchanging one. Organizations need staff who are able to adapt quickly as the demand to deliver more services with fewer staff continues. Recruitment is a vital way of ensuring that the workforce is ready and able to manage such change. Goulding et al. refer to the various warnings of recruitment crises in some areas of the sector.[4] In such an environment, employers need to ensure that sufficient effort and resources are dedicated to recruitment and selection. Mistakes are hard to rectify, and can have a considerable effect on the organization. That is why selection must be seen as something more than describing existing posts and filling them. Potential sources of information are dealt with in more depth in the remainder of this chapter.

STAGES IN THE SELECTION AND RECRUITMENT OF STAFF

ADVERTISING

It may be appropriate to consider making an internal appointment. Where there has been a lack of mobility among staff, there is likely to be a reasonable field for promotion, especially in a large library, and internal promotion can be an important motivating factor in such circumstances. In addition, the person's performance and potential will already be known, and less training and induction into the procedures and culture of the organization will be required. Different organizations have different policies on internal appointments, and usually the library will need to adhere to the policy of the parent body. For example, any appointment which would entail a promotion for an internal applicant, or which is for more than a length of time prescribed by the parent body, may have to be advertised externally.

Where jobs are advertised externally, it is important that information is also circulated internally, and our view is that for motivation purposes alone, it should normally be the case that all internal candidates are interviewed. However, the decision not to interview an internal candidate may be taken if it is clear that the applicant is far from suitable for the post. This decision will then avoid unfairly raising the expectations of the internal candidate. If such a decision is taken, or if an internal candidate is interviewed but not appointed, then it is vital that constructive feedback is given to the unsuccessful candidate.

Internal appointments save on some of the costs of recruitment, provide motivation for staff, and have the benefit of reducing the induction period. However, as Parry reminds us:

> an internal appointment always generates a vacancy elsewhere. It may be at a lower level if a promotion has taken place but an internal appointment can actually have the effect of lengthening, rather than shortening, the recruiting process overall.[5]

This should not be taken as reason not to appoint internally, but the transition of the successful applicant from their original post to their new post requires careful management, and thought will need to be given as to how all the various duties can be most effectively prioritized.

There are a number of standard advertising outlets used by libraries for the recruitment of staff. Certain constraints may be laid down by the parent body, such as advertising a post internally as a first step, or the use of particular publications such as local newspapers. It is unlikely that a search for new outlets will be worth the effort, since librarians seeking posts will regularly peruse familiar sources. In Britain, such sources include:

- the Library Association's *Library and Information Appointments Supplement*
- *The Guardian*
- *The Times*
- *The Times Literary Supplement*
- *The Times Educational Supplement*

- *The Times Higher Education Supplement*
- *The Daily Telegraph.*

Local newspapers are frequently used for para-professional posts, and Job Centres can also be used.

The Internet is increasingly being used to advertise jobs. Research conducted by the Institute of Personnel and Development found that: 'Nearly half – 45 per cent – of employers now use the Internet when recruiting to certain posts … this represents an increase in Internet usage of more than 10 percentage points compared with just 12 months ago'.[6] Details of vacancies can be made available on Websites such as <http://www.jobs.ac.uk> and e-mail lists such as lis-link.[7] Parent bodies may also have a policy of advertising all vacancies on the organization's Website, if one exists.

There are also a number of specialist recruitment agencies, for example:

- Aslib Professional Recruitment Ltd
- INFOmatch, the Library Association recruitment agency
- Keep Informed Recruitment Services, a division of Informed Business Services
- Instant Library Recruitment Ltd
- Sue Hill Recruitment & Services Ltd
- TFPL Recruitment Ltd.

Hill and Jago have described what a good specialist recruitment agency is able to do. Such an agency should provide a totally confidential and professional service, which can include:

- offering access to a wide range of candidates, all of whom will have been interviewed by the agency
- assistance with, and advice on, drawing up a list of the skills the job requires
- preparing a shortlist of potential candidates
- advertising on your behalf.[8]

Some organizations make use of advertising agents, who normally receive a fee from the medium. They will design advertisements, and can also provide response analyses, which can be useful for future recruitment.

Specialist staff may need to be recruited through sources such as specialist publications or group contacts.

Search consultants are sometimes used to 'headhunt' senior staff. The consultants will find out as much as they can about the requirements of the client before researching into likely candidates, who will normally be approached first by telephone and encouraged to meet the consultants to discuss the position further. Eventually, recommended candidates will get together with the client, and negotiations can take place. Roberts describes the benefits and disadvantages of using search consultants. The main benefits are that this method is 'more targeted and more proactive than simply relying on the appropriate people to apply'. The disadvantages are the cost, which is likely to be high, and the fact that the success of the process is 'very dependent upon the skills and the network of the "head-hunter"'.[9]

The first 'message' about the library is conveyed to the potential applicants by the advertisement, therefore it needs to be planned carefully. The objective is to attract those potential applicants the library would wish to attract, and discourage those who would be unlikely to make a success of the job. The advertisement should be drafted with that objective in mind, and to help to achieve it, the person compiling it ought to be aware of the sort of information the potential applicant would like to have. Use should be made of the job description and person specification to provide such information as:

- the name of the organization
- the title of the post (in the professional press titles will be understood; advertisements placed elsewhere may need explanations)
- salary and grade
- main purpose and duties
- the essential qualities being sought
- special conditions, such as awkward hours of work, and also positive features, such as approved training schemes.

Figure 5.2 is an example of an advertisement which conveys these facts and gives some flavour of the organization.

Unlike other stages of the selection process, advertising is carried out in public, and therefore has an important public relations dimension, giving the library an opportunity to present its image to the profession and beyond. Many librarians make a habit of reading through advertisements, whether they are looking for a post or not, and their attention can be held by the information and design of a carefully thought out advertisement. There are obvious constraints of space and money, but very short advertisements or ones which use small type can give the impression of a penny-pinching organization.[10]

When a library wants to fill a vacancy quickly, various options are available. In some cases, the library may have employed a person as a trainee or as a placement student, and may have systematic appraisal records which can suggest those who would be fairly certain to prove a success in the post. Speculative letters requesting employment can be kept to build up lists of individuals interested in posts. Part-time staff may be willing to work addi-

Subject Librarian
(Health Sciences)

Up to £20,892 with
possible progression to £22,782

We are looking for an experienced and enthusiastic librarian to join our well established Science, Engineering and Health team. Working in our innovative, purpose built library, you will be dealing with one of the largest schools covering a wide range of science disciplines. You will be responsible for collection development, enquiry work, classification and for continuing the links between the school and the library. You will also be developing the growing involvement in information skills work and contributing to the delivery of information through our web pages.

You will be a chartered librarian with either a degree in an appropriate subject or with substantial experience in delivering information services in a relevant subject area. Excellent communication skills and an ability to work well on your own as well as working effectively in a team will be essential requirements for succeeding in this post. **Ref No: CA50/01**

For an informal discussion please contact Sub Librarian, Science, Engineering and Health, telephone 024 7688 7534 or email

For further details and an application form please telephone the Personnel Department on 024 7688 8120, or ♪ Minicom 024 7688 8100;

Email futures.per@coventry.ac.uk

Closing date: Friday 23 March 2001.

www.coventry.ac.uk

We would particularly welcome applications from black/ethnic minority groups and people with disabilities who are under-represented in the University.

Higher Education for all

C O V E N T R Y
U N I V E R S I T Y

Figure 5.2 Advert for post at Coventry University Library

tional hours for limited periods. Recruitment agencies can often provide suitable applicants in a short space of time. If a means to fill a post quickly is found, it is advisable to offer the post on a temporary basis while the usual recruitment process is followed. This ensures that the rigour of the recruitment process is applied equally to all posts. The person appointed on a temporary basis would be eligible to apply for the post on a permanent basis, if they so wish, and should be in a good position to make a strong application.

SHORTLISTING

When a number of people apply for a post, it is normal to draw up a list of those whom the selectors consider strong contenders. At this stage, the sources of information are the application form or Curriculum Vitae (CV, also known as a résumé) and any supporting letters which candidates have sent. It is usual to wait until the shortlist is drawn up before requesting references, so these are unlikely to be available. Candidates may also supply testimonials, which can be used. The available information from each candidate should be measured against the person specification in order to ascertain those applications which most closely match the stated criteria. As well as content, presentation is important. Is the application form or CV roughly thrown together, badly laid out, full of errors? Does it ramble on inconclusively? Are there unexplained gaps? Is it legible?

When vacancies become scarcer and the number of applicants is very large, selectors tend to search more assiduously for disqualifying data, and sometimes this will represent a further refinement of the original specification. Care needs to be taken if this approach is adopted as, whilst one candidate may have supplied additional useful information, for example experience of a relevant software application, other candidates may also have this experience but may not have referred to it if it was not detailed in the original person specification they received. It is therefore vital that all stages of the selection and recruitment process, from the design of the job description to the methods used for selection, are designed to gather appropriate and sufficient information to enable an informed decision to be reached.

Application forms

Application forms should be designed to facilitate analysis against the person specification, although, as members of larger organizations, libraries are frequently obliged to use less helpful forms.

The basic information should include:

- name

- qualifications
- employment history
- work experience (main duties and responsibilities)
- training
- health
- current salary and period of notice required
- relevant practical information (for example, is a current driving licence held?).

There should also be sufficient space for candidates to provide further information in support of their application.

Many forms require candidates to declare criminal records. The Rehabilitation of Offenders Act (1974) provides that certain convictions should be regarded as 'spent' after specified periods of time. Spent convictions need not be declared for the purpose of employment. The length of 'rehabilitation' varies, and is dependent upon the penalty. Custodial sentences of over two-and-a-half years can never become spent. There are various exceptions to the Act: for example, where a post involves working with children, spent convictions must be declared if the post is designated as such.

Application forms are assumed to be part of what the Sex Discrimination Act describes as 'arrangements made for deciding who should be offered employment'. Some questions on application forms could be unlawful if:

- they are asked only of women (or men)
- it can be shown that the asking of them constitutes 'less favourable treatment'.

In the UK, the Equal Opportunities Commission has produced guidelines:

> Questions on application forms should not suggest that the employer wishes to take into account any factors which would, or might, discriminate on grounds of sex or of marriage. Such questions undermine the confidence of applicants that they will be treated fairly and without prejudice, even where there is no intention to discriminate.[11]

The Equal Opportunities Commission gives examples of questions which might deter some applicants from completing the forms and cause suspicion that the answers might be used in an unlawful manner. These are questions dealing with families, ages of children, married/single/divorced status, intentions about engagement and/or about having children, or intimate personal questions.

Many employers collect information on areas such as gender, marital status, ethnic origins and disabilities for monitoring purposes. The Equal Opportunities Commission recommends that in these cases this information should be collected on 'a separate sheet or tear-off slip, which is not made available to those making decisions at any stage of the recruitment or selection process'.[12] Further, applicants should be reassured that this approach will be taken. The applicant pack supplied by Essex Libraries contains a form entitled 'Recruitment Monitoring Information'. This clearly states: 'This form should be returned with your application form, but will be removed from your application prior to shortlisting.'

Curricula Vitae

The use of CVs can cut the cost and the time scale of the process as there is no need to supply an application form and wait while this is returned. However, it can also remove the opportunity to supply additional information about the post, the job description and the person specification. This will result in less focused applications, and the information presented will differ between applicants. Consequently, the process of shortlisting and comparing candidates becomes more difficult. The combination of a CV and covering letter is more useful than a CV alone.

Biodata

Research has shown that biodata has higher validity than interviews, and is particularly useful where very large numbers of applications are received. Roberts provides a concise definition of biodata:

> Biodata is an abbreviation of 'biographical data' and is the process by which the story of people's lives will hold keys to their future. It uses the simple assumption that past actions, behaviours, etc. will be the best predictor of future behaviours, patterns, etc.[13]

Using the criteria defined in the person specification, a pool of biodata items is drawn up which is related to success in the job. There is insufficient research in library and information work to provide a list with high prediction levels, so initially a library may look at biodata provided by successful applicants who have been effective in their posts. Available research suggests biodata items will normally come under the following categories:

- demographic details (sex, age, family circumstances)
- education and professional qualifications
- previous employment history and work experience
- positions of responsibility outside work
- leisure interests
- other information, such as career/job motivation.

137

Data would be provided in application forms, designed as biodata question-naires. The biodata is then weighted according to importance, and items combined into groups. The idea is to end up with a single score. Caution must be exercised, particularly with background data, to avoid discrimination. This factor may account for the fact that the research undertaken by the IPD found that just 7 per cent of respondents used biodata as a selection method.[14]

INFORMAL INTERVIEWS

Informal interviews can take various forms, and the approach will be influ-enced by the post which is being filled, the management style of the organization, and the number of candidates being interviewed. There are two main forms of informal interview: the *tour* and the *informal meeting*.

Many selection processes now include a tour of the library. The candidate is given a chance to ask questions informally and look around, whilst a member of the library staff can make an assessment and feed this back to the selection panel. The tour needs to be conducted by someone who can answer questions posed by candidates, and as with all other stages of the process, the tour should convey a positive impression of the service. Parry argues that above all, the member of staff giving the tour must be 'a good communicator who can emphasize the strong points of the organization'.[15] Candidates may be unaware that an assessment is being carried out, though the perceptive ones will realize that they are being assessed from the moment they arrive.

The second type of informal interview, the informal meeting, tends to be used more frequently in the selection of senior staff. For example shortlisted candidates may be invited to meet with a group of senior members of the organization. The group may be made up of a mixture of people with whom the successful candidate will work closely, and those who are senior to the advertised post within the staff structure. Informal meetings such as these do help to simulate the situations in which the successful candidate would find themselves after appointment.

For some people, informal discussions are a welcome and relaxing contrast to the formal interview, whilst for others, as one respondent remarked, 'a too detailed preamble to the interview can cause confusion or make candidates ill-at-ease in interview'. In particular, this can happen during 'lunch with the candidates' or when candidates are taken round the library together and feel they must be observed asking sensible questions.

When informal meetings or tours are to be used in making the final deci-sion, it is desirable that the criteria used are directly related to the person specification and are similar to those being used by the selection panel. There will need to be timely feedback to the decision-makers by those involved in facilitating the informal interviews. In instances where the decision will be given on the same day as the final assessment is made, communication has to take place fairly quickly. If it is the practice for a longer period of time to elapse between the interview and the final decision, for example to enable outstanding references to be collected, there will be more leeway in the timing of this feedback. Even in such cases, those involved should be provided with the opportunity to communicate their impressions as soon as possible, while the event is fresh in their mind.

FORMAL INTERVIEWS

The favourite – and in many cases, the only – face-to-face method used in selection is the formal interview, although studies have frequently found that it is the most unreliable. Roberts suggests that the reason for the popularity of the interview is also the reason for its unreliability:

> It [the interview] is a very natural process; being able to sit and talk to others is a skill which is not confined to the professional recruiter and is shared by the candidate and the line manager or client. It may also be the downfall of many interviews which are designed as an opportunity to talk rather than as a technique for gathering data on a candidate in order to be able to make a decision.[16]

With due attention to the person specification and the post that is being filled, the interview can be a productive selection method. Dewberry concludes that 'designed appropriately and used correctly, the interview is good!'.[17] It is for this very reason that the interview requires careful planning. In this section, suggestions are made which should improve the performance of the interviewer.

The use of an interview form which is directly related to the specification helps to ensure that the interview keeps on relevant lines. The example from the Royal Society of Medicine demonstrates how such a form can be laid out (see Figure 5.3).

As far as possible, interviewers should want accurate information to be communicated to both 'sides' – directly through the information given, and indirectly through the process itself. Factors that inhibit the flow of relevant information should be minimized in favour of those that facilitate it.

In librarianship, the number of interviewers can range from one to many. In the private sector, smaller numbers are the norm, with two-level interviews, one with a member of Human Resources staff and one with the manager, being quite common. In the public sector, a panel of interviewers is the usual format. In addition to library staff, the panel may include a member of the Human Resources section or members of the parent organization: for example, a member of academic staff may be included in the panel interviewing for

139

LIBRARY ASSISTANT: GRID

CANDIDATE'S NAME:

INTERVIEWER:

INTERVIEW START: END:

QUESTION	CRITERIA	COMMENTS	GRADE	SCORE
				Grade x WF
1. What makes you a good communicator?	1		6 x	
2 What makes a team work well?	3		6 x	
3. How do your organise your own work?	5		4 x	

Figure 5.3 Interview assessment form from the Royal Society of Medicine Library

LIBRARY ASSISTANT: GRID

CANDIDATE'S NAME:

INTERVIEWER:

INTERVIEW START: END:

QUESTION	CRITERIA	COMMENTS	GRADE	SCORE Grade x WF
4. Why do we need deadlines at work?	4		6 x	
5. What have you used a computer for & what packages did you use?	6		4 x	
6. What kinds of material have you had to retrieve? How was it arranged?	7		2 x	
7. Is there any health reason which would prevent you from retrieving and shelving the type of materials you've seen on your tour?	9			

Figure 5.3 continued

141

142

LIBRARY ASSISTANT: GRID

CANDIDATE'S NAME:

INTERVIEWER:

INTERVIEW START: END:

QUESTION	CRITERIA	COMMENTS	GRADE	SCORE
				Grade x WF
8. You know that The RSM has an equal opportunities policy. What does this mean to you?	10		2 x	

N.B. Chair asks Qs 1-3, MJ 4-5, SB 6-8.
Well Met scores 3; Met scores 2; Partial scores 1; Not Demonstrated scores 0.
Criteria 2 and 8 assessed in selection. The test also assesses criteria 3, 4, 5 and 7.
Total score = 90. Questions 1-3 have WF of 6, 4-5 have WF of 4 and 6 and 8 have WF of 2. Question 7 is not scored.

Figure 5.3 concluded

a subject librarian in a university library. The Commission for Racial Equality recommends that more than one person should be involved in the shortlisting and interviewing processes.[18]

Attention should be paid to a number of factors.

The environment of the interview

Candidates should be properly received. Their names and times of appointment must be known by the first person they will meet, even if this is not a member of library staff, for example a security officer or company receptionist. If they have to wait a long time, tea, coffee or a cool drink could be offered. Attention should be given to the place in which candidates wait before being called into the interview room. It should not be within earshot of the interview room, but should be a comfortable area in which it is easy for candidates to compose themselves. If other selection procedures are taking place on the same day as the interview, for example tours or tests, thought needs to be given as to how the processes interleave, and all the staff involved need to be properly briefed as to where candidates should be asked to wait between the various stages. Interruptions and outside noise should be avoided in the interview room, and seats should preferably be at the same level for interviewers and interviewees. Some interviewers dislike physical barriers between themselves and the interviewees, whilst others prefer to acknowledge the formality of the occasion, and also provide a resting place for documents and notes.

The pattern of the interview

Interviews often follow established lines, and if these norms are followed, interviewees are likely to be more relaxed, especially when they become used to the experience. It is helpful to inform candidates beforehand about the form of the interview, who will be interviewing, and what will happen afterwards. The length of the interview will vary greatly, depending on the post which is being filled. It is advisable to allow at least 20 minutes in order to allow a good rapport to develop between the interviewers and the candidate. More time is likely to be needed for the recruitment of senior staff. In such cases, the job will be complex, so more questions will be necessary in order to determine which candidates most closely match the person specification. The candidate will have more experience to draw upon, and so should be able to give fuller answers. It is worth remembering that interviewing is a tiring process for all participants, and that an over-long interview is likely to result in both the interviewers and candidates performing below their optimum. Rather than simply extending the interview to enable more questions to be asked, it is advisable to consider using other selection techniques to complement the interview. Once the maximum length of the interview has been decided upon, it needs to be used to determine the timetable for the whole process. It is important to build in some time between candidates in order to allow the interviewers to make notes once a candidate has left the interview room and to prepare the papers relating to the next candidate.

Before the questioning starts, candidates should be introduced to the selectors and the plan of the interview should be explained. Candidates should always be given an opportunity to ask questions at the end of the interview, and this should be explained during the introduction.

It is usual to begin the interview gently and lead up to more difficult questions. There may still be some who believe in making the interview a stressful experience, perhaps in order to simulate the stresses in the job. There is no evidence to suggest that a confrontational approach will identify candidates more able to withstand the pressures of the post. We are inclined to agree with Parry that 'aggressive interviewing techniques are unlikely to generate an atmosphere of trust and are generally discouraged'.[19]

Interviewers should get together well before the interviews and plan the progress they want to make. This does not mean that the interview will not move spontaneously, but it should ensure that it progresses in a logical manner and covers all key points. Keeping to the timings for the interviews is important. Hill and Jago refer to a survey published in 1990 by the UK employment agency Reed Employment, which showed that whilst 4 per cent of candidates said they had been late for interviews, 33 per cent of employers admitted being late.[20] This shows a lack of courtesy, and presents a very poor image.

Questioning

Obviously, the questions should not be unnecessarily complicated or vague. Interviewers may feel that this form of questioning can be used in a deliberate way to test candidates, but must always remember they are communicating their own vagueness to candidates, and that the outcome will be of little or no value: 'The purpose of the interview is to clarify and supplement the information already given by each shortlisted candidate, and to help each to appear in their best light. Therefore, questions designed to trip up or confuse candidates serve no purpose other than to massage the ego of the interviewer.'[21] As far as possible, the wording of the questions should be decided in advance, to ensure that the question is an effective vehicle for discovering whether the skills in the person specification are present or not. 'Closed' questions, requiring no more than 'yes' or 'no' answers, should be avoided because the selectors' object is to hear what the candidate has to say, and therefore to ask questions which invite the candidate to do this. Useful approaches include relating questions to experience ('What experience have you had of dealing with difficult users?'), asking for a discussion of principles or beliefs ('What have you found to be the best way of dealing with difficult users?') and introducing hypothetical situations ('What would you do if a lecturer refused to pay a fine?').

Fear, who has written a comprehensive work on interviewing, says that when interviewers are thoroughly trained in his methods, they do only 15 or 20 per cent of the talking.[22] He suggests a number of ways to ask open or exploratory questions, including the use of 'laundry lists' – listing a number of possible responses, and giving a choice to the interviewee. This method can help, particularly where an interviewee is having difficulty with a question which requires considerable analysis or in following up a 'clue' provided in previous questioning. For example, the interviewer may want to discover a person's strengths and weaknesses by saying: 'Some librarians like working with readers best, others like working with books and others like classifying and cataloguing. What gives you most satisfaction?' Another way is to offer two views that are more or less opposites, and to ask which the interviewee supports. For example: 'In your last post, did you publicize the library as much as you would have liked, or in hindsight, would it have been better to have spent more time on it?'

The opportunity should often be taken to follow up general questions with a request for more detail by the use of probes such as: 'Tell me more about ...' and 'Why does that appeal to you?' However, interviewers should avoid 'grilling' the applicants, which could cause them not to respond freely. Regard must be given to the race relations, sex discrimination and disability discrimination laws, and questioning should therefore avoid discrimination on grounds of race, sex or disability. Questions about personal matters present the most difficulty, because 'an employer must be able to satisfy him/herself whether the potential recruit is likely to serve for a reasonable time, come to work with reasonable regularity and meet the demands of the job in such matters as mobility, overtime and spending nights away from home'.[23]

The Equal Opportunities Commission offers the following advice:

> No questions should be based upon assumptions regarding women's roles in the home and the family. There was, perhaps, a time when all such responsibilities were met by women, with men being the sole breadwinners and doing nothing domestically. That situation is no longer true and questions should not be based upon any such assumptions.
>
> Questions regarding intentions about marriage and having children are, rightly, regarded as impertinent, are resented and should never be asked.
>
> Any questions which are asked to find out whether the individual can meet the needs of the job on hours, overtime, mobility etc. should be asked equally of men and women.

> Questions should be about job requirements and not about domestic intentions or arrangements.[24]

There is concern in some organizations that exactly the same questions should be asked of all candidates, without variation. The authors are of the opinion that following a 'script' precisely will lead to an inflexible and unresponsive approach which is unlikely to put candidates at their ease or enable them to demonstrate their skills and abilities fully. It is our view that interviewers should decide upon a core list of questions to ensure that all relevant points are covered, and that these should be put to all candidates. These core questions should be complemented by supplementary questions as necessary, and these may differ from candidate to candidate.

Listening and responding

Selection interviews are rarely tape-recorded, so the only chance to hear what is said is at the interview itself. Careful listening is very important, because it also indicates the interviewers' interest in the candidate. Salient points should be noted as soon as possible, although it is difficult to make notes without appearing not to be listening. In addition, interviewees can be disturbed if notes appear to be taken when information of a highly personal or unsatisfactory nature is imparted. Fear sensibly recommends that interviewers wait until favourable information is given before writing unfavourable information previously given.[25] If the interview is being conducted by a panel, it may help if the members come to an arrangement to take notes for each other. This avoids the conflict of needing to write down the responses given by candidates while maintaining the flow of the interview by interacting with the candidate.

When interviewing a series of candidates, it is easy to confuse one with another. It is a good idea to write a brief description of each person alongside assessment notes, to ensure no mistake has been made. What candidates fail to say is as important as what they say. Interviewers should be careful to listen to, and if necessary wait for, all answers, and not give a 'halo' to those candidates who start well or have certain outstanding qualities. Nor should one or two early mistakes disqualify a candidate for the rest of the interview. It is well known that interviewers often make decisions after only a short time in the interview. The estimate of how long a candidate has to make an impression varies, and research reported in *The Guardian* revealed that interviewers may make decisions within a minute. The article argues that instinct informs the quick decisions, and necessitates these in order to ascertain whether or not a situation is a threat.[26] Interviewers need to be aware that such reactions take place, and to guard against the effects of snap judgements. Involving more

146

than one person in the interview and combining a variety of selection processes will assist with this.

The response that is made to answers is known to influence interviewees. The interviewer can control the pace of the interview, and through indicating approval or disapproval of responses, affect the course of it. At worst, this can cause interviewees to withhold information and try to please the interviewers by telling them what they believe the interviewers would like to hear.

Although the primary focus will be on what is said, non-verbal cues will be playing a significant part, and the competent interviewer will be aware of them. In particular, facial expression and body movement are important, especially where they conflict with what is being said. There are some difficulties in applying kinesic analysis to selection interviewing, because interviewees are often nervous, and betray that nervousness under stress. On their part, interviewers can ease that stress by responding facially to information given. It is well known that the raising of eyebrows and smiling helps to indicate interest and friendliness.

In spite of its popularity, the traditional interview has often been criticized because of its artificial nature and its bias in favour of those who 'interview well' but may not be good at the job. Selectors should therefore not ignore the written evidence when coming to their conclusion. A number of librarians have been sufficiently dissatisfied as to devise additional methods which simulate more closely the actual work which the successful applicant will have to perform.

GROUP SELECTION

The simplest form of this method is to give the group of candidates a topic to discuss, and then observe them. Stoakley believes that 'the technique can reveal valuable information on group problem solving, confidence, assertiveness, influencing skills, communication, empathy, leadership and teamwork'.[27] In some cases, current topics such as income generation or the management of electronic journals are sent to candidates before the selection event. Other topics may be suggested on the day. A trained assessor should carry out the observation and analysis. A second form is that of the case study or command exercise, in which candidates take the chair in turn and outline their solutions to a problem given to them some time before, and defend it before the other candidates.

Group exercises can be presented in written form by individual candidates, can be carried out with the selection panel or with the other candidates, or most realistically, they can be performed with the staff with whom the successful candidate will be working, and the case studies can simulate actual problems encountered in the post for which they have applied.

147

Assessment of work in groups presents problems, but the type of analysis described in Chapter 8 could be used with profit.

PRESENTATIONS

An increasing number of posts involve making presentations. These may be in the form of training sessions for colleagues or readers, or presenting ideas to library staff or to other staff in the organization. If successful candidates are going to need to make presentations in the course of their work, it is useful to include a presentation from applicants as part of the selection process.

The post which is to be filled will determine the topics. The presentation may be made to just the interview panel, or other staff may also be present. Timely feedback from any other staff who attend will be required, just as with the informal interview.

Candidates should be informed in advance of the topic, the length of time the presentation should take, and the audience which will be present. Unless the presentation is also intended to test the applicants' use of particular equipment or software packages, a choice of audio-visual aids should be offered to candidates. Figure 5.4 reproduces the guidelines supplied to candidates required to give a presentation as part of the selection process. As with all methods of selection, the presentations should be measured against the person specification.

Presentation topic for ALSM interviews

You are required to prepare a five minute presentation to be given to the panel at the start of the interview.

A lecturer approaches you at the library counter and briefly mentions that she thinks they may need a few more books when the course she leads is upgraded from a part time diploma to a full time MA. Briefly outline what you think the Assistant Library Services Manager should do.

- The presentation may not last any longer than five minutes. Candidates who exceed the time will be asked to stop speaking as soon as the time limit is reached.
- You may not use any aids or handouts other than a single side black and white A4 handout, but this is optional.
- You are not expected to know the circumstances at CSSD, but should make your comments based on your library service experience.

Figure 5.4   Topic and guidelines for presentation given by candidates for the post of Assistant Library Services Manager at the Central School of Speech and Drama Library

TESTS

Tests fall into two main types. Ability tests are directly related to the job, for example shelving tests or tests involving a particular software package which is used frequently in the post holder's work. This might be the library catalogue, a certain database or a software application such as a word processing program. Secondly, there are personality tests. Roberts draws a distinction between the two types:

> Although ability tests are tests in the true sense of levels of performance and of pass/fail, the same is not true of personality tests, which aim to gauge the innate traits and characteristics of people, codify them, and compare them with others.[28]

Since all tests can be somewhat threatening, it is good practice to inform candidates beforehand, and to reassure them that the tests are relevant and are only part of the selection procedure. In order to comply with the Data Protection Act (1998), individuals should be provided with their results if they so wish.

If tests are to be successful, they should enable the selectors to measure how far candidates possess the various attributes required by the person specification, and like other methods, they should be good predictors of performance in jobs. The validity of any test is therefore very important, and is essentially the extent to which it measures what it purports to measure. Selectors will also be concerned with 'concurrent validity' – how scores correlate with some other measure of the quality being assessed – for example, students' scores on a verbal ability test matching the ratings made already by their tutor. Predictive validity is even more useful, as it compares test scores with performance measures on the job taken at a later time. We are not aware of such measures being taken in library and information work. Whilst it is normally not difficult with most methods for candidates to appreciate what the selectors are trying to do (its 'face validity'), some tests appear at first acquaintance not to be related to the job for which the candidate is applying. In these cases, candidates can feel alienated and resentful. Jones states that even tests that are scientifically valid and reliable will fail if they lack face validity: 'If no one wants to do the test because it seems to be a waste of time, then the test has failed the public relations test, however scientifically proven it may be.'[29]

The user of tests should also have confidence in their reliability, which means that the test is consistent in the results it produces. For example, a verbal reasoning test that gave wildly differing scores for the same people from one week to the next would be of no value. Fletcher et al. state that in ability tests, 'a reliability of +0.75 or above based on a sample size of at least 100 should be expected', and that for personality tests, 'a reliability of +0.65 or above based on a sample size of at least 100 may be considered acceptable'.[30]

Most of the popular tests are supplied with information on their reliability and what they purport to measure. The British Psychological Society emphasizes that untrained people should not use tests. It describes testing as 'a social contract in which all parties should seek a common shared understanding of the process'.[31] In the UK, all reputable test publishers maintain registers of trained test administrators, and will only supply tests to those administrators who are registered with them.

The British Psychological Society is aware that factors such as 'sex, ethnicity or social class may act to obscure, mask or bias a person's true score on a test'. It advises users that: 'Test manuals should state whether the test has been evaluated for potential bias.'[32] Clearly, users could be breaking the law if the test would lead to discrimination. The reasons for using the test must be carefully thought out. The attribute that is being tested must be essential for the post which is to be filled, and the test should be the most effective way of exploring this attribute. The test chosen should have norms for groups as similar as possible to those you wish to test. Normative information which describes the groups tested and the range of scores is available in the manuals which accompany the tests. The Equal Opportunities Commission warns that whilst it might appear that tests cannot introduce sex bias, this is not always the case, and that safeguards are necessary.[33]

Ability tests are used in recruitment for a wide range of posts. There are various tests that can also be used to test mental ability, such as verbal reasoning, numerical ability and spatial ability.

Libraries also make use of tests of attainment, such as numeracy, spelling, grammar and keyboard skills, often by devising simple tests of their own. For example, The Central School of Speech and Drama gives a test to potential shelvers. This requires the candidates to put 50 books in Dewey order followed by the alphabetical suffix within a time limit of 10 minutes. The test is designed to check:

- ability to work rapidly yet accurately
- ability to cope with numerical and alphabetical filing systems
- ability to listen to and follow simple information given when working under pressure.

Others require library assistants to do mental arithmetic with fines and giving change, or to use the library catalogue to answer questions about items which the library holds.

Personality tests were originally designed as diagnostic aids in clinical and psychiatric medicine, and are probably the most controversial of all. The majority pose questions which prompt the candidates to describe themselves in some way which is then related to scores for some known group. Goulding et al. identified Cattell's Sixteen Personality Factor (16 PF) Inventory as the 'most appropriate for assessing the personality traits demanded by LIS employers'.[34] The scores in this test are computed from the analysis of answers to around 200 questions, and personality is measured on a ten-point scale for each of the personality factors. Table 5.1 lists some of them:

Table 5.1   Selected personality factors from Cattell's 16 PF Inventory

Low-score description	High-score description
Reserved	Outgoing
Less intelligent	More intelligent
Humble	Assertive
Shy	Venturesome
Tough-minded	Tender-minded
Trusting	Suspicious
Self-assured	Apprehensive
Group-dependent	Self-sufficient
Relaxed	Tense

We often refer to 'personality' in everyday speech, but it is difficult to pin down its meaning in any precise way. In the past, personality was viewed as a characteristic mode which a person consistently chose to deal with the world – 'same old Bill' – but more recently it has been recognized that responses can change with experience, and that the way people behave will vary with the different situations in which they find themselves. The selector tries to predict how a person will behave in the future, and it has to be said that personality tests are of dubious value, although Smith and George believe that there is emerging evidence for the validity of personality tests which are job-related.[35]

There is greater doubt about tests which aim to explore the values and psychological states which lie beneath thorough projective tests. Most of these are visual, and subjects are asked to explain pictures which are usually ambiguous. Probably the best-known of these is the Rorschach Ink-blot Test. Kline, a strong critic of the use of personality tests in employment selection, asserts that responses to projective tests: 'are believed to show the deepest levels of personality. However, there is, in fact little firm objective evidence that projective tests can reveal anything of the sort. Indeed, there is often little agreement between examiners or the same examiner on different occasions.'[36]

A third type of test which seems to be used rarely in the field of librarianship is those tests which aim to identify and draw conclusions from interests and motivation. Interests are defined as a liking for doing something, and may be asked about in interviews. However, research has shown a low relationship between interests and job performance, and consequently the once common trend of asking for details of interests on application forms or at interview has decreased in use.

Two examples of these sorts of tests are the Strong-Campbell Interest Inventory, which tests interests, and the Thematic Apperception Test, which via the use of black-and-white pictures, aims to identify motivation.

In the past, it was usually the case that books on psychological testing were written by professional psychologists and tended to be full of professional jargon and detail incomprehensible to non-psychologists. In contrast to such texts, an excellent introduction to testing with information on 19 tests has been written by Jones,[37] and the work by Fletcher et al.[38] is similarly accessible and practical. Both can be used by managers thinking of using tests, and by candidates required to take tests.

ASSESSMENT CENTRES

An assessment centre may be a physical place, but the term more accurately describes a particular approach to selection. An assessment centre combines methods such as interviews, tests, and presentations. Different assessors then apply criteria to the performances. Combining various methods helps to increase the validity of the overall process. Morgan makes a good case for the use of assessment centres, and also describes some of the things which can go wrong and jeopardize the process. He suggests that:

> Perhaps the success of the assessment centre approach depends upon good old-fashioned qualities like treating people with courtesy and care and making them feel valued. Too often selection is done *to* people rather than *with* them. The more you carry the candidates with you, the more likely they are to give of their best and, in the end, the more accurate will be the predication.[39]

REFERENCES

A certain amount of doubt exists concerning the value of written references. Under the Data Protection Act (1998), applicants can insist upon seeing any information which a prospective employer holds in relation to them. This, of course, includes references received from current or previous employers. Further, the legal requirements placed upon reference writers mean that it is common for them to highlight strengths rather than weaknesses. The care which employers need to exercise when writing references can be seen in the case, *Spring* v. *Guardian Assurance plc and others.*[40] Spring was dismissed from his job as an insurance salesman following the sale of an unsuitable policy to a prospective customer. After two years of unsuccessful job hunting, Spring discovered that his former employers had supplied an unsatisfactory reference. The High Court found in Spring's favour on the count of negligence, overturning the decision of the Court of Appeal, which had held the view that employers owe a duty of care only to the recipient of a reference, and not to the subject of it. In a commentary on the matter, Howard concluded that the lesson that employers must learn from this case is that 'if they prepare and send an inaccurate reference which subsequently harms the ex-employee's employment prospects, they will be in breach of their duty of care and liable to be sued for negligence'.[41]

Despite the fact that a reference is likely to be written in a bland fashion to avoid breaching the (possibly contradictory) duties of care to the potential employer and the subject of the reference, the practice of requesting references appears to be universal. A writer of references needs to be asked about the knowledge, abilities, skills and personal qualities that are considered important for the particular job. This is precisely what the person specification aims to do, and it is increasingly common to provide the person specification with the request for the reference. If one is not made available, it makes the job of the reference writer more difficult, and the resulting reference will be less useful to the selectors. We have found two questions particularly useful to ask of referees:

- 'How many days' sick leave has the applicant had in the last twelve months?'
- 'Would you employ the applicant again?'

It is common practice to ask for two references, and to insist that one is from the applicant's current employer, if there is one. In many cases, the current employer will be a librarian, and it is reasonable to assume that opinion on performance in a job, which has similarities with the one for which the person is applying, is more helpful than a reference from a personal acquaintance.

Many applicants will be unhappy about revealing their interests in another job to their current employer, and some application forms acknowledge this by allowing the applicant to indicate if they would prefer the approach to their current employer to be delayed until after the interview stage. On the other hand, it is not unknown for employers to look more favourably on those seeking employment elsewhere if they are valuable members of staff. Nonetheless, it is good practice to offer candidates the choice of when references are taken up.

In most public sector institutions, references for shortlisted candidates are requested prior to the interview, and are considered alongside other evidence. In the private sector, it is common to make appointments subject to satisfactory references, and to request them after the interview. An offer subject to references may also be necessary if the references are not available, either because they have not arrived, or because the applicant has indicated that they should not be requested until after the interview stage. Gould is particularly critical of this practice because it 'puts the referee in the invidious position of being able to exercise a veto on the appointment by giving a critical reference or refusing to give one at all'.[42] Our experience has been that almost all written references are good, and rarely affect the decision.

Since doubt exists about the value of written references, selectors may choose to obtain verbal references in addition, or instead. Verbal references should not be used as a means to by-pass the protection of an individual's privacy. When seeking or providing a verbal reference, care should be exercised over the information sought or given. Nonetheless, a telephone conversation with a professional colleague can be quite revealing, as it provides a more informal means of gathering information. In fact, it is our experience that selectors ask the very questions and provide the very information which they fail to provide when seeking written references.

Testimonials are written without a particular job in mind, for use by the person about whom it is written whenever an appropriate occasion arises. They are only of minor value, and are rarely asked for by selectors, though applicants may provide them as additional evidence.

THE FINAL STAGES

Decision-making

The reason for carrying out recruitment and selection is, of course, to find someone who most closely matches the requirements of the vacant post. Once the final stage of the process has been completed by all candidates, all the evidence provided by the candidates throughout the selection process will need to be gathered together and evaluated against the person specification, and a decision reached. The time spent on setting up and administering a selection process can easily be undermined if the evidence-gathering and decision-making is rushed. The evidence from each candidate should be considered in turn, to ensure that the final decision is reached as objectively as possible.

In some organizations, the chair of the interview panel will need to submit a formal report which outlines the reasons why the successful candidate was chosen, and also why the other candidates were unsuitable. If a report is not a requirement of the parent organization, the chair should keep a record of test results and other evidence which contributed to the final decision. These notes will prove to be useful in the event of any complaint about the process or a request for feedback.

Informing candidates

Informing someone that they have been successful is perhaps the most pleasant part of the whole process. As with other stages, the way that this is done may depend on the parent body. At some point during the interview, the candidates should have been informed of how they will hear about the outcome. A statement like this ensures that candidates are clear about this part of the process:

> We intend to reach a decision today and the successful candidate will be informed by telephone either tomorrow or the next day. Unsuccessful candidates will be informed by letter in the next week.

This also provides the opportunity to check where the candidate can be contacted. It may be that they would prefer not to be contacted at their current workplace, or if the interview has involved travelling some distance, that they are staying locally. Once the decision is reached, it is vital that the interviewers are clear about how to contact their chosen candidate. Whoever is responsible for this will need to have prepared certain information. This is likely to include:

- starting salary
- starting date
- whether there are any conditions, such as the offer being subject to references
- relocation expenses.

It is also advisable to ensure that the candidate has a contact telephone number for someone within the organization, so that if they need to check or clarify any point before they start, they are able to do so. It is usual for the offer to be made by telephone, and for this to be followed by written confirmation and then the appropriate paperwork, such as the contract. It is important to remember that a verbal offer is a binding contract, and as such should only be made when the panel are sure of their decision. Any salary offered verbally should also be considered binding, therefore such discussion should only be entered into if the chair is in a position to guarantee the agreed amount.

It is always possible that the chosen candidate will decide not to accept the post, or to withdraw before they sign the contract. In such an event, there may be a clear second choice, or it may be necessary to revisit the evidence from the remaining candidates. If the latter is necessary, then any notes or reports made at the time will prove useful.

Contacting unsuccessful candidates is obviously far from pleasant. It may be that an organization chooses to do this by letter rather than telephone. If the contact is made by telephone, preparation is again vital. Candidates may ask for immediate feedback, so this information needs to be to hand. It is sometimes the case that there has been little to choose between two (or more) candidates, and that a future application from an unsuccessful candidate would be welcome. If this is so, the candidate should be informed of this, rather than just receiving a short phone call or standard letter.

The request for feedback can seem daunting, but Roberts argues that in fact, such a request indicates that a candidate was comfortable with the selection process.[43] Constructive feedback can greatly assist candidates with future applications, and any such request should be met as fully as possible.

Induction

Recruitment and selection does not end with the decision and the acceptance of the chosen candidate. When the new member of staff arrives, the investment in their recruitment needs to be fully realized by providing a thorough induction. Induction training is covered in detail in Chapter 7, but here are a few key points:

- Provide clear directions about when and where the person should report on their first day.
- Ensure that they are expected by the first person they will meet.
- Ensure that their immediate colleagues are prepared for their arrival.
- Plan a programme which provides familiarization with their work environment and role.

6   Staff appraisal

Staff appraisal illustrates very well the nature of management and the reasons why it is a complex activity with a variety of consequences. In a sense, management takes place in all organizations, otherwise very little would be achieved. Modern management has emphasized the need to be systematic in deciding clearly the objectives of any activity, how it could best be carried out, and how it should be monitored and changed in the light of experience and a changing environment. Both practitioners and management theorists are sharply divided about the merits of staff appraisal. Proponents typically believe it to be 'the cornerstone for all training and development programmes, and the subsequent development programmes are central to keeping and motivating staff',[1] whereas W. Edwards Deming has described it as 'one of the six deadly sins afflicting American management',[2] with writers on librarianship displaying 'a noticeable attitude of scepticism' towards the effectiveness of evaluations.[3]

Those who employ formal staff appraisal systems have three main reasons for doing so. These reasons are so interconnected that even where only one or two of them are formally recognized, the other(s) will be partly present. Randell et al. have distinguished the three main objectives,[4] and their ideas are drawn upon in the list below:

1. **Performance reviews** – to improve the performance of the library, and in particular the performance of individual members of staff. This incorporates the discovery of training needs, the motivation of staff, counselling, and shaping behaviour by praise or punishment.
2. **Potential reviews** – to predict the level and type of work the individual will be capable of performing in the future.
3. **Reward reviews** – to allocate and distribute rewards more fairly.

Like most management techniques, formal appraisal is a systematization of an activity that already exists less formally. The secret of much successful management lies in formalizing existing practices without destroying the natural strengths of the informal system. Appraising people is a natural and popular activity. Inside and outside places of work, people are stating their opinions about others. At work, such appraisals are most likely to concentrate on personal strengths and weaknesses, and upon job performance. In fact, trainers are often pleasantly surprised by the quality of written appraisals produced by good managers unpractised in the art.

Over the last decade or so, there has been a considerable increase in the number of library and information services employing staff appraisal systems, often because it has become the policy of the parent body. They have long been a feature in the private sector, especially in large companies, but now they are also prevalent in the public sector.

The most obvious change has been in the academic sector, influenced initially by the Jarratt Report of 1985 on efficiency studies in universities, which recommended 'a regular review procedure, handled with sensitivity' which 'would be of benefit to staff and to the university as a whole'.[5] Greater impetus was given in 1987 in the *Twenty-third Report of Committee A*,[6] which recommended appraisal systems 'directed towards developing staff potential, assisting in the improvement of performance and enhancing career and promotion opportunities'.

Andrew Green's survey of university libraries in 1993 discovered that nearly all had adopted schemes, though 'to most libraries appraisal came as a novelty'.[7] The survey provided a good deal of information about schemes and the reactions of staff to them. Detailed information about schemes adopted by 11 former polytechnics has also been collected and published by Revill.[8]

As a result of her research into appraisal schemes, Judith Stewart came to a number of conclusions about the success of schemes,[9] and we shall be drawing upon these in discussing approaches to appraisal.

IT MUST BE APPRECIATED THAT STAFF APPRAISAL IS A VERY PERSONAL AND INDIVIDUAL EXPERIENCE

Most staff are apprehensive when asked to see their supervisor, and in most appraisal schemes a special period is put aside for the two to meet and talk frankly. However, for this to happen, careful planning is needed, and a high degree of sensitivity on the part of both participants: 'All managers face a dilemma in that identifying, discussing and doing something about weaknesses involves treading a very fine line between successful development and seriously damaging the reviewer/reviewee relationship.'[10]

Because the event is so personal, most schemes make it clear that records of the interview are only available to those who really need access. Thus, for example, the booklet explaining the London Borough of Sutton's Appraisal and Employee Development Scheme states that:

> The content of the meeting is confidential between you and your manager. Any notes made in preparing for the meeting or taken during the meeting will not form part of the paperwork. The Appraisal Record Form will be the only record of the discussion. There should only ever be two copies of the form – one for you and one for your manager. Managers must make sure they have a lockable storage place for appraisal records.
>
> Training Managers may receive information about training and development needs to help them plan the service area training programme. They may also use this information to compile reports for the service area Management Team, and to identify trends. They will not share any information about you personally.

It is inevitable that the people involved in such a personal, stressful experience will seek the relief of recounting the experience to friends and colleagues, and appraisers need to be mindful of this when they are talking to appraisees. Equally, appraisers may wish to discuss the interview with others. This will be necessary in cases where improvements are needed, such as additional training, as the Sutton example illustrates, but it should always be made clear to the appraisee that this will have to happen if progress is to be made.

THE IDEA AND BENEFITS OF APPRAISAL NEED TO BE SOLD TO STAFF

When schemes are introduced, the aims must be clearly stated and explained. A good summary of benefits is described by Bentley in guidance offered by him to those being appraised: 'What you get is recognition and appreciation; guidance for how you can improve; a sense of goodwill towards your appraiser and the organisation; increased motivation and commitment; encouragement, and increased confidence.'[11] Sheffield Hallam University's appraisee preparation notes provide a suitably bold statement (Figure 6.1).

On the other hand, Brigden and Bolton found that 'for many in education the threat, as it is seen, of appraisal, is a chimera, looming large and foul over our shoulders; for others it is a fantasy that cannot come to pass' but 'for some it is a practical part of institutional autonomy and individual professionalism'.[12] Both Stewart[13] and Ruffley[14] discovered negative reactions in academic libraries, where there was the suspicion that systems were being introduced because it would be jumping on a management bandwagon. In particular, they were seen to be connected with a new businesslike approach being adopted, and there were fears that there would be possible misunderstand-

---

Sheffield Hallam University
Learning Centre

Appraisal Scheme
Appraisee preparation notes

Introduction to Appraisal

1. What is Appraisal?

Appraisal is a process, rather than a single event. Every member of staff will have an appraisal meeting at least once a year, but the process of development, planning and the achievement and revision of objectives goes on all year round. The purpose of the appraisal meeting is to:

- look back at the last year and review past objectives
- discuss any present issues and concerns
- look forward to the forthcoming year and agree objectives
- identify development activities required to carry out the objectives

The meeting is a two way discussion. It is open and honest, free from any ambiguity and should result in a clear action plan for the next year.

2. Why is appraisal useful for me?

Appraisal is useful for a variety of reasons. The benefits include:

- better communication between staff and managers - your one to one meeting is an opportunity for you to discuss your progress and plans for the future with your manager
- increased understanding of your skills, aspirations and contributions to the team
- better understanding of the teams plans and priorities - you will be able to see where you fit in to the team and have a clear idea about what will be expected of you over the next 12 months
- a chance to raise any concerns and worries you may have and an opportunity to ask for the support you need to help you feel more confident about them
- an opportunity to discuss training and development events that may benefit you and your team

Figure 6.1 Appraisee preparation notes (extract) – Sheffield Hallam University

ings and misinterpretation of views expressed during the appraisal interview. The worst approach, Pollitt reminds us, is 'to introduce an essentially managerialist scheme whilst claiming it is developmental'.[15]

PEOPLE PREFER APPRAISAL SCHEMES WITH FIRM STRUCTURES AND FRAMEWORKS

It has been our experience that participants in meetings like to understand the structure of the meetings. That is why it is desirable to signal progress from time to time, to ensure everyone knows what is happening. This is also the case with appraisal. The form which might be used for a preparatory self-appraisal is a good basis for the interview. Pennington and O'Neill sum up the requirements quite neatly: 'a consistency of process based on clearly defined public criteria, documentation, joint formulation of reports for subsequent action and an open appeals procedure'.[16]

There is, however, difficulty in achieving uniformity of standards. In many areas of staff management we are judging other members of staff, so appraisal is not alone in having to deal with this problem. Some variation in standards is inevitable, but our own experience in receiving differing reports on the same person from different managers is that it is often the different jobs, and therefore the different abilities required, that account for variation. Most managers are remarkably good at judging, and with training and a form of appraisal which provides some structure and guidelines, a reasonable uniformity of standards can be achieved. Where there is a definite clash of personalities or philosophies, managers have to be encouraged to recognize and admit these difficulties so that a third person can be made aware of the problem when assessing performance. Strategies described in Chapter 8 are highly recommended for improving relationships, and in particular, for carrying out effective appraisal interviews.

TRAINING FOR INTERVIEWERS AND FOR THOSE TO BE INTERVIEWED IS OF PRIME IMPORTANCE

This requirement is strongly supported by Myland:

> Implementing a new or revised appraisal system is almost certainly doomed to failure if the correct emphasis is not placed upon training appraisers. An appraisal training programme will often focus upon the meaning of appraisal and what the organisation aims to achieve from implanting it in terms of primary and secondary benefits. The training might also address the system itself, explaining paperwork

and procedures, and probably most important of all, it will develop some of the special interpersonal skills required to help appraisees towards agreeing an appropriate plan of action.[17]

Greater emphasis is likely to be placed upon appraiser training than upon the training of appraisees, as the initial impetus would almost certainly have come from senior management. Green found that all but one of the universities surveyed provided training for appraisers, but in almost half the interviewees received no such assistance.[18]

THE APPRAISAL INTERVIEW IS AN IMPORTANT OCCASION

Where appraisal systems are seen to be imposed, there is the danger that staff will 'go through the motions' and that the exercise will be a waste of time. A degree of formality in the interview is therefore necessary, with no interference by telephone or personal callers. Stewart recommends a neutral room for the interview,[19] and the interview will be considered more serious if both parties are required to prepare before the interview. A good example is the 'Personal Preparation Checklist' used by appraisees before interview at the library of De Montfort University, Leicester (Figure 6.2).

Personal Preparation Checklist

1. How has my job changed over the last year or so?

2. What did I achieve?

3. What prevented me from achieving what I wanted to achieve?

4. Which aspects of my job give greatest / least satisfaction? Why?

5. What does my past work performance tell me about my strengths and weaknesses?

6. What does this tell me about my needs for training and development?

7. Do I have additional skills which I am not currently using in my job?

8. What is my main career interest?

9. In what work area could my next job be in the next 2 - 5 years?

10. Has the lack of any.skill or knowledge limited me progressing in my job or career?

Figure 6.2   Personal preparation checklist – De Monfort University

162

What will happen?

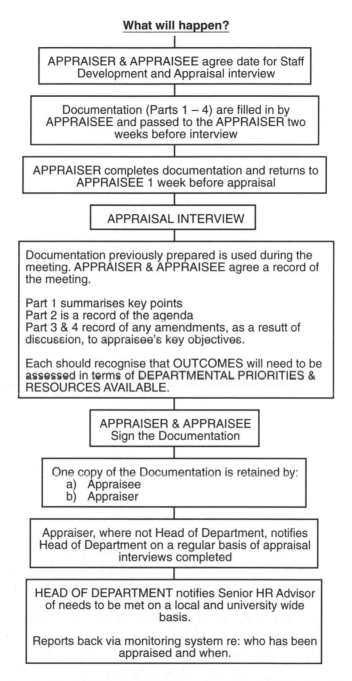

APPRAISER & APPRAISEE agree date for Staff Development and Appraisal interview

Documentation (Parts 1 – 4) are filled in by APPRAISEE and passed to the APPRAISER two weeks before interview

APPRAISER completes documentation and returns to APPRAISEE 1 week before appraisal

APPRAISAL INTERVIEW

Documentation previously prepared is used during the meeting. APPRAISER & APPRAISEE agree a record of the meeting.

Part 1 summarises key points
Part 2 is a record of the agenda
Part 3 & 4 record of any amendments, as a result of discussion, to appraisee's key objectives.

Each should recognise that OUTCOMES will need to be assessed in terms of DEPARTMENTAL PRIORITIES & RESOURCES AVAILABLE.

APPRAISER & APPRAISEE Sign the Documentation

One copy of the Documentation is retained by:
a) Appraisee
b) Appraiser

Appraiser, where not Head of Department, notifies Head of Department on a regular basis of appraisal interviews completed

HEAD OF DEPARTMENT notifies Senior HR Advisor of needs to be met on a local and university wide basis.

Reports back via monitoring system re: who has been appraised and when.

Figure 6.3 Staff appraisal scheme summary – University of Northumbria

163

In some cases, there are preliminary interviews followed by final interviews, but this can be time-consuming.

A helpful summary of a typical scheme (University of Northumbria) is shown in Figure 6.3.

THE RELATIONSHIP BETWEEN THE APPRAISER AND THE APPRAISEE IS CRITICAL

Most schemes list an improved relationship between supervisors and subordinates as an objective, largely through the requirement for managers to talk to their subordinates about matters which are very important to both of them. However, the appraisal interview cannot be viewed in isolation. We have always agreed very much with Fletcher's findings, which 'suggest that relatively little is achieved by the appraisal where existing communications are poor, though – paradoxically – this is where the need is greatest and the potential gains highest'.[20]

It is especially difficult for effective appraisal to be carried out openly where a subordinate has little professional regard for the appraiser. The two people may have personal differences which are difficult to change, though the onus is upon the senior person to establish a good working relationship. It is more likely that appraisal is simply highlighting poor management, and only considerable effort on the lines recommended in other sections of this book can hope to bring about desirable changes. It is our experience that those managers least willing to operate appraisal schemes tend to be those who are managing staff least well.

From their review of the literature, Aluri and Reichel identify many other non-performance-related factors that 'confound the outcome of performance-related evaluations', such as task complexity, clarity and predictability, and organizational characteristics such as task independence, observability of task performance, the structuring of the authority system, power differentials and the nature of communicated appraisals.[21] O'Neilly has highlighted the way in which appraisals can easily become racially biased, where, for example, temporary promotions, for which there is no open competition, are less likely for ethnic groups, and although 'appraisal is now mostly welcomed by staff … it can never be wholly objective, and it can swiftly become sinister if it reduces the self-confidence of the appraisee and produces the judgment that they are not yet capable of managing staff, without any way putting this to the test'.[22]

The style used by individuals will reflect their management styles, which in turn will be influenced by the style prevalent in the organization, which may, of course, differ in different parts of it.

In a library managed on mechanistic lines, as described in Chapter 2, a formal appraisal scheme is most likely to be instituted as a useful device for checking that staff are doing what they are told to do, though McGregor feared that an appraisal scheme in the hands of a Theory X (a mechanistic style) manager could prove a 'devastating weapon'.[23] Mechanistic managers may, however, reject the use of formal appraisal where controls are already tight enough or where management fear that their own competence may be called into question.

In an organismic system, a scheme might be welcomed if it could be shown to improve staff performance, but reservations would be likely concerning the constricting nature of a formal scheme because, in a truly organismic structure, appraisal of each other's performance would be taking place all the time. In fact, Stewart found that library staff who 'expressed satisfaction with their present access to senior managers and to staff development opportunities' could see 'little benefit in formalizing the process'.[24] A formal scheme could easily stifle spontaneous action designed to meet problems as they arise, one of the main reasons that Deming, an advocate of Total Quality Management, opposed staff evaluation as 'management by fear', with employees fearful of risk taking.[25] The mechanistic organization would be more likely than an organismic one to accept a method employing simple trait or numerical ratings, as job performance would be viewed by the latter as a complex matter not amenable to simple ratings. Angiletta states clearly the sort of organismic system he prefers:

> One which focuses not on a given event, which gives rise to given documents employing universal and formal language, but on a continuous horizontal relationship between professional colleagues which, while punctuated by time-bound control documentation directed at grades and accountability – a kind of necessary quick dose of vertical power relations – might best be termed 'performance consultation' rather than 'performance evaluation' or 'performance appraisal'.[26]

IT IS VITAL THAT DISCUSSIONS ARE ROOTED IN REALITY AND FACT

Our experience has been that appraisees are most concerned about their weaknesses as perceived by their managers, even if their overall performance has been appraised as excellent. It is therefore essential in these instances that managers have the correct facts before them on which the judgement has been made. Appraisees will almost always ask for specific events that have led to the criticism. It is also very important for the appraiser to be realistic. For example, most schemes are concerned with encouraging staff development, so it is counter-productive to advise and offer development when it is known that resources are inadequate.

THE REAL BENEFIT OF STAFF APPRAISAL LIES IN REGULAR AND EFFECTIVE FOLLOW-UP OF AGREED ACTION PLANS

In most schemes, performance over the past year will be reviewed in the light of goals set the previous year. Both appraiser and appraisee should have committed themselves to action, and the appraisees need to assume ownership for their performance and for the agreed plans: 'If agreed action is not forthcoming or even seriously attempted then the situation can be worse than if the whole exercise had not taken place at all.'[27]

IT IS NECESSARY TO MONITOR, EVALUATE AND DEVELOP APPRAISAL SCHEMES FOR THEIR CONTINUED SUCCESS

The starting points will be the objectives of the scheme. Using these as a basis, the system should be evaluated regularly. All participants will be able to give their views (for example, each year) on the success of the scheme in meeting its objectives and how it might be changed.

PERFORMANCE REVIEWS

The starting point for an appraisal system should be the desire to improve the performance of the library, which in turn requires improvement of the performance of individual members of staff. A number of ideas have already been introduced in this book on participative management and objective approaches designed to encourage staff to participate in decision-making and decide what they and the library wish to achieve in the future. Performance appraisal aims to improve the performance of individuals at work by first of all reviewing their existing performance in the light of previous reviews, if any, and deciding on future goals and desirable support, such as training needs, to enable the goals to be reached.

Naturally, staff have to be informed of the manager's view of their existing performances in order to be stimulated to improve upon them, and in some ways the most important objective of an appraisal system turns out to be the communication of such information to staff. It is surprising how few staff have any accurate knowledge about senior management's view on their performance. Indeed, if they had known, their careers might have developed quite differently, and most important of all, they could have improved their performances if only they had been aware, especially if help had been forthcoming.

Our own experience has been that many younger librarians welcome systematic feedback on their performance, and help and advice on improving it.

Appraisal should be viewed together with training and development of staff, because it helps to identify training needs which have to be met if staff are to improve their performances. For many commentators, staff development is seen as the major function of appraisal: 'the key to successful appraisal is focusing on the educational need and developmental goals of the individual',[28] 'appraisal has a valuable function in developing people, and that is where its motivational value lies'.[29] A noticeable feature of many of the schemes adopted by libraries is the emphasis on staff development, to the extent that a number have given their schemes such titles as 'Staff Development and Career Review' and 'Professional Development and Review'. Possibly, this has been done to provide a softer but more positive image than staff appraisal, even though the schemes may also incorporate performance reviews. Bolton Metro's guidance notes not only state what their Staff Development Review is, but also state that it is not performance appraisal, but is intended 'to promote communication to clarify the nature of current and future work and to explore development needs'. If appraisal is to be successful, a library must be able to offer training opportunities to staff who are formally appraised. If it cannot do this, then appraisal is more likely to bring into question other areas of management for which appraisers are responsible, such as staffing structures, recruitment, deployment of staff and the management information system. There is a danger that appraisers will be drawn into discussing these wider issues which are claimed by individuals to affect their performances, and so lose the focus of these appraisals. Nonetheless, appraisees' views should be listened to, and subsequent action taken where necessary.

In our opinion, too much emphasis has been placed on individual performance, and insufficient on the context in which a person operates:

> Various commentators have raised the point that few appraisal schemes in existence at present make a conscious effort to take organizational factors into account when assessing performance ... Very few people work in isolation, yet we try to single out each individual as though he were totally responsible for the results.[30]

In assessing performance, it would seem natural in a profession like librarianship, in which most people work in groups, that appraisal should start in the work group. Group appraisal implies an objectives approach, the objectives being agreed by the work group led by the library manager with the support and involvement of senior management. An annual group appraisal system is employed at Manchester Metropolitan University. Before each summer vacation, senior management of the library meet the professional staff of each section of the library. The meetings last about two hours, and the most pro-

167

ductive pattern has been to begin with the annual report, which is worked through systematically. The list of objectives agreed at the previous meeting is then reviewed. In practice, most of the objectives will have been covered in the annual report, and discussion will then centre around those that have not been achieved for one reason or another. It is recognized, for example, that circumstances change, and therefore a rigid adherence to objectives determined a year ago would not be in the interests of the library.

The meeting then discusses the list of objectives being proposed for the coming academic year by the section, and when these have been agreed they are documented and both the senior managers and the section heads agree on the final version. In practice, a number of the objectives develop from the discussion of the annual report at the beginning of the meeting. Only decisions which have been made about the future are documented. There is deliberately no attempt to write minutes of the meeting. Although most of the objectives are to be achieved by the section, senior managers usually end up with a number of matters they have to address at a general level.

Where group appraisal operates alongside formal appraisal of individuals, the relationship between the two must be thought out carefully: 'Standard performance appraisals are conducted on an individual basis and do not contribute to the team-building efforts that are an important element in today's participative management style.'[31] Performance appraisal judges individuals who are frequently enjoined to improve their performances, sometimes in order to obtain a new job, promotion and/or an increase in pay. We have probably all worked with individuals who seemed intent on developing themselves rather than the service, perhaps at the expense of others who 'carry the burdens of the day'.

If this conflict is to be avoided, individual appraisal needs to encourage and reward those who develop in those areas of most use to the library. Such a practice is normal, for example, when decisions are made about attendance at training events, and it is our experience that staff respond best when encouraged to work on projects, often with a qualification at the end, which are of value to the library as well as to themselves. Equally, encouragement should be given to the development of teamworking skills, and contributions to the team should be rewarded as much as individual achievements.[32]

POTENTIAL REVIEWS

In a period when the number of posts is reducing rather than expanding and there is low mobility among staff, promotion policies within organizations are likely to be scrutinized more thoroughly than usual. The traditional policy in most libraries has been to advertise internally and externally, and for the person who performs 'best on the day' to obtain the post. Chapter 5 has described some of the difficulties in selecting staff on the basis of interview only, and a great advantage in evaluating internal candidates is that their present performance is well known to the selectors. If there is a regular appraisal system, information will be even more reliable. With low mobility, in large systems it is likely that there will be staff very able to take on posts at a higher level without requiring the basic training and induction needed by external appointees. It must be particularly galling for staff of a library which appoints mainly externally to find many others appointing mainly internally.

Many organizations deliberately set out to identify staff potentially able to work effectively at a higher level, and to prepare them for the future (see also Chapter 3, p.94). Identification is frequently carried out by means of a *potential review*. Most libraries shrink from such a positive step, partly because internal promotion is not encouraged, but also because, as Randell et al. observe:

> It is probably the most dangerous in possible psychological effects, for statements about an individual's potential, or lack of it, can be psychologically disturbing. There are also social problems such as identifying 'crown princes': someone may have been labelled as heir-apparent and may start behaving in that role even though he may not have the capacity for the work for which he is being groomed. There is also the 'self-fulfilling prophecy': making a prediction about a person's potential and publicly announcing it can bring about the prophecy.[33]

Difficulties can arise, for example, when shortlists are being drawn up and applications are received from internal candidates who are not considered suitable for the post. If they are not shortlisted, it could be perceived as a public statement of their lack of potential, which could be highly demotivating, especially if it happens frequently. On the other hand, not being appointed following several interviews would also have a demotivating effect. Our own view is that internal applicants should normally be interviewed, but if they are rejected frequently, then the situation should be discussed with them.

Such problems would almost certainly deter most managers from spending time on potential reviews in addition to the constant difficulty of basing judgements about future performance in general on performance in a different job at a lower level.

Although few British libraries operate a systematic potential review system, they do frequently involve themselves in discussions with individuals about their future and try to help them through their existing jobs. As librarians move up the hierarchy, they inevitably move from professional work towards managerial work, and this has to be tackled effectively if the library is to function well. Research has shown that managers' choices increase as they obtain higher-level posts, and this also seems to be the case with librarians. If

169

they shy away from managerial tasks because they are more comfortable with professional ones, the library is bound to suffer. A survey of librarians moving into senior management posts has shown the following areas of managerial skills to be most important and therefore the ones upon which potential counselling might concentrate:[34]

- **Management of staff** – motivating; supervising and allocation of work; delegation; working as a team; counselling; problem-solving; selection-interviewing; training
- **Planning** – objectives definition; making best use of resources; preparing evidence; financial management; time management; confidence-building
- **Boundary maintenance** – other chief officers; authority members; learning new professional jargon
- **Communication** – communications; public speaking; public relations.

REWARD REVIEWS

In the private sector, appraisal systems are often used for assembling information to enable organizations to share out rewards. Reviewing the research, Fletcher reported that a 1991 survey found that 75 per cent of organizations had adopted performance-related pay, with appraisal usually playing an important role.[35] Rewards include bonuses, increments and increased pay. Two factors dominate the criteria to be used. First, there is the correct rating for the job, and in this respect most public sector employees also have a system of review. Usually, this consists of an annual review within which managers can propose a change in grade for a subordinate and individuals can apply for a regrading of their own jobs.

The main reason for regrading will normally be a change of duties since the last time the post was graded, in which case the original job description is no longer accurate. In recent times, computerization and amalgamations have been major reasons for changes in duties and responsibilities, though many organizations have been reluctant to accept them as justifications, since they affect so many staff and both are expected to result in reductions in staffing costs.

Comparisons with other posts in the organization or with posts in other libraries are also used to justify regrading, although organizations have been more reluctant to accept such arguments as they have tried to reduce staffing costs.

In practice, all these reasons are used by managers, individuals and by the trade union representatives, who act as advisers and often support a case in the event of an appeal.

The second important factor in reward appraisal is the performance of the individual. In the private sector and in libraries in the USA, for example, making an extra payment for good performance is common. In the public sector in the UK, it is much less common, though it is being introduced to reward good teachers in schools, and it is interesting to note that cash incentives were used in both British universities and polytechnics to persuade staff to agree to annual performance appraisals. As Farmer points out, there is little literature on performance pay for librarians, and she is only able to cite American literature.[36] The difficulties of measuring performance in a library, its effect on working relationships and team work are all factors which must be taken into account. However, some librarians feel that appraisal is not worth carrying out unless the payment of financial rewards is possible in recognition of achievement. Some fear that unless 'there is some consequence of appraisal it is likely to fizzle out in a year or two as many will get bored with it'.[37]

WHO DOES THE APPRAISING?

Most personnel management textbooks, and more recently library management textbooks, list and discuss available methods of appraisal. There is now a considerable periodical literature on the subject, and we have also obtained recent material from libraries.

In most schemes, it is the senior librarians who formally appraise the librarians who work directly for them. In some cases, the next person above in the hierarchy ('the grandfather') plays some part. In the British Civil Service, for example, some departments have three layers. The reporting officer reports on performance, but promotion markings in those departments that give them may be assigned by either the reporting officer or a countersigning officer, and in some cases there will be a third signatory.

The trend in recent years has been towards involving in the appraisal an increasing number of persons who have working relationships with the appraisee. Redman and Snape[38] report a trend in the United States and also in the United Kingdom involving the use of multi-raters who can provide what is being referred to as 360° feedback, whereby:

> Different aspects of work can be assessed best by different groups of people. So, for example, peers can judge teamwork, clients and users can judge service quality and individuals can judge management and leadership skills. The main purpose of these unique forms of appraisal is to encourage communication between the manager and the job holder. One skill which managers may have to acquire with an upward appraisal system is the ability to take constructive criticism.[39]

Peer evaluation is based on the idea that peers are potentially good judges of each other's performance because they work with each other at the same level and frequently interact. Aluri and Reichel discuss a number of problems which can arise with peer evaluation, the major one being 'that peers are actually competing for the same rewards, such as merit raises and promotions'.[40]

Although still rare in the UK it is claimed that subordinate or upward appraisal will improve managerial effectiveness, particularly in relation to leadership and people management, and will contribute towards a more participative management style, including the 'empowerment' of lower-level employees. Redman and Snape have thoroughly reviewed the current situation, and conclude that:

> There is a tendency among some of its proponents to claim a lot for upward appraisal. After reading some of the literature, one could be forgiven for thinking that upward appraisal is the answer to all the personnel department's problems. Such wide-ranging claims deserve the level of scepticism that many UK personnel practitioners traditionally reserve for 'flavour of the month' innovations. However, it seems likely that more UK organizations will consider adopting upward appraisal in order to obtain some of the potential benefits that the technique has to offer, particularly as part of a broader strategy to enhance employee involvement and commitment.[41]

Our own experience in appraisal sessions in which subordinates make reference to wider matters has led us to agree with Rubin, who has developed an instrument for upward appraisal at the Dayton-Montgomery County Library, whereby appraisal of subordinates 'should encompass all relevant activities that pertain to the performance of the supervisor in the capacity of supervisor. Asking subordinates to evaluate their supervisor on other matters such as their ability to deal with administrators, or their general budgeting skills'[42] is unhelpful, as they are activities seldom experienced or observed by the subordinates, nor do they possess sufficient information to make a judgement.

Most British librarians, we are sure, would consider multi-rater systems too complex and time-consuming. In fact, the time required to introduce a scheme, train appraisers and appraisees, carry out the appraisals and provide follow-up support has been a major problem, in our experience. The more complicated the scheme, the greater the likelihood that additional work will be created. For example, a number of managers at BP Exploration involved with upward appraisal who experienced SARAH (Shock, Anger, Rejection, Acceptance and Help) were encouraged to seek counselling, and at W.H. Smith's, up to 300 managers required retraining.[43] We surmise that a major reason for not extending appraisal to all staff is the time factor, although keen clerical staff, for example, are known to feel left out and demotivated – not an intended outcome of the scheme!

The most desirable outcome of appraisal is for staff to appraise their own performances with the help of others. In many schemes, self-appraisal is considered so important that it is the starting point. Green's survey of British university libraries found that 73 per cent made use of a preparatory or self-appraisal form,[44] and Ruffley found it to be the most popular method – 'the form is completed by the appraisee and then comments are added at the interview following discussions and agreement by both parties'.[45] She believes that 'the use of self-appraisal transfers the sometimes contentious issue of assessment to the individual concerned. The professional status is not impugned and the interview allows constructive guidance to be given.' Similarly, Bentley believes that self-assessment before an appraisal meeting 'enables a meaningful dialogue to take place, with both you and your appraiser in a position to speak clearly, openly and honestly about events'.[46] Bentley suggests that there are four main questions that need answering in the self-assessment phase, and most examples we have seen follow a similar pattern:

1. How well have I achieved my objectives?
2. How well have I improved my performance criteria?
3. Have I performed my operational/job requirements as expected?
4. How well have I contributed to my team?

A great deal is made of the concept of 'ownership' in present-day management, and self-appraisal does enable individuals to 'own' their appraisals. A self-assessment form used by the British Library of Political and Economic Science at the LSE (Figure 6.4) and Wrexham County Borough's 'Questions to help you prepare for the meeting' (Figure 6.5) are good examples of self-assessment documentation. Where there is no formal self-appraisal, good managers, like good teachers, begin discussion of performance from the position of the appraisee, and only later introduce their own assessments, otherwise management views are taken into account and colour subordinates' reactions.

FORMS OF APPRAISAL

The major criticism levelled against a scheme devised for the Shoe and Allied Trades Research Association by Knibbs and Swailes was that it was 'form-dominated'.[47] Some staff had seen the exercise as one of form-filling, and the forms had constrained thinking and discussion. Similarly, Bentley advises that completing the appraisal form 'should be done as a by-product of the meeting and not as the purpose of the meeting'.[48] Careful thought is therefore needed when designing forms, and they should be pre-tested and their use monitored to ensure they are supporting the aims of the scheme.

173

STAFF APPRAISAL FORM
Year: 2000 - 2001

NAME:

GRADE:

DATE OF APPOINTMENT TO LIBRARY:

DATE OF APPOINTMENT TO PRESENT POST:

DATE OF APPOINTMENT TO PRESENT GRADE:

APPRAISEE TO FILL IN SECTIONS 1 & 2 AND RETURN TO APPRAISER ONE WEEK BEFORE THE DATE OF THE APPRAISAL DISCUSSION

SECTION ONE   LOOKING BACK - THE YEAR 1999-2000 IN REVIEW

1. **Job Title and brief description of responsibilities**

2. **What objectives were set for the year 1999-2000?**
    (enter those set in last year's appraisal)

3. **Which objectives have I achieved/not achieved?**

4. **What factors contributed to any objectives not being achieved?**

5. **Other Tasks or Projects Undertaken in the Year 1999-2000:**
    (enter other achievements not mentioned above)

PERFORMANCE 1999-2000:

6. **Which areas of your job have given you most satisfaction?**

7. **Which areas of your job have given you least satisfaction?**

8. **What can both of us do to improve those aspects of your work that have given less satisfaction?**

Figure 6.4   Staff appraisal form – British Library of Political and Economic Science at the LSE

SECTION TWO: THE YEAR AHEAD – 2000-2001:

9. TARGETS FOR NEXT YEAR
What do ou see as your objectives for the coming year?
(No more than 6 objectives which can realistically be achieved in the coming year)

10. FUTURE PLANS:
How do you see your career developing?

11. OTHER SKILLS:
Indicate any other skills you have which are currently not being used and which you feel
could be applied to your work now or in the future.

Figure 6.4 concluded

The earliest form of appraisal used by libraries appears to have been *trait rating*. The American Library Association published a standard rating form in its 'personnel organization and procedure' manual,[49] in which raters were required to score staff on 33 traits using a five point scale, each point being denoted by a cue such as a phrase or adverb (see Table 6.1).

There are many variations on this system, both in layout and scoring. It is a form of appraisal which has a number of advantages. Completing the form is relatively easy for the appraiser. A cynic might say that they don't have to think up their own pet phrases because they have already been prepared by someone else. Because values are being assigned, trait scoring does give the impression that the process is scientific, and in some libraries the scores for each trait are aggregated and a total score given for each appraisee. This may leave the appraiser with a comfortable feeling of a job neatly completed, but critics would argue that evaluating staff is more a complicated matter, and that a person does not consist simply of the sum of the traits chosen for an appraisal scheme. McDonagh expresses unease about the method, and criticizes it because it concentrates on looking backwards, can be highly subjective, and tends towards the choice of middle positions on scales.[50] In addition, often 'gradings reflect the boss–job holder relationships rather than achievement', and if they are to be used, he recommends that that gradings be substantiated by written comments and guidelines on grading definition, and should be related to performance, not personality.

Any scoring system faces the problem of standards. Aluri and Reichel discuss some of the problems:

> Standards, despite their wonderful sound, are not really standards. First, it is virtually impossible to define precisely the tasks in terms of how they should be carried out and what should be their quantitative outcomes. The more complex

175

■ Questions to help you prepare for the meeting

These questions are designed to help you prepare for your PRD Interview/Review meeting. Some questions may not be applicable to your particular job or situation, but others should help you to assess your performance at work and any training and/or development needs you may have.

■ Your present job
- Am I in the right job?
- Which parts of my job do I enjoy most, and why?
- What part of my job do I least like doing, and why?
- What resources/materials/equipment am I responsible for?
- What additional resources would enable me to do my job better?
- What are the main tasks involved in my job?
- How effectively is my time allocated between these tasks?
- What other tasks do I undertake? (Eg. tasks I do which are not part of my job but which I do to help colleagues.)

■ Your performance
- Do I discuss my performance with a more senior colleague throughout the year?
- Are areas which I need to work on/develop brought to my attention as soon as they become apparent?
- Do I need advice, guidance and/or practical support to help me improve my performance at work?
- Do I return telephone calls/eMails promptly and as requested?
- Do I respond to correspondence quickly?
- Do I get my various tasks completed reasonably quickly and/or produce as much as I should in the time available?
- What stops me working productively?
- What is preventing me from developing my area(s) of responsibility?
- Has the team of which I am a member set its objectives for the next year? (If so, who knows about these?)

■ Time management
- Do I plan my work programme well in advance? (Am I able to?)
- Do I think ahead about the various steps in a task I am working on, and estimate the time and resources I will need for each of these?
- Do I have sufficient time in the week to do my job properly (and, if not, what can I do about it?)
- Do I work at home regularly, and/or work unsocial hours?
- Is taking work home really essential for me to keep up-to-date?
- When I'm away, how can I prevent tasks from building up and not being dealt with until I return?
- Do I use support staff as effectively as I can?

■ Your training and/or development needs
- Who helps me with my T/D?
- What skills and knowledge do I use in my current job?
- What part(s) of my job would I like to do better/need to do better?
- What have I gained, and what do I need from, training and development?
- Have I identified my personal development needs for the coming year?
- What initiatives is the Council launching which will effect my job? Have I discussed these with my manager?
- Have I done all that I can to keep up-to-date with the knowledge needed to do my job effectively'?
- How do I think my job might change over the next two years?
- What new skills/knowledge will I need to gain because of these changes?

■ Your next job
- What would I like to be doing in 3 years' time?
- Do I discuss my career with a more senior colleague from time to time?
- Do I have a Personal Career Development Plan?
- Do my current tasks prepare me for greater responsibilities?
- Have I expressed interest in working in any other team, Department or Directorate (what happened as a result?)

Figure 6.5   Appraisal preparation questions – Wrexham County Borough

Table 6.1   Cues used in American Library Association standard rating form

---

Thoroughness

Meticulous in checking.	Usually thorough.	Moderately careful
Always sees things through.	Sometimes skips details under pressure.	Inclined to take too many short cuts.
Superficial. Does not follow through if difficulties arise.	Does not complete assignments satisfactorily.	

---

and professional the tasks are, the more difficult it is to define them in such a manner. In addition, factors such as the introduction of new technologies, new personnel, new managers, and new policies and procedures make such standards quickly obsolete. Precise definition of tasks tends to destroy creativity on the part of employees by freezing how certain tasks are conducted even when employees can identify ways in which such tasks can be improved, enhanced or eliminated altogether.[51]

For example, when appraisers try to rate individuals on the trait of 'Dependability', shown above, how do they take into account the constraints under which they work, and although some guidance is given, what is the standard against which they are making the comparisons?

In all the current academic schemes we have seen, and those reproduced by Revill,[52] there is no attempt to score performance. In some public library forms, there is the facility to rate staff as satisfactory, below satisfactory or above satisfactory in key areas. It does appear that organizations are trying to avoid the threat of rating in order to give appraisal a positive image. Thus, a partially 'controlled written report' has become the most popular format. The form itself will carry only a few headings, leaving appraisers the freedom to write what they wish. The Birkbeck College Appraisal Record form (Figure 6.6) is typically open. Like most of the schemes, however, guidance notes are provided, with recommendations on how the process should be carried out, including the completion of the report.

Many schemes like the Birkbeck one require both the appraiser and appraisee to sign the appraisal report. Areas of disagreement can be recorded on the form, and where there is dissatisfaction with the outcome of the meeting, it is normal for an appeal to be allowed and an interview arranged with the reviewer's immediate manager

ACADEMIC-RELATED STAFF

APPRAISAL RECORD-SUMMARY

CONFIDENTIAL (to appraiser and appraisee only)

Name of appraisee: ....

Name of appraiser: ....

Date of appraisal: ....

Future action(s)
(Please describe which tasks the appraisee will need to undertake during the next year to improve his or her performance and to further his or her development. An agreement on how the appraisee should go about the tasks and what support (if any) he or she will need to achieve them, plus a deadline, is necessary)

Task   **How**   **To be done by**

APPRAISER'S COMMENTS ON THE APPRAISAL MEETING

APPRAISEE'S COMMENTS ON THE APPRAISAL MEETING

Signatures: .... (Appraiser) .... (Appraisee)

Figure 6.6   Appraisal Record Form – Birkbeck College

APPRAISAL INTERVIEWING

Earlier in this chapter, we referred to the importance of good relationships between appraisers and appraisees. One of the aims of appraisal is frequently stated to be the improvement of this relationship, so communication in the interview itself must be successful to achieve this objective. The questions listed in Figure 6.7 have been used by the authors as an analytical tool for training purposes. Many organizations video-tape role-played interviews or provide training videos themselves. In addition, some schemes provide valuable advice to interviewers (Figure 6.8).

Objectives
1   Is the purpose of the appraisal made clear by the appraiser, and does it appear to be understood and accepted by the appraisee?

Procedure
2   Does the appraiser make clear what pattern it is hoped the interview will take?
3   Do the participants appear to understand the points made by each of them? Is clarification sought where necessary?
4   Does the appraiser summarize what progress has been made in the interview from time to time, and receive confirmation that the summaries are accurate?
5   How far is the discussion a two-way one, and how far is it dominated by one of the participants? Are they both good listeners?
6   Is sufficient time given for each person to explain their position to their own satisfaction?

Relevance
7   Does the interview keep in step with the purpose of the appraisal or does it wander off into irrelevant side-tracks?

Conflict
8   Is disagreement used constructively, or does it lead mainly to dissatisfaction?
9   When one criticizes the other, is it done in a constructive way, producing suggestions along with every criticism?
10   Do participants admit it when they are in the wrong or inadequate in some way, rather than pretend to be right or adequate all the time?

Non-verbals
11   Are there any contradictions between the verbal and non-verbal behaviour? Do the non-verbal behaviours of the two persons help to create an atmosphere of trust and openness?

Action
12   Are the participants clear about action that is required before the next appraisal interview, and is there a firm commitment to carry it out?

Figure 6.7   Typical questions used to evaluate an appraisal interview

Hannabuss has devised 'a simple form by means of which judgements from both people can be identified'.[53] The form is reproduced in Figure 6.9. Appraisers and appraisees can each complete the form after an appraisal, and compare perceptions.

Chapter 8 of this book provides guidelines on interpersonal skills relevant to appraisal interviewing, including Transactional Analysis. Brigden and Botton sum up the requirements:

179

LISTENING

DO

Pay attention:

- – by looking at the reviewee
- – by inclined body language towards him/her
- – by minimizing distractions

Gather information:

- – by observing reviewee's body language
- – by listening for his/her feelings

Test for understanding:

- – of facts
- – of feelings

Hold your fire:

- – by suspending judgement
- – by not responding too quickly
- – by allowing silences

Express understanding:

- – by reflecting back key phrases
- – by showing empathy

DON'T

Interrupt or show impatience

Jump to conclusions

Give advice

TRY

To keep an open mind

To recognise your own blind spots and prejudices

To be responsive more than initiating

Figure 6.8   Reviewer interviewing skills – Napier University

---

INTERVIEW ANALYSIS FORM 1

Name of Appraisee:
Name of Appraiser:

In the questions below appraiser should write an X and
appraisees should write an O.

1 How satisfied are you with the other person's response to you during the
appraisal interview?

        Very dissatisfied   1   2   3   4   5   6   Very satisfied

2 **For the appraisee only**:
What is your view of the appraiser during the interview?

                    Rigid 1 2 3 4 5 6 Flexible
                    Open 1 2 3 4 5 6 Reticent
        Considerate 1 2 3 4 5 6 Inconsiderate
       Indifferent to 1 2 3 4 5 6 Concerned about
mutual problems   mutual problems

3 **For the appraiser only**:
What is your view of yourself during the interview?

                    Rigid 1 2 3 4 5 6 Flexible
                    Open 1 2 3 4 5 6 Reticent
        Considerate 1 2 3 4 5 6 Inconsiderate
       Indifferent to 1 2 3 4 5 6 Concerned about
mutual problems   mutual problems

4 **For the appraisee only**:
How satisfied are you with the appraiser's performance during the interview?

        Very dissatisfied   1   2   3   4   5   6   Very satisfied

5 **For the appraiser only**:
How satisfied are you with your own performance during the interview?

        Very dissatisfied   1   2   3   4   5   6   Very satisfied

6 **For the appraisee only**:
In your view, was the interview an effective way to achieve your aims?

        Completely   1   2   3   4   5   6   Not at all

7 **For the appraiser only**:
As 6.

From: Stuart Hannabuss (1991), 'Analysing appraisal interviews', *Scottish Libraries*, **30**, November/December, pp.13–15.

Figure 6.9 Appraisal analysis form

The ability to listen, support, counsel and ask appropriate questions is essential … follow constructive feedback practices … non-judgmental, specific, directed towards performance rather than personality, checked with recipient, outcome based, problem-solving and in the form of suggestions rather than prescriptive comments.[54]

7 Staff training and development

For training to be effective, it must be viewed as an essential element in the management cycle (see Chapter 1), thus the starting point really lies in the changing needs of the communities which libraries serve, and the different responses which can be made to fulfil those needs by utilizing new skills and technologies. The rapid pace of change in information technology (IT) and the move towards recognizing that libraries must be customer-driven in the serv ices which they deliver have resulted in changing roles for library staff. There is no indication that this pace of change is likely to stop, or even slow, and the statement that 'the only constant is change' has become a truism. Training and development enable staff to cope with acquiring the new skills which they need today, and also, ultimately, to be comfortable with the fact that this skill set will change and evolve continuously throughout their working lives.[1]

Some managers have been nervous of providing staff with training and development opportunities, in the belief that they would see none of the benefits, as this would merely equip staff to move on to other jobs. This attitude cannot be sustained, and the emphasis on lifelong learning and the need to be able to deliver services in an increasingly competitive marketplace (both within the private and public sectors) mean that those organizations, managers and staff who have a positive approach to training will have the edge over those who still regard it as a luxury to be indulged in, not terribly frequently, by the privileged few. The recent public library workforce study *Recruit, Retain and Lead* 'confirmed the view that there is a link between retention and training and that success in retaining high quality staff derived from a combination of the qualities of the job itself and a structured approach to training'.[2]

Several reports have recognized the key roles that training and development play in the delivery of effective library and information services. The Fielden Report prompted libraries in the higher education sector to re-examine their approach to this aspect of staff management.[3] In the further education field, *Networking Lifelong Learning Making it Happen: An Implementation Plan* stated that training and continuing professional development (CPD) are vital to the success of Information Learning Technology initiatives.[4] *New Library: The People's Network*[5] and *Building the New Library Network*[6] have led to a reassessment, both from without and within the sector, of the role of the public library. The funding for staff training from the New Opportunities Fund is linked to this reappraisal. Each report emphasizes the impact of IT developments, and there is undoubtedly a critical need for training, at all levels and across all sectors, in this area. In the midst of the urgency to improve IT skills, there is also recognition that people skills remain as vital as ever.

Changes in the profile of the workforce have also had an impact on the approach to training and development. The increase in the number of staff with part-time and temporary contracts has been discussed in Chapter 3. The needs of these staff must be considered at each stage of the training cycle, shown in Figure 7.1. Failure to extend training and development activities to staff in these groups has far-reaching implications. Goulding and Kerslake state that 'legal and quality issues demand that managers develop an understanding of flexible worker demands and requirements'.[7] Research into the provision of training to flexible workers, such as the British Library-funded project conducted by the same researchers,[8] can help managers to achieve this understanding.

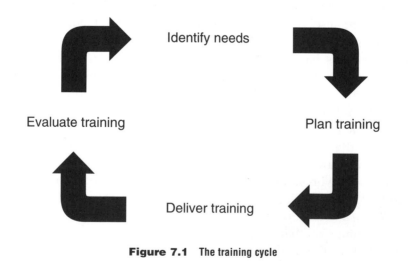

Figure 7.1 The training cycle

TERMINOLOGY

The lifelong learning culture has led to a blurring of the distinction between training activities which are directly related to work, and more diffuse development or 'continuing education' activities. There has been a shift towards regarding participation in high-quality learning activities, whether these are specifically related to the participant's current job or more wide-ranging in their applicability, as a valuable use of staff time which is likely to result in benefits for the organization. CPD is a term which is frequently used in the literature, although the activities to which it applies vary. Whilst some distinction may be made between specific training and CPD, we are in agreement with Parry's observation that: 'In fact, CPD is a broad concept that includes staff development, training and personal development'.[9] The main methods used in CPD are listed in Figure 7.2. For the purposes of this chapter, training activities have been treated separately from staff development activities. Specific training activities are those which fall in the lower, right-hand quadrant of the table in Figure 7.2, and staff development activities are the remaining activities listed in the figure.

THE RESPONSIBILITY FOR TRAINING AND DEVELOPMENT

The responsibility for training exists at every level within an organization. Ultimately, training and development are the responsibility of the individual, and an effective organization is one which recruits and supports staff who actively want to learn. For staff to realize this aspiration, there needs to be a commitment to training from the top down. A training culture cannot exist without the support of senior managers. As well as leading by example and demonstrating full commitment to training, 'it [is] incumbent upon the senior management to ensure that all managers and supervisors accept responsibility for their staff's training and development'.[10] It is often line managers and supervisors who carry out staff training, and they are the ones who need to ensure that the service is still delivered when staff are participating in off-the-job training. Further, they have day-to-day contact with staff, and are able to encourage participation in training by assisting staff with identifying appropriate activities, providing opportunities for staff to put what they learn into practice, and ensuring that staff evaluate the process effectively.

Whilst responsibility for training needs to permeate an organization, such a critical activity requires co-ordination. The Fielden Report stressed the importance of assigning responsibility for training to a single individual, preferably a senior manager.[11] More recently, the IMPEL2 project listed 'the appointment

```
┌─────────────────────────────────────────────────────────────────────┐
│                    Development of diffuse capabilities                │
│                                                                       │
│         20  Teamwork              8   Academic education              │
│                                                                       │
│         19  Delegation                7   Research                    │
│                                                                       │
│              18  Visits to                6   Professional education  │
│                  libraries                                            │
│                                                                       │
│                                   5   Writing and publishing          │
│                                                                       │
│         17  Involvement with          4   Reading professional literature/ │
│             professional association      e-mail discussion lists     │
│                  16  Appraisal            3   External courses        │
│                                                                       │
│  Implicit      ─────────────────────────────────────         Explicit │
│  development   15  Consultancy                             development │
│                  14  Job rotation         (a)  Written instructions   │
│                                           (b)  Lectures               │
│                                           (c)  Case studies/          │
│                  13  Job exchange              simulations            │
│                                    2  In-house  (d)  Role-playing     │
│                  12  Staff meetings   training  (e)  Seminar/discussion │
│                                     programmes       groups           │
│                                           (f)  Audio-visuals          │
│              11  Objectives approach      (g)  Self-teaching          │
│                  to management                 packages               │
│                                           1   On-the-job training     │
│                  10  Projects                                         │
│                  9  Working parties                                   │
│                                                                       │
│                    Development of specific capabilities               │
└─────────────────────────────────────────────────────────────────────┘
```

Figure 7.2 The main CPD methods

of a senior member of staff as Staff Development Officer to oversee and co-ordinate staff training and development activities' as a factor in delivering successful staff training and development.[12] Many services have taken the step of making training the responsibility of a single individual. This person may be employed solely to organize and administer training and develop-ment, or the responsibility may be part of a wider remit. In the latter model, which is more common in small libraries, the person who has overall responsibility for staffing often also has responsibility for training. In order for such a post to be fully effective, the training officer should be a member of the senior management team, and should be acknowledged as the link with training personnel of the parent body. The approach will vary between organizations, and as we have seen with other management activities, for example recruitment, the culture of the parent organization will result in differing levels of autonomy for library services.

Whenever a special responsibility is created, there is a natural tendency for other staff to leave that specialism to the specialist, and neglect it themselves. It cannot be emphasized too strongly that it is not the training officer's job to carry out all the training. The job of the training officer is to operate as a 'fulcrum of training activity' and the 'catalyst for training change and development',[13] and in this role the person should aim to create a training atmosphere in the library, and an acceptance by line managers of their training responsibilities. Thought must be given to the exact nature of the duties of the training officer, whether it is a dedicated post or part of a wider remit. Will the person be responsible for the training budget? To what extent will they be expected to deliver training? Will they represent the organization on any co-operative training groups, or other external committees?

Some libraries, particularly in larger organizations, have created a training group to support the work of the training officer. The group can provide information and ideas on training needs and assist with evaluation or training needs analysis, and in itself, membership of such a group provides a development opportunity for staff. Where a training group exists, the function and membership of such a group should be considered, as well as the relationship between the training officer and the group. It is good practice to aim to represent the range of staff in the library by ensuring that the members come from different sections and different grades within the service.

The extract from the Staff Development Policy of the library at the University of Bath reproduced in Figure 7.3 shows one way in which the responsibility for training can be organized and expressed within an institution.

TRAINING AND DEVELOPMENT POLICIES

Many libraries have produced written staff development and training policies. The Fielden Report listed the areas which should be included, as a minimum, in a training policy. Whilst the Fielden Report concentrated specifically on the higher education sector, this list would be of use to any library service wishing to draw up a training policy. A checklist for the contents of a training policy,

187

5. ORGANISATION

5.1   Final responsibility for staff development lies with the University Librarian
5.2   General management of staff development is the responsibility of the Staff
      Development and Training Officer. This entails:

- identification of organisational and individual needs
- organisation of staff development
- promotion of staff development
- support of the Staff Development Group
- management of the budget
- external liaison

5.3   The Staff Development Group will implement the staff development programme.
5.4   The Staff Development Group will consist of the Staff Development and Training
      Officer and six other members of staff representing all grades and all areas of the
      Library. [The objectives of the Staff Development Group are detailed in Appendix A
and its composition in Appendix B.]

APPENDIX A:

OBJECTIVES OF THE STAFF DEVELOPMENT GROUP

The Library Staff Development Group meets regularly to arrange meetings and events
designed to encourage Library staff to acquire new skills and expertise. The Group has
the following objective and aims:

To provide a comprehensive, structured programme of continuing devlopment for all
Library staff to promote the growth of a high quality Library service that can provide
effective support to the University in pursuance of its objectives as defined in the
Charter.

- To contribute to the maintenance and improvement of the Library service through
  a programme of continuing staff development.
- To encourage individual recognition of the need, and responsibility for, staff
  development.
- To encourage corporate recognition of the need for staff development and the
  University's responsibility to provide adequate resources for staff development.
- To promote the career development of Library staff.

Figure 7.3   Extract from Staff Development Policy – University of Bath Library

APPENDIX B:

COMPOSITION OF THE STAFF DEVELOPMENT GROUP

The composition and constitution of the Staff Development Group has been ratified by the Senior Management Team as follows:

- The Staff Development Group will consist of 7 members of the Library staff representative of all grades, and all floors of the Library, and including the Staff Development and Training Officer (SDTO).
- Membership of the Group will normally be for a two year term.
- Two members of the Group will resign each year.
- New members will be encouraged to join the Group by the Chair and the SDTO, in consultation with Group members, so as to maintain its representative balance.
- The Chair will be elected annually from amongst Group members, and may not be held by the same person for more than two consecutive years.
- Minutes will be taken by each member of the Group in turn.
- The year will run from 1st January to the 31st December.

Figure 7.3 concluded

derived from this section of the Fielden Report,[14] is given in Figure 7.4. The development of such a document is a means to provide all staff with access to useful information on those policies of the institution which relate to training. As such, it is vital that the training and development policy is easily accessible, and it should be given to all new staff during their induction period. Figure 7.5 reproduces the policy of Bolton Metropolitan Borough Council Education and Arts Department.

RESOURCES FOR TRAINING

The training officer, or training group, will need to ascertain what resources for training exist in the organization. In particular, a position statement should be drawn up concerning accommodation, equipment, expertise, and of course, available funds.

- Aims and objectives of training and development within the service.
- Funding for training and development.
- Existing priorities for training and development.
- Methods which will be used to achieve these priorities.
- The staff who have responsibilities for training and development.
- The details of these responsibilities.
- The possibilities for undertaking formal study and the support which is provided in such cases.
- The possibilities for undertaking S/NVQs and the support which is provided in such cases.
- The extent to which membership of professional associations is encouraged and supported.
- Forms of senior support.
- Details of mentoring schemes.
- Details of whether training is compulsory or voluntary.
- Methods for evaluating training and development activities.
- Methods for evaluating the training and devlopment policy.
- Links to the appraisal process.

Figure 7.4 A checklist of points to include in a training and development policy (derived from the Fielden Report)

ACCOMMODATION

Rooms for large and small groups which allow flexibility of use are desirable. The following measures, adapted from those used by Peter Smith to evaluate accommodation,[15] provide a helpful checklist:

- acoustics – reverberation, background noise, sound levels
- eating and drinking facilities
- furniture – tables, chairs, writing facilities, flexibility of seating
- room layout – size and shape, ease of vision, nature of exit and entry
- teaching aids – sockets, access to computer network
- thermal – air temperature, air movement, ventilation
- toilet and washing facilities
- visual – natural and artificial lighting.

EQUIPMENT

This includes screens, overhead projectors, equipment for projection from computer screens, computer terminals, network points, laser pointers, video recorders and monitors, film and video projectors, flipcharts.

BOLTON MBC EDUCATION AND ARTS DEPARTMENT

TRAINING AND DEVELOPMENT POLICY

Policy Statement

The Department of Education and Arts recognises that its most important asset is the skill and dedication of its staff and is therefore committed to supporting them through a structured and planned approach to staff development.

In training and developing staff, the Department aims to:

- enhance the quality of its services through continuous improvement
- ensure that all employees have the skills and knowledge to meet the increasing demands made upon services
- support staff in times of change

Principles of the Policy

1. All employees have an equal right to access to training and development opportunities, regardless of grade or length of service.
2. All new employees and those transferring to new areas of work will be given induction training which is appropriate to their role.
3. Staff development is a continuous process recognising the need for constant updating as staff roles and responsibilities change.
4. Each employee will have access to a regular review meeting with their manager when their training and development needs can be discussed. The outcome of this will be an agreed Personal Development Plan relating their needs to those of their Service or Unit plan.
5. Where possible and appropriate, training will be linked to professional qualifications, award bearing courses or National Vocational Qualifications.
6. Attendance on formal courses is not the only form of training. Team meetings, job shadowing, job exchanges, mentoring or other forms of staff development can and should be employed where appropriate.
7. All training activities will be monitored and evaluated against their contribution to the development of individual staff, to their Service or Unit plan and to the work of the Department.

Responsibilities

1. All staff are responsible for their contribution to the Personnel Development Planning process, in identifying their own development needs and taking action to ensure that the training they receive is used to its maximum benefit.
2. Managers have the responsibility for developing themselves and their staff, ensuring that Personal Development Plans are agreed that opportunities are available for staff to develop and resources are allocated on a fair and equitable basis
3. The Training Unit has the responsibility of providing guidance and support on good practice to managers and staff. This could include; information on new developments, advice on suitable training events, the creation of a Departmental training programme or the organisation of training on behalf of Divisions or Services.

Figure 7.5 Training and development policy – Bolton MBC Educational Arts Department

4. The Departmental Policy Team (DPT) has the responsibility of promoting training and development throughout the Department. This will include continuing commitment to the importance of training, action to meet the Policy's aims and to ensure fairness and equality for all staff. DPT are also responsible for ensuring that training and development activities contribute to the overall aims of the Department.

Resources

1. Each Division has access to a training budget and will allocate its resources on an equitable basis according to identified and prioritised needs, based on the requirements expressed in Service and Unit plans.
2. The Strategic Plan will outline the continuing commitment to the development of staff and ensure that resources are allocated for that purpose.
3. Each Service or Unit plan will outline the training needs required to ensure the plan's success.
4. The effectiveness of the resources spent will be evaluated within the context of Personnel Development Planning process and the aims and objectives expressed in Divisional, Service and Unit plans.

Figure 7.5 Training and development policy – Bolton MBC Educational Arts Department

EXPERTISE

Two main types of expertise are necessary. The first is knowledge of the areas in which training is required. Here, the range of methods shown in Figure 7.2 can be combined with a checklist of training activities, such as those in Figure 7.6, and names attached where expertise is available. The second type of expertise relates to the skills required to teach and train, and this may be more difficult to discover. Staff may have had teaching experience, or they may be known as good instructors, but on the other hand, expertise may be lacking, and in that case an important early consideration will be how to train the trainers – it would be detrimental to launch a programme only to have it poorly delivered.

FUNDS

Money must be available for training in the library budget, or from other funds, such as those of staff development units.

The mechanistic/organismic paradigm (Figure 2.1) shows how staff training and development claims a larger share of resources in a library managed in an organismic style. Therefore, a library which acts positively in the areas discussed in this chapter will, almost by definition, have organismic characteristics. Staff training and development are intimately affected. Not only will training flourish under certain management styles, but training will itself

1   *Induction*
    Aims of the host organization
    How the library/information unit serves these aims
    Service objectives

2   *Professional skills*
    Collection management
    Selection of materials
    Arrangement of materials to facilitate retrieval
    Maintenance of the stock, physically and in terms of currency
    User education
    Provision of information in response to enquiries
    Use of IT
        1   for housekeeping
        2   for information retrieval
        3   for daily work
    General administrative procedures

3   *Management skills*
    Staff management skills
    Priorities and work organization
    Problem-solving/decision-making
    Budgeting and financial management

4   *Analysis and evaluation*
    Evaluation of the service offered
    Evaluation of managerial practices
    Evaluation of policy
    Production of evaluative written work

5   *Communication*
    Working as part of a team
    Supervising staff
    Communicating with users
    Publicity and promotion
    Written communications and instructions
    Committee work

6   *Training*
    Attendance on short courses
    Day to day training and monitoring
    Evaluation and discussion of training received and future development
    Assessment of training needs

7   *Professional involvement/awareness*
    Visiting other types of service
    Attending professional meetings
    Discussing general concerns of the profession
    Meeting other professionals

Figure 7.6 Checklist of training activities

affect that organization and its style of management in the way it is meant to in an organismic library.

IDENTIFYING TRAINING NEEDS

If training is to be effective, both for the individual and the organization, it should be planned and relevant. Any organization contemplating qualifying for the Investors in People (IiP) standard will need to make the link between training needs and the strategic aims of the organization. Principle 1 of IiP is concerned with commitment, and states: 'An Investor in People is fully committed to developing its people in order to achieve its aims and objectives.'[16] IiP combines this approach with an emphasis on evaluating all training activities and feeding the results back into the strategic planning of the organization. Even if there is no plan to apply for the IiP standard, the principle is a sound one. Establishing a link between training needs and organizational objectives helps to avoid the *ad hoc* delivery of training. The cyclical nature of the training process is demonstrated in Figure 7.1. This does not mean that training experiences have to be narrow, and the importance of CPD in the widest sense is discussed later in this chapter.

Identifying training needs means identifying areas in which performance is at odds with the organization's aims. However, poor performance may be due to low morale, lack of motivation or poor working conditions. Such factors need to be addressed appropriately, and whilst training may be the solution, it should not be assumed that this is always the case. In addition to ensuring that training is not presented as the panacea for all workplace difficulties, care should be taken not to raise staff expectations to an unrealistic level. The process of identifying training needs requires staff to consider their own development. In times of diminishing budgets, it will not always be possible to act upon the needs which are identified. Therefore, the process must be handled sensitively. Staff must feel able to be honest about their training needs, but must also be aware that these will be viewed within the context of the organization's priorities and funding.

APPRAISAL

As we saw in Chapter 6, the appraisal process presents an excellent opportunity to identify training needs. A well-developed appraisal process will incorporate many of the activities which can be used to assess training needs. These include:

- analysis of job descriptions
- discussions with library staff
- observation of performance
- feedback from library users
- correlating individual responsibilities with the overall objectives of the organization.

Appraisal will usually indicate the training needs for a particular individual, but an analysis of the outcomes of the appraisal process will reveal training needs which exist across the organization. It may also be appropriate to use group appraisal to ascertain the needs of certain groups. Group and individual appraisal systems are discussed in Chapter 6.

Appraisal is far more than a means to identify training needs, and one critical factor to the success of an appraisal process is the assurance of confidentiality. Therefore, schemes need to ensure that whilst confidentiality is preserved, the training needs can be analysed and acted upon. This can be done simply by detailing the training needs on a separate sheet which can then be copied to the staff with responsibility for training. Appraisers and appraisees need to be aware that this will happen.

PERSONAL APPLICATIONS FOR TRAINING EVENTS

Many organizations now provide structured application forms for participation in training events. These provide a means for staff to apply to attend events, and as such complement the training and staff development aspect of the appraisal process. It is common for such forms to prompt the applicant to explain how the activity relates to the organization's objectives. Figure 7.7 shows an example form that is used within Essex Libraries, which demonstrates an interesting approach. The applicant is asked to outline their learning need *before* explaining how this will be met. As such, the member of staff is encouraged to focus on the outcome of the activity from the early stages of considering training. The evaluation process is also highlighted from the start. As part of the application, the line manager needs to state how the activity will be evaluated. Further, the reverse of the application form is an evaluation form which details areas which need to be covered when the line manager discusses the activity with the member of staff.

EXIT INTERVIEWS

Exit interviews with staff who resign can also reveal deficiencies which can be addressed through training. Where there is a high turnover of staff, exit inter-

---

LEARNING REQUEST

for staff from Libraries, Information, Heritage and Culture Service Group

Surname: .... Forename(s): .... Date: ....

Location: .... Post held: ....

What do I hope to learn? ....

....

On a score of 1–10 (1 is low 10 is high)
I would describe my existing skills/knowledge in this area as:

How does this relate to the Business Plan? ....

....

....

What is my preferred learning method? (e.g. course title, learning package title etc.) ....

....

....

What do I intend to do as a direct result of this learning? ....

....

....

Do you have any special dietary needs?: Yes/No Details..

Do you have any mobility needs?: Yes/No Details..

TO BE COMPLETED BY THE LINE MANAGER:

What will the learning cost?   Course cost.. £...

Peak relief backffll (No. of hours)................   Travel and subsistence £..........................

Will there be an opportunity for this member of staff to deliver any cascade training?
Yes/No

How will this learning be evaluated?..

....

....

Line Managers
Signature.. Date:...

Ageed by ADM/Service Lead........................ Date:...

Training Unit only
Date received..Date training attended................................

Figure 7.7 Learning request/post-learning evaluation form used by Essex Libraries

POST LEARNING EVALUATION

Your member of staff has now completed this training. You need to evaluate how effective this has been at the next Development Review progress report meeting or sooner if needed. Listed below are some questions you will need to ask and make notes on. This will form the basis of future discussions with your own line manager.

How would you rate your skills/knowledge now?
    on a score of 1-10 (1 is low 10 is high)

How confident are you in the new skills acquired? ....

....

....

How have you been able to transfer the learning to your job? ....

....

....

How have you started using these skills in your job? ....

....

....

Looking back at the Learning Request form and the course programme how have all the outcomes been achieved'? ....

....

....

Were there any obstacles which prevented you from achieving these outcomes and how can we overcome them? ....

....

....

As your line manager, can I help you any further with transferring and practising this learning? ....

....

....

....

....

Date discussed

Figure 7.7 concluded

views are especially important. Exit interviews are normally carried out with those who have resigned voluntarily. They are interchanges 'between the employee who is leaving the organization and a manager or staff person of that organization conducted close to the time that the employee leaves the organization'.[17] It is recommended that the interview should take place during the last week of employment, but not on the last day. There can be a problem of confidentiality, especially in small libraries, even if only objective statistical information is made public. In many organizations, therefore, personnel officers rather than line managers carry out the interviews. The intention is to find out why staff have resigned. This is not always easy. Our experience has been that staff are often loath to tell managers the real reasons, therefore skilful and tactful probing needs to be employed.

The training needs which are identified may not just relate to the post which is being vacated. The departing post holder may also provide information which indicates that their line manager has certain training needs. This is a further reason for someone other than the line manager conducting the exit interview. When such information is provided by a departing employee, thought must be given to whether it is appropriate to convey this to the line manager in question, and if so, how this can be done most effectively. As well as providing valuable information for the improvement of training programmes, exit interviews can help to improve working conditions and solve staff problems. Some organizations also, or instead, employ 'post-separation surveys' conducted by post or telephone about thirty days after the departure of the employee.

TRAINING NEEDS ANALYSIS

The increased emphasis on training combined with the need to demonstrate that training is good value has led some libraries to undertake full training needs analyses. Williamson identifies two interpretations of training needs analysis (TNA):

> Some managers will refer to it as the complete process of identifying the basic training needs and then following all the necessary steps until these needs have been analyzed and addressed in the best possible way. The pure interpretation of the term describes the final process only.[18]

We are in agreement with Williamson, who uses the first definition throughout his guide.

TNA should not be carried out lightly. It is a time-consuming exercise, and if it is poorly conducted, the result will be a disillusioned workforce. Whetherly warns against TNA which generates vast quantities of information which cannot be matched to individual and organizational needs. In such a scenario, it will be difficult to act upon the data. This can lead to staff feeling frustrated: 'staff have had their expectations raised yet hear nothing more. In subsequent years it becomes difficult for the library and information service to regain staff interest in training.'[19] On the other hand, TNA which has been carefully planned and which is clearly linked to organizational objectives can be beneficial, and may be particularly effective when there are 'reasons for wanting to examine and review demands, performance and priorities'.[20]

There are a variety of methods and information sources which can be exploited when an organization decides to carry out a full TNA. Whilst the appraisal should not be used as a substitute for a full TNA, as has been discussed earlier, the training and development element of an appraisal process generates data on training needs, and this can be fed into a TNA. Other ongoing activities such as applications for training events and exit interviews can also provide information for a TNA. These sources can be augmented by data gathered through means such as:

- questionnaires
- interviews
- observation of staff
- self-observation
- analysing activities in light of organizational objectives
- feedback from library users.

The TNA questionnaire used by University College London (UCL) Library Services is shown in Figure 7.8. The questionnaire was followed up by one-to-one interviews conducted between the Assistant Librarian, Staff Development and all Library Services staff. As can be seen from Williamson's definition, TNA does not stop with the identification of training needs. Once this data has been gathered, the most effective means to meet these needs must be given consideration. In the UCL example, recommendations based on the data gathered through the questionnaires and interviews were presented to the senior management team, and led to various developments, including, for example, the piloting of a training hour and the investigation of staff shadowing schemes.

TRAINING NEEDS OF GROUPS

The evidence obtained from the analysis of both individual and organizational needs will show that particular groups have their own training needs. In large organizations, this is so likely, and makes training so much easier, that analysis by group should be an essential part of training needs identification.

199

200

TRAINING NEEDS ANALYSIS 2000

SECTION 1 TRAINING ACTIVITY TO DATE

Q.1   How far has the training you have received to date met the needs of your job?

Q.2   Were training sessions held that might have been useful to you, but which you were unable to attend? If so, what were they?

Q.3   How successful do you think the publicity for training has been?

Q.4   What could the Library Services Staff Development & Training Committee do to improve your personal development?

SECTION 2: FUTURE TRAINING - SPECIFIC NEEDS
Please assess your familiarity with and need for training in the following skills on a scale of 1 -4
(1 = fully confident; 2 = reasonably confident; 3 = need more training; 4 = no need in job)

2.1 IT SKILLS

Q.5   Basic PC housekeeping & good practice

Figure 7.8   Training needs analysis used by University College London Library Services

TRAINING NEEDS ANALYSIS 2000

Q.6   Microsoft packages

       Access   Powerpoint

       Eudora   Word

       Excel   Other (please state)

Q.7   Web searching

Q.8   Web design

Q.9   Database searching

Q.10   Aleph modules (e.g. Circulation, Items, Cataloguing). Please list.

2.2 MANAGERIAL AND INTERPERSONAL SKILLS

Q.11   Recruitment / selection skills

Q.12   Appraisal skills

Q.13   Communication skills

Q.14   Customer care/ Dealing with difficult people

Q.15   Time management

Q.16   Teamwork

Q.17   Managing change

Q.18   Supervisory skills

Q.19   Motivating staff

Q.20   Training skills

Q.21   Managing your career

Figure 7.8   continued

201

TRAINING NEEDS ANALYSIS 2000

2.3 PROFESSIONAL AND ADMINISTRATIVE SKILLS

Q.22   Presentation skills

Q.23   Project management

Q.24   Proposal and bid writing

Q.25   Financial and budgeting skills

Q.26   Writing reports

Q.27   Chairing meetings

Q.28   Participating in meetings

Q.29   Taking minutes

Q.30   Enquiry desk skills

SECTION 3: FURTHER COMMENTS

Q.31   What other areas would you like to see covered in the training hour?

Q.32   Would you be willing to deliver a training session as part of the training hour programme? If yes, on what topic?

Please add any further comments on training and staff development.

Figure 7.8   concluded

Where group members are working closely together, it is particularly desirable for them to put forward what they believe to be their training needs as a group. In this way, training can much more easily be perceived as being intimately connected with the work, rather than an extra that can be indulged in when there is an excess of funds, which is almost never.

Many libraries now have team-based structures, and clearly an analysis of the training needs of individual teams is one way to ascertain group needs. There are also other groups which may be identified. For example, all senior library assistants may have line management responsibilities, and as such can be considered to form a group of staff. This group will require certain skills which will differ from the skills needed by individual senior library assistants when they are working in their functional team.

A structured approach to identifying training needs will ensure that training is available to all groups of staff. Corrall and Brewerton highlight the fact that:

> Historically, some groups of library staff have fared far better than others when it came to opportunities for development ... as Fielden recognized, some staff have been neglected in the past: senior staff are often expected to rely on common sense and experience; while paraprofessional staff and library assistants have had fewer opportunities than the professionally qualified.[21]

Scottish/National Vocational Qualifications (S/NVQs) have been embraced by many organizations, more so in the public library sector than by academic or special libraries, as a means to address the training needs of library assistants and to accredit the range of skills which are now needed by these staff. S/NVQs are dealt with in more detail later in this chapter.

Training for senior managers can be particularly difficult for institutions to deliver, as, by definition, there are few people in these posts within particular departments. This can be overcome by using outside agencies for training. Such an approach enables senior managers to meet with colleagues in the same profession, and so benefit from shared experiences. The need for training for management roles has been recognized by SCONUL (Society of College, National and University Libraries). In the mid-1990s SCONUL worked with UCoSDA (Universities' and Colleges' Staff Development Agency, now part of the Higher Education Staff Development Agency, HESDA) and Aston Business School to develop a customized course in strategic management for senior managers. The course continues to run, and has evolved in response to feedback from participants and input from UCISA (Universities and Colleges Information Systems Association).

The difficulties in providing training to this group of staff are not confined to the higher education sector. *Recruit, Retain and Lead* uncovered a need to identify and support the public library leaders for tomorrow. The study recommends that 'the Society of Chief Librarians, together with BAILER and the LA investigate the provision of leadership programmes, fast tracking schemes and a staff college for the public library sector'.[22]

STAGES OF TRAINING

As we investigate the various groups and their training needs, we can distinguish:

- induction training
- maintenance training, which enables the library to maintain its existing procedures
- basic updating and improvement training, for example in new services which are being offered by the library or parent organization
- staff development (see pp.233–8).

INDUCTION

Even libraries which provide little other training involve themselves in induction training. In a sense they have to, otherwise new staff would be unable to perform existing tasks adequately, but many induction programmes are more systematic and acknowledge that all new staff need a general introduction to the service. It has to be recognized that induction introduces staff to the social and cultural aspects of the organization as much as to the job itself:

> Above all, [induction] provides an early opportunity to establish a positive relationship between employee and employer. First impressions are often the most lasting, so the way in which new or promoted employees are treated by the organization may well have a significant impact upon their attitude and performance for many years to come. If managers and supervisors fail to use this formative stage to promote corporate values the informal grapevine will almost certainly do the job for them.[23]

Induction of new staff really begins when the person is appointed. The information which is sent out immediately conveys a message to that person. It should therefore be welcoming, and should contain the basic details the person needs before commencing the job. The practice followed by many manufacturers in their service manuals, congratulating purchasers on their judgement in selecting products, might well be copied by employers welcoming staff to an institution or authority. It can be quite difficult to do this when it is also necessary to ask appointees to declare any previous criminal convictions and to complete medical questionnaires. It is thought best to refer to these requirements briefly in the welcoming letter, but to provide the details separately. Basic information will normally include the place and hours of work, where and when to report on the first day, the name of the person to whom they should report, and what they need to bring with them.

Planning the induction programme should also begin at the appointment stage. Webb groups the content of the induction programme under four headings: 'the organization (what it does), the people (who does what), the surroundings (what is where), and the job (what the individual will be doing)'.[24] It is now common for organizations to use induction checklists as a basis for drawing up induction programmes. These have a dual role. On the one hand they act as an *aide-mémoire* for the manager, ensuring that all aspects of the process are organized before the arrival of the new employee; on the other, they provide the new recruit with some structure and a means of gauging their progression through the various elements of the induction process.

The great danger with induction is providing too much information, usually with the best of intentions, in too short a time. Here, as in many management activities, the manager should try to see things from the point of view of the newcomer. It is important to build into the induction programme some time for consolidation and reflection on the part of the new employee. Ideally, the new recruit should be given the opportunity to carry out some tasks on their first day. This enables them to feel that they are contributing to the service from the outset, and reduces their sense of being overwhelmed by information.

Some parts of the induction process will be common to all staff, for example health and safety training. Others will differ depending on the nature of the post. Figure 7.9 shows the general induction list used by Essex Libraries for all staff and Figure 7.10 contains an extract from a checklist for specific posts. It is likely that the Human Resource section or Staff Development Unit will provide material to assist with induction of a new employee. Thus, a parent organization can ensure that the training of staff is handled efficiently from day one.

On the first day, the new employee should be welcomed formally. If possible, a senior person should do this, whatever the position of the employee, to indicate immediately that every member of staff is considered important. Attention to practical details such as ensuring the new arrival has a locker and a pigeonhole will help to convey a positive impression and 'will engender a sense of belonging which will ease his/her transition into the new post'.[25]

Many institutions and authorities provide induction packs for new employees which contain a wide range of information about which staff should be aware. Some of these packs are very large and require at least some oral

Induction Checklist

General

When		Trained Date & initial	Completed
	Vision of the Service		
FM	Business Plan		
FM	Marketing Strategy		
FM	Training and Development Plan		
FW	By laws/Rules and Regulations		
FM	PDR		
	Customer care		
FM	Policy		
FM	Acceptable behaviour		
FM	Handling difficult or angry readers		
	Health and safety		
FM	Policy		
FW	Manual Handling - basics		
3M	Manual Handling course		
	Training and Development		
FM	Learning Log		
FM	IiP		
FM	NVQ's		
FW	Dates for - Induction course - Customer Care Course		
	General information		
FW	Conditions of service		
FW	Pay		
FW	Hours of work		
FW	Timetabling arrangements		
FW	Annual leave		
FW	Reporting sick		
FD	Meeting staff		
FD	Tour of building		
FD	Tea/lunch breaks		
FW	Union		
FD	Evacuation procedures		
FD	Dress code		
FW	Staff privileges		

Figure 7.9   General induction checklist – Essex Libraries

	Elan		
FM	Checkout		
FM	Checkin		
FM	Membership		
	- Proof of address/identity		
	- Confidentiality/Data Protection		
	- Conditions		
	- Tickets		
	- Privilege tickets		
	- Replacement tickets		
	- Notes on tickets		
	- Suspended readers		
FM	Renewals		
FM	Screen messages		
FM	Fines		
FM	Charges		
FM	Printouts		
FM	Holds		
	- Placing a hold		
	- Checking progress		
FM	OPAC's		
3M	Backup		
	Information Technology		
6M	Explanation of Hardware/Software		

Key: FD = First Day   FW = First Week   FM = First Month
         3M = Within 3 Months   6M = Within 6 Months

Figure 7.9 concluded

explanation if they are not to be consigned to the top shelf or the waste-bin. A typical pack will contain documents on:

- health and safety procedures
- conditions of service
- appraisal procedures
- discipline procedures
- grievance procedures
- equal opportunities policy
- maternity benefits
- dealing with threats or violence
- special leave provisions

Induction Checklist

Library Manager/Assistant Library Manager/Mobile Library Manager/Senior Library Assistant

When		Trained Date & initial	Completed Unsuper-vised
	Structure		
FM	County Structure		
FM	Role of District team		
FM	Role of Core teams		
FM	District Manager and Assistant Distict Manager Role and Visits		
FM	Library Manager's role		
FM	Learning Logs		
FM	Links with professional team		
FM	Mobile Library staff (where appropriate)		
FM	Headquarters Support		
	Staff Management		
FM	Timetables and rotas		
FM	Peak relief and attendance record		
FM	PDR and training needs		
FM	Annual Leave (+ formula for part time staff)		
FM	Absence return		
FM	Absence records		
FM	Sickness regulations		
FM	Overtime return		
FM	Accidents		
FM	Incident reports		
FM	Personnel Handbook		
3M	Recruitment - Appointments - Resignations		
FM	Staff supervision		
FM	Role of DAA		
	Finance		
3M	Managing budgets		
FM	Banking		
FM	Float		
FM	Petty cash		
FM	Dealing with invoices		
FM	Travel claims		
FM	Newspaper invoices		
FD	Safe keys		

Key: FD = First Day FW = First Week FM = First Month
3M = Within 3 Months 6M = Within 6 Months

Figure 7.10 Extract from post-specific induction checklist – Essex Libraries

- career break schemes
- aims and objectives of the parent body
- recent copies of the staff newsletter.

New staff learn most by working closely with other staff, talking, observing, asking and listening. Encouragement can be given, for example, by involving them in joint projects with other staff. The most important persons both inside and outside the library have to be identified, and arrangements made for the newcomer to meet them, and where desirable, to visit the places where they work. During this period of acclimatization, it is a great advantage if a colleague can take on the role of mentor. Mentoring within organizations is discussed further in Chapter 8.

The more senior the post, the more likely there is to be a considerable amount of choice by the post holder in determining how their time is spent. Most important in the first few months will be talking and listening to key persons in the library and in the organization, assessing strengths and weaknesses, and working out a role. At the same time, relationships will be built up with senior staff, colleagues and staff for whom the new recruit has management responsibility. A great deal can also be learned through reading reports, statistics, minutes of meetings, circulars, guides, manuals, memos and so on. New staff can do this themselves, though important documents can be identified and provided. Within the first year, many undertake their own surveys and investigations where they feel they require more information. Throughout this early period, they need to be aware that they are making some impact immediately they take up the post, and should therefore think about and prepare activities carefully. There is not necessarily a 'honeymoon' period during which mistakes will be easily forgiven. The most important managerial skills required are discussed in Chapter 8, and once again a mentor can be crucial for successful self-development.

Goulding and Kerslake have found that flexible workers are frequently excluded from induction training. They identified two central issues regarding induction for flexible staff:

- extensive induction for temporary and casual staff is not generally considered cost-effective; and;
- part time workers may wait a considerable time for induction if periodic sessions take place on days they do not work.[26]

As we have seen, comprehensive induction training is vital if services are to maintain the standards which their users demand. Making it clear from the start of the recruitment process that flexible staff will need to take part in induction activities, combined with a flexible approach on the part of the manager and the trainers to the timing of the induction sessions, will help to overcome some of the barriers which flexible staff can face.

Induction training is necessarily conservatively biased, therefore there is a need both for updating and improvement training and for the general development of staff if innovative and positive work practices are to be developed.

MAINTENANCE TRAINING AND BASIC UPDATING

In order to deliver an effective service, library staff will need access to training which will:

- reinforce existing procedures and policies – for example, registering students at the start of the academic year
- provide information on new or changed services – for example, new databases
- explore innovations which the library is interested in considering – for example, self-issue systems.

In the main, these needs can be met by the training methods in the lower half of Figure 7.2 – those methods which develop specific capabilities. As with so many aspects of training, there is a fine line between developing specific capabilities and developing diffuse capabilities. For example, attending external conferences and visits to other libraries are ways in which staff can become familiar with innovative means of meeting the needs of readers.

ASSESSING COMPETENCY

The skills which staff acquire through their daily work and by taking part in maintenance training or basic updating represent a major investment on the part of both the employee and the employer. For many, the opportunity to achieve formal recognition of this investment is an attractive one. In some sectors, for example engineering, staff can work towards such recognition through apprenticeship schemes. In the library and information sector, the most widespread form of assessing job competency is the Scottish and National Vocational Qualification (S/NVQ) scheme.

The concept of demonstrating competence is fundamental to the S/NVQ system. As such, 'these qualifications – unlike many that are more traditionally exam- or test-based – are about the practicalities of how you perform when faced with a task to do or a problem to solve'.[27] There are five levels within the S/NVQ system (5 being the highest), and to date Information and Library Services (ILS) S/NVQs have been available at levels 2, 3 and 4. At each level there are a certain number of units, some of which are mandatory and some of which are optional. The number of optional units from which candidates may choose increases with the complexity of the level. This enables staff

210

from the full range of sectors to identify elements which are relevant to their own work context. As reported by Oldroyd, even within a single organization the units which staff select and the order in which they follow these will differ. Thus, the structure provides staff with the ability 'to make their own choices to fit individual and team needs and to attempt units in an order to suit themselves and to fit their opportunities to collect naturally occurring evidence'.[28] This approach results in a very flexible qualification which can be tailored to fit individual circumstances.

The second way in which S/NVQs are flexible is in the fact that there are no time limits or timetables for submission. Candidates may set their own pace and may take breaks from working towards the qualification if their circumstances necessitate this. In practice, candidates can be affected by the revision of standards. When substantial revisions take place, 'a candidate who has some but not all of the Units for the full VQ has only a limited period in which to continue to achieve the rest of the old Units to achieve the (outdated) VQ'.[29] It may be possible for the candidate to change to working to the new standards by submitting additional evidence to upgrade their existing units.[30] This flexibility of pace and choice of content make S/NVQs particularly appropriate for part-time and temporary staff. Goulding and Kerslake have identified that S/NVQs, with positive support from managers, present a potential opportunity to overcome some of the constraints which flexible workers face when aiming to participate in training activities.[31]

Opinions on the applicability of S/NVQS to the library and information sector differ widely. Take-up has been strongest in the public library sector, whereas in the special and higher education sectors, the response has been patchy. This is due in part to the debates about competencies versus knowledge. There is a view (expressed by Sykes,[32] for example) that competencies quickly become outdated, and that which is measured by S/NVQs soon ceases to be relevant. Further, some argue (Wilson,[33] for example) that S/NVQs are mechanistic, and at the higher levels, that they do not encourage the qualities which are required of managers. The way in which the standards are written and presented has also led to caution on the part of potential candidates and their employers, although authors such as Arundale[34] and Herzog[35] go a long way towards demystifying the process.

The benefits of the S/NVQ approach are many, and the potential for flexible workers should not be ignored. Even if staff do not enter for assessment, the standards which have been developed for ILS-NVQs have a variety of uses. Dakers has identified three areas in which the full potential of S/NVQs has yet to be realized. These can be summarized as:

- human resource management – the standards provide an off-the-shelf source for job descriptions, and a framework for many staff management activities
- influencing higher education qualifications – the required underpinning knowledge could be embedded within Library and Information courses
- establishing our position within the overall labour market – S/NVQs are a *national* vocational qualification, and Dakers reminds us that 'we will only survive as a sector if we are part of the mainstream, seen as relevant to others and comparable to them'.[36]

The future of ILS NVQs went through a period of uncertainty when, following a long wait for revised standards, Oxford Cambridge RSA Examinations (OCR) withdrew as the validating body for England, Northern Ireland and Wales. The ensuing lengthy hiatus while the Chief Verifier and the Information Services National Training Organization (isNTO) worked to find a new verifying body led many in the sector to predict the demise of ILS NVQs. The authors are in agreement with Stauch, who identified such an outcome as representing an opportunity lost.[37] The agreement by City and Guilds to become the Awarding Body for Levels 1 and 2 and the submission of the revised standards to the Qualifications and Curriculum Authority (QCA) for accreditation reaffirmed the future of the qualification.

MEETING TRAINING NEEDS

Training needs may be met through training which is delivered in-house or externally. It may be that a specific course can be found which meets the requirements that have been identified, or there may be a need to develop a series of workshops which will benefit a range of staff with a variety of needs. In some cases, it may be appropriate for a member of staff to follow a formal course of study, in other instances self-paced learning using on-line packages will be more suitable. There may be regional training groups which can be tapped into. These can be particularly useful for smaller libraries, where regular training programmes are not feasible, and for addressing the needs of distinct groups of staff. Participating in such events provides added value, as staff have the opportunity to network with colleagues from elsewhere in the region. Job exchange may be appropriate, either internally (job rotation) or between organizations. The training officer will need to ascertain which methods are most suitable and how cost-effective they are in terms of time and money. In order to do this, it will be necessary to first consider the nature, and number, of the staff to be trained (their experience, existing knowledge, articulacy, motivation and different learning styles), and then to examine the range of options which are available.

In practice, it will often be necessary to combine a variety of training methods, often from different providers. Figure 7.11 reproduces the introduction and first part of a skills checklist from the British Library of Political and Economic Science at the LSE. Training which is delivered within the library is complemented by sessions delivered by other departments within the organization and external training. Meeting the training needs of Chartership candidates will also involve bringing together a variety of training methods and activities. Organizations which offer Route A to candidates need to submit their programme to the Library Association (LA) for approval. This can be a standard programme which can be used by an employing organization on a regular basis for a number of candidates, or a tailored programme designed for a named individual in a specific post. The LA provides a pro forma which requires supervisors to describe how training will be delivered in areas common to most posts in library and information work.[38] This prompts the person designing the programme to consider a variety of training activities. The checklist in Figure 7.6 is derived from this pro forma, and can also serve as a checklist of training activities for all staff.

ORGANIZING IN-HOUSE TRAINING PROGRAMMES

In order to provide staff with a means to keep their skills and knowledge up to date, many services have developed in-house training programmes. These may be delivered by other staff from the library or parent organization. If the necessary expertise does not exist within the organization, then an external trainer may be brought in to deliver the required training. Once it has been decided that training will be delivered in-house, the training officer will need to choose the methods that will be used. It may be that there are suitable published materials, such as case studies, self-teaching packages and videos produced by libraries, commercial organizations and Departments of Library and Information Studies. Practical training methods such as discussion groups and computer-based training can be used, and these are considered later in this chapter. As we saw in identifying training needs, effective training must be linked to organizational objectives, and these must be kept in the foreground when designing an in-house programme.

By looking at a specific training need, we can discuss the way training might be organized in an effective way. Imagine, therefore, the following situation. There has been a considerable increase in the number of attempts to remove material from the university library without permission. Culprits are usually caught at the exit from the library when they pass through the security

SKILLS CHECKLIST – LIBRARY SERVICES STAFF

Library Assistant
Public duties
No line management responsibilities
(LA) July 2000

How to organise the training activities in the checklist

Basic skills and identified task skills to be achieved by the end of probation, remaining skills by the end of Year 1 or as agreed.

As a rule of thumb an evaluation form does NOT have to be filled Out for these short courses but use the Personal Development Plan to keep a record.

From The Library
Information Services, User Services and other sections of the Library run regular rolling training programmes that new staff can be booked on to. Existing staff who may have missed elements of the programmes can be slotted in —just talk to the programme organisers.

From IT Services
IT Services provide a monthly list of courses covering all the training in the checklist plus for example task based training. If you do not have a copy ask the Library Administrator. Booking forms are contained in the list.

From The Staff Development and Training Section
The Staff Development prospectus will be issued annually in January. All the Staff Development training courses noted in the checklist will be available plus a number of others. Use the prospectus to choose the appropriate courses — booking/evaluation forms are then available from the Staff Development and Training Section.
As these courses are currently free to the Library try to use these rather than an external one on the same topic.

1 – BASIC SKILLS to be completed by all staff by the end of probation unless otherwise agreed			
Customer Care awareness	O	Half day	Rolling programme via Library Administrator
Disability awareness	O	Half day	Staff Development rolling programme
Equal Opportunities awareness	O	Half day	Staff Development roiling programme
IT competence with Windows packages (basic courses)		3 hours each	ITS rolling programme
word processing	O		
spreadsheets	O		
Outlook / email / public folders	O		
database	O		
internet searching	O		
Telephone skills		Half day	Problem solving workshop via (linked modules in one day programme via Staff Development)
dealing with callers	O		
using the telephone system	O		
sending faxes	O		
Communication skills		Half day	Effective reading techniques / writing with impact / (linked modules in one day programme via Staff Development)
effective reading	O		
writing skills / basic note taking at meetings	O		
Ability to work as an effective part of a team and on own initiative	O	1 day	Facilitated bespoke training via Staff Development as required
Health and Safety awareness	O	1 hour	Staff Development rolling programme
Fire procedures / disaster planning	O	1 hour	IS rolling programme
Awareness of structure / senior management / departments	O	Documentation only	Induction Pack Section 3 and via School web page

Figure 7.11 Extract from skills checklist – British Library of Political and Economic Science at the LSE

214

device. The librarian made representations to the directorate, and the matter was put to the governors, who agreed to an increase in penalties. The secretariat of the university drew up a recommended procedure to be followed at disciplinary hearings, which would be attended by alleged offenders. The librarian was keen to ensure that the library staff knew what to do when users were caught, and how to conduct themselves at hearings. The training officer was asked to organize a training programme, and the following steps were worked through to meet this training need:

- **Step 1 – Establish needs**
  - Analyse incidents between library staff and users caught trying to remove material without authorization.
  - Ascertain the correct disciplinary procedures with the university secretariat, including the role of library representative and witnesses.
- **Step 2 – Determine aim**. Write down the aim of the training as clearly as possible. For example, the ultimate aim is to ensure that:
  - the library staff behave correctly and document incidents accurately
  - the library staff understand disciplinary procedures, and perform effectively at disciplinary hearings.
- **Step 3 – Determine specific objectives**. Decide on methods and the trainers responsible (see Figure 7.12).

'TRAINING HOURS'

In-house training, such as that described in the above scenario, can be delivered as a one-off, or it may form part of a rolling training programme. Time is often cited by staff as one of the major constraints on taking part in training activities. For example, Sharpe states that the main difficulty in spending the allocation of money from the New Opportunities Fund aimed at reskilling the public library workforce is 'finding the staff time ... while at the same time maintaining services'.[39] Offering protected time in the form of a 'training hour' is an approach which has been adopted by many organizations. The IMPEL2 project found that training hours 'demonstrate management commitment to training and can help to support the growth of an ethos of staff development within the workplace'.[40] Ideally, the library service should be closed during the training hour. This ensures that all staff may participate in the training, and also enables the trainer and the trainees to use resources which may not be available when the library is open. Whilst it is accepted that shops and banks will close for training, persuading parent organizations that training is sufficiently important that the library or information service should close can be difficult, and conflicts with the customer service ethos of offering

	Method (see Figure 7.2 p.186)	Responsible staff
Knowledge required of:		
1 Disciplinary rules and regulations	2(a) 2(e)	Secretariat
2 Methods employed by users to remove material without authorization	2(b) 2(c) 2(d)	Circulation librarian
3 Documentation required when reporting incidents	2(a) 2(e)	Secretariat. Deputy librarian
Skills:	2(c)	
4 Communication skills in dealing with users and meetings skills in disciplinary hearings	2(d) 2(e)	Training officer
Attitudes:	2(c)	All trainers
5 Objectivity in dealing with users. Belief in need to take action against attempted theft	2(d) 2(e)	

Figure 7.12 Setting training objectives

long opening hours. Possible compromises are to open the building with restricted or no staffed services, or to repeat the sessions in order to enable staff on duty to attend.

Spurred on by the Fielden Report, staff at the University of Reading Library took the decision to implement a training hour. This was developed in the context of a library which was already carrying out training, but as Paterson and Munro report, 'except for induction training, most of this training benefited professional staff (and particularly academic-related staff) more than library assistants'.[41] The resulting programme consisted of eight modules, and the extract from the programme for the summer term in 2000, reproduced in Figure 7.13, shows that in any given week, five sessions are available. Staff are encouraged to undertake self-paced learning in the training hour if they do not wish to attend any of the structured sessions.

This method of providing training can redress the imbalance between the training which is available to para-professional staff and that which is offered to professional staff. Care needs to be taken to ensure that part-time staff can benefit from such an approach. The Training Hour Group at University of Reading Library recognized this, and reached the following solution:

Summer Term 2000 Training Hour

	Session 1	Session 2	Session 3	Session 4	Session 5	self paced
Friday 19 May 2000	OPAC searching	Staff training and development	Effective meetings	Archives Introduction	What is Knowledge Management	
Co-ordinator Venue Module	RM MLW PC Lab IT	JP MLW Training Room Customer care	MG & HS MLW Finzi Book Room Management	MB MLW Archives Our Library	SC Bulm Lib Seminar Room Issues in Librarianship	
Friday 26 May 2000	Tables on MS Word	Awkward colleagues	ECS Dean	Minimal service for Attendants	Geography of Whiteknights	
Co-ordinator Venue Module	MG MLW PC Lab IT	KP & KP MLW Training Room Customer care	DM Bulm Lib Seminar Room Faculty team topic	IB MLW Staff Room Our Library	MB MLW Staff Room University in context	
Friday 2 June 2000	Self-paced with advice	Open & Distance Learners	Rare books in the sciences	First Aid for Minimal service	The Trust Library	
Co-ordinator Venue Module	CA & RS MLW PC Lab IT	LM MLW Training Room Customer care	CS MLW Firzi Book Room Faculty team topic	HS & DS Bulm Lib Seminar Room Our Library	JD Royal Berks Hospital Beyond RUL	

Figure 7.13 Extract from 'Training Hour' programme – Reading University Library

The staff whose normal working hours do not include the Training Hour, have been encouraged either to rearrange their hours on that day if possible, or to come in and be compensated with time off in lieu. Most such part time staff have been extremely flexible and positive about this.[42]

In addition to devising the weekly programme, the Training Hour Group have produced a training hour handbook and an evaluation sheet for training hour sessions. Not all organizations will be able to make the commitment in terms of the necessary staff time to organize a programme on the scale of that in place at the University of Reading Library. Nonetheless, a structured programme, albeit on a smaller scale, taking place in protected training time can be of enormous benefit to a service.

PRACTICAL TRAINING METHODS

Some training methods demand more participation from the trainees than others. In general, those which involve input from the participants are likely to result in a more effective and satisfying training experience for all concerned. However, when they are poorly managed, they can be counter-productive. Research by Jones has helped to provide guidelines for trainers which, if followed, should ensure a positive outcome in most circumstances.[43] Fuller treatment can be found in Part 1 of *Case Studies in Library Management*.[44] Not all the information which needs to be conveyed lends itself to participatory methods. Where it is necessary to use methods which permit passivity on the part of the audience, this should be compensated for by including some form of activity, for example by including a short quiz at the end of a set of written instructions. If trainees are encouraged to tackle the quiz in small groups, it will become less exam-like and may spark questions related to the procedure which is being conveyed.

LECTURES AND TALKS

Lectures and talks, whether or not accompanied by audio-visual aids, are normally dominated by the speaker and give minimal opportunity for contributions from the audience, who are cast in a passive role. Careful consideration should therefore be given to the kind of information conveyed in this way. It is satisfactory for communicating ideas and introducing topics, but is poor for conveying detailed information, unless various handouts are issued by the speaker so that the audience may follow up a general introduction with written guidelines or instructions for action.

An easily followed structure is essential, and it is helpful if the speaker sets this out at the beginning (orally, on a handout, or by using projection equipment) and refers to it at various intervals. It is important to decide in advance the key points which will be communicated, and to recapitulate in order to reinforce them. These may also be reinforced by illustrating with audio-visual aids (presentation software, overhead projectors and videos are the most common). When these are used, make sure in advance that all the equipment works, that it is all plugged in, and that the trainer is knowledgeable about the various controls. This may sound obvious, but it clearly needs to be reiterated, as anyone who frequently attends professional or recreational meetings, or who is an *aficionado* of the John Cleese Video Arts Production on the use of (or rather, the hazards of) audio-visuals will know.[45]

Talks which last for much more than half an hour are not likely to keep the attention of the audience. If it is necessary to go on longer than that, it can help to have a 'break-out session' to enable small groups of trainees to talk to each other about points made. Alternatively, people can be asked to write down their views or experience as a break from just listening. Both these methods are often more productive than saying hopefully, 'Are there any questions so far?', which nearly always draws a negative response.

The level of language and the tone used (littered with witticisms or sonorously earnest, chatty and informal or sermon-like and portentous) is only partly a product of one's personality. Try to match it to your audience. Check whether they think it does, by sensing their response as the talk proceeds. Look at their faces and talk directly to them, rather than to the ceiling or the back wall, or worst of all, your own notes. In training, new words and terminology may be necessary, and if you are in doubt as to whether your audience understands these terms, give out a glossary. Acronyms now abound in many topics, and should be de-mystified by providing the audience with the relevant definitions.

The most common problems trainers experience with this method are trying to communicate too much detailed information, and delivering their talks in a manner which is dull or distracting because of perhaps unconscious mannerisms. To overcome these problems, it is advisable to establish how much of the information would be better communicated in handouts, or in a loose-leaf staff manual for staff to look up later. As for personal mannerisms, among the most distracting are speaking too fast or too slow, in a monotonous unvarying rhythm, waving hands about all the time, or wearing out the carpet by walking around in small circles while talking. The analysis sheet shown in Figure 7.14 has been used successfully by the authors to obtain feedback from audiences.

Brewerton has provided some useful checklists under the headings:

- planning presentations

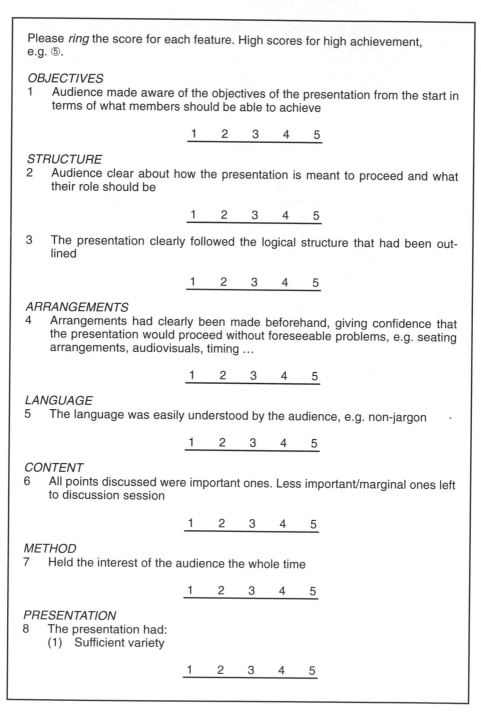

Please *ring* the score for each feature. High scores for high achievement, e.g. ⑤.

OBJECTIVES
1   Audience made aware of the objectives of the presentation from the start in terms of what members should be able to achieve

        1   2   3   4   5

STRUCTURE
2   Audience clear about how the presentation is meant to proceed and what their role should be

        1   2   3   4   5

3   The presentation clearly followed the logical structure that had been out-lined

        1   2   3   4   5

ARRANGEMENTS
4   Arrangements had clearly been made beforehand, giving confidence that the presentation would proceed without foreseeable problems, e.g. seating arrangements, audiovisuals, timing ...

        1   2   3   4   5

LANGUAGE
5   The language was easily understood by the audience, e.g. non-jargon

        1   2   3   4   5

CONTENT
6   All points discussed were important ones. Less important/marginal ones left to discussion session

        1   2   3   4   5

METHOD
7   Held the interest of the audience the whole time

        1   2   3   4   5

PRESENTATION
8   The presentation had:
     (1) Sufficient variety

        1   2   3   4   5

Figure 7.14   Checklist of features of a good presentation

220

(2) Correct pace

    1   2   3   4   5

(3) Good voice delivery – easy to understand and 'kept up' at end of sentences

    1   2   3   4   5

(4) Energy and enthusiasm.

    1   2   3   4   5

(5) Emphases which were appropriate.

    1   2   3   4   5

(6) No offputting mannerisms

    1   2   3   4   5

(7) No barriers between the audience and the presenter, e.g. presenter looked directly at audience, no unnecessary physical barriers.

    1   2   3   4   5

(8) Adaptations were made to the audience's response as the presentation proceeded

    1   2   3   4   5

AUDIOVISUALS
9   Audiovisuals were:
    (1) Legible/audible

    1   2   3   4   5

    (2) Fitted in well

    1   2   3   4   5

    (3) Equipment worked

    1   2   3   4   5

HANDOUTS
10   Handouts were effective

    1   2   3   4   5

Figure 7.14   concluded

- delivering presentations
- evaluating presentations.[46]

Attendance on a presentation skills course is a wise investment for anyone who is in the position of giving talks and lectures on a regular basis. These are offered by a range of training providers, for example the LA and Aslib. Parent organizations also often run such events. It is likely that the course will involve being filmed while giving a presentation. This is a daunting prospect, but it does represent an excellent way of discovering hitherto unknown and probably distracting mannerisms!

WRITTEN INSTRUCTIONS

The most common forms of written instructions are leaflets, cards, loose-leaf manuals, notices containing flowcharts or diagrams for a particular section of the library, or a particular process. Use of these enables the trainer to be certain that the trainee can check and refer back to the instructions when the trainer is no longer there to explain. Thus, they are economical in saving the time of the trainer. Also, people learn at different speeds, and many staff find it a comfort to be able to remind themselves of procedures at their own speed, and without a trainer asking them whether they understand fully. In the early stages of training, it is very hard for trainees to tell whether they understand or not, so that may not be a meaningful question unless it is checked by asking them to carry out an activity to demonstrate their understanding.

In preparing written instructions, it is important to provide a clear logical structure, and this should be reflected in the layout, headings and subheadings, numbers of pages and sections, and in the use of diagrams (often more appropriate than long paragraphs of prose for explaining, for instance, a staffing structure, or the stages in book processing). The more practical examples there are, the better, as in the early stages of training abstractions will be bemusing for many trainees. The form and level of language must be relevant to the trainee group, just as in oral communication.

DISCUSSION GROUPS

The purpose of discussion groups is to let all members express their views on an issue, so the size should be limited to twelve. The groups may be led by a trainer or by a group member, or may remain informal and leaderless. Inevitably, if the trainer leads, group members will talk less to each other and the trainer will talk for a quite high proportion of the time. Therefore, if the objective is for the group to talk more, it is better for the trainer to let the group get on with it, or only join it after the halfway mark.

Discussion groups should be used when the topic lends itself to a variety of opinions and alternative solutions. They should be avoided when there is nothing much to talk about and the topic is straightforward and does not lend itself to a number of different interpretations. It can be useful for developing the interpersonal skills of staff in a safe, professional context, where most people should have some view to put forward and are willing to listen to others' views so as to modify their own starting position. It is particularly appropriate for influencing people's attitudes, rather than for imparting knowledge or skills. It is, for instance, widely used, along with role-play, in local authority equal opportunities courses.

Three factors tend to make discussion groups work well. First, the objectives must be clear. Are group members agreed on the task before them, the problem to be solved, and the outcome that the trainer expects? Second, the group needs to have some structure to get through the task, and that requires a chairperson to review and summarize and mark progress towards goals, and a reporter to keep a record of the group's decisions. The record is better kept in some visible form for all to see, rather than only in the notebook of the reporter. Main ideas can be summarized and subheadings and criticisms of ideas noted on a board or flipchart. Third, the group will be most satisfactory when everybody takes part and there are no members being carried by the rest. A good chairperson can help by bringing everyone in, or going round the table in turn, but so can other group members by engaging in building and supporting behaviour (see Chapter 8 on interpersonal skills for meetings).

The mix of people in the groups affects the success of this method, and the trainer may wish to assist with this by arranging the groups beforehand. A common problem is the domination of the group by one or two monopolizing individuals, and a corresponding retreat into passivity by other group members. Dividing groups into two, one consisting of the higher contributors and the other of the lower contributors, so that everyone will feel more in their element, can alleviate this. It is also possible that groups will be affected negatively if the trainer participates in the activity. To avoid leader dominance, trainers should organize the session so that they are not in the group all the time, inhibiting the others, but are only present at the beginning and end to explain, to hear views, and to comment and summarize. Aggressive and obstructive behaviour is uncommon in groups of library and information workers. On the rare occasions when it happens, in our experience, it has had its origin outside the immediate activity, perhaps because people have been compulsorily sent on the training course, or because they have an issue which they wish to air before they do anything else. Some people find that the training discussion group is the only opportunity they have for expressing their grievances. In that case, it may be worth the trainer taking ten minutes out of the programme specifically for that purpose.

CASE STUDIES

Case studies are particularly useful in management and interpersonal skills training, because they simulate real-life problems and give trainees a chance to find solutions in a low-risk situation, where they can try out ideas and see what happens, without the possibly disastrous effects which might, if the ideas are half-baked, accrue in real life. The assumption is that this is a learning experience which will develop judgement, and make people into better decision-makers. The method is related to discussion groups, in that case studies are usually tackled by a group, though they can be used with individuals as well, who write up their ideas and give them to the tutor or trainer. In the group setting, they give trainees practice in interpersonal negotiations with colleagues, as well as thinking things out for themselves. This is useful for real life, where ideas remain pretty futile unless they can be implemented, and that means persuading other people that they are viable and valuable.

It is preferable for trainers to write their own case studies, or to adapt existing ones to their own context. It saves time to use existing cases, but they should be chosen carefully to ensure they are relevant to the trainees' level of expertise and experience. It does not go down well to set problems which in real life would be the responsibility of senior management, and impose them on new professionals. When the trainer draws on their own experiences, proper attention must be paid to ensuring that the people and environment on which the case is based cannot be identified.

The trainer's task is to write or adapt case studies that are credible and do not go 'over the top', otherwise the result will be to entertain rather than to instruct. In addition to designing the case studies, the trainer will need to draw up a programme of instructions on running the case study. For example, the trainer may organize the group into fours or sixes, give them half an hour to come up with solutions by discussion, ask for a report at the end (verbal, or in the form of overhead projector transparencies or wall posters), and leave time for feedback on the solutions of the mini-groups, and how they compare with classic solutions as set out, say, in management textbooks, or practised in more progressive libraries. In addition to all this, the trainer needs to work out how the trainees will absorb the case study material. It should ideally be given to them in advance, or sent out with the course programme, so that they will come to the discussion with some prior knowledge, and not have to spend the first half hour trying to grasp what the problem is.

If case studies are being written by the trainer, remember that too much detail will confuse and overwhelm the learners, whilst too little will mean that they will spend the first session asking for more information. Requests for more information should be approached warily. This is often an excuse for not using the actual information given. One of the reasons why the case study method is so valuable is that it tests people's ability to apply ideas and strategies, and to make use of information sifted from working documents. Reluctance to do this, and slowness in developing these skills, are an unfortunate aftermath of formal, teacher-centred education systems. The trainer needs to explain why the method is being used, and equally the trainees should be helped by being given some ideas and theories to apply, in an introduction or handout. Otherwise, they will chat around the problem, and come up with rule-of-thumb solutions which make no reference to relevant management or communication ideas.

The most common problems trainers encounter in using the case study method are pragmatism and regression to teacher-centred, 'right answer' stances. Trainees may sit around chatting about the problem situation, without any incisive analysis or ability to get to the crux, in the hope that in half an hour they will be told the solution by the trainer. In order to avoid this, trainees should work individually or in pairs, writing down ideas and listing points on what the problem is, and how it may be solved. If no preparation has been done, it may be necessary to issue a handout containing some basic management strategies which could solve the problem. For example, if the case study were about deciding on a formal staff appraisal system, one or two examples of appraisal interview forms used in other libraries (see Chapter 6) plus a ten-point checklist of what appraisal is meant to do from the management literature would be helpful.

A further problem in using case studies is that people need group skills to work with others in solving a problem. They may be unused to any other kind of work besides individual work, and it may be difficult to gain co-operation to reach a consensus without individuals feeling mortified because 'their' idea got lost and a 'worthless' solution was accepted just because a dominant group member kept pushing it rather aggressively. It should be pointed out that people have a choice of behaviour in groups, and can learn to modify their own, and indeed other people's, by practising the helpful group behaviours (proposing, building, supporting, openness, summarizing, seeking and giving information, and bringing in) and developing strategies for coping with the unhelpful group behaviours (blocking, shutting out, stating difficulties, negative disagreeing, defending/attacking). Case studies offer an opportunity to try out some of these behaviours, and to learn from the experience.

225

ROLE-PLAY

Role-play is an optional extra to the case study method. Rather than discussing a problem from the outside, the trainees play the roles of the people in the case study, and try to reach a solution which takes account of feelings as well as rational analysis. It is used to explain, demonstrate and sensitize, most often in the interpersonal skills areas of staff–user relations, or supervisor–staff counselling and appraisal, and in the area of recruitment and selection.

In setting up a role-play the trainer must write the scenario, making sure that the incident corresponds to the teaching aim (how to conduct a counselling interview, how to open up a reference interview), and that it is sufficiently realistic and close to the trainees' experience to be credible to them. A handout may be given to each player, containing details of their position in the library, what they believe to be the circumstances surrounding the incident, and the problem incident itself. The best way to run role-plays is to have groups of threes, with two role-playing and the third observing their behaviour and commenting at the end of the ten-minute role-play. Role-swapping is useful, so that each member of the trio has a chance to play both sides of the situation (for example, from the supervisor's view, and from the junior assistant's view) and to observe. At the end of the role-play, it is important to gather comments from all the participants, and to draw out general conclusions about what has been learnt, in order to encourage learning transfer.

The usual problems experienced in using role-play are that people worry about having to act, or enter into the role-play as if it were just acting, by 'hamming it up'. Emphasize that they are being asked to play *themselves*, and to try to imagine how they would behave in the kind of situation they are given. If trainees are diffident about starting, feeling shy and embarrassed, the trainer may help to break the ice by doing a dummy run with a colleague or one of the extroverted group members. It is also possible to use 'shadows', where each trainee has another person backing them up whom they can consult on how to play the role, or take turns to share the same role. In a really tongue-tied group, a helpful strategy is 'group role-play', in which three or four people talk to each other about how the role should be played, and only one of them has to play it. A real-life outsider (maybe someone who conducts appraisal interviews in everyday life) may be invited to attend, and give a demonstration of how they would have handled the problem in their own job. It is beneficial to make the situation as close to real life as possible. For example, in large organizations there may be employees, or in the education sectors, students, who are keen to practise being interviewed. Thus, if the purpose of the role-play is to practise recruitment and selection techniques, a 'stranger' can act as an interviewee, and this will help to create a situation similar to that which the trainees will experience when they interview external candidates.

COMPUTER-BASED TRAINING

There are various advantages in using computer-based training (CBT) – electronic means such as Web packages or computerized tutorials – to deliver staff training. Biddiscombe summarizes these as:

- increased flexibility
- reduced costs
- more efficient use of time
- self-paced learning.

He goes on to list some of the disadvantages:

- the need for a networked environment
- the need to provide an adequate introduction to the technology
- making sure the training is being undertaken by the trainees
- measuring results
- providing supervisory help
- the costs of the software.[47]

It is clear from these summaries that using IT to deliver training is not without its difficulties. In particular, it is worth noting that the matter of cost appears in both lists. It is easy to assume that delivering training via computers will be a cheap option, but as Biddiscombe stresses: 'even if this method is chosen for the cost savings that can notionally be made, the provision of this type of training should not be undertaken simply for that reason'.[48] There will be costs in terms of the trainer's time, or fees if an external trainer is used. The trainees will be absent from their day-to-day work, and there may be equipment costs to consider. Nonetheless, the potential of this means of providing training is enormous. The use of online packages as a means to overcome the difficulty of releasing staff on a regular basis is recommended by Garrod and Sidgreaves.[49] Use of this method can also help to provide training for part-time staff who are not present when training is usually delivered. The Training the Future project found that 'developments in new technologies are making the possibility of a Web-based framework for learning increasingly possible'. A networked learning environment could enable staff to access online training materials, maintain contact with tutors, mentors or other staff, monitor their own progress, and record their achievements.[50]

One obvious use of computers to deliver training is in the area of IT. Many off-the-shelf software packages include built-in tutorials. The quality and use-

227

fulness of these can vary, and they will not be tailored to the specific needs of the organization. It is important to remember that if IT is going to be used to deliver staff training, the staff who are using the computer-based packages will need to have had sufficient training in using the relevant IT applications that they feel confident about learning online.

The development of the European Computer Driving Licence (ECDL) offers a means for organizations to provide accredited IT training to their staff in an online environment. Following the provision of £230 million from the UK government's New Opportunities Fund (NOF) to improve the IT skills of teachers and school and public library staff, many public library authorities have taken this route as a way to meet the NOF expected outcomes. Indeed the guidance from NOF identified the ECDL as an appropriate package for this training. The British Computer Society (BCS), which administers the scheme in the UK, has ensured that the standards represented by the ECDL are tied in with other nationally recognized qualifications, for example S/NVQs.

The ECDL will not be appropriate for all organizations: 'the seven modules and associated practice time and examinations represent a major commitment of staff time'.[51] Sharpe recommends considering alternative approaches, for example the Computer Literacy and Information Technology (CLAIT) training course. This, combined with supplementary sessions, can be used to develop the skills listed in the NOF expected outcomes. Sharpe's article highlights the need to remember that the delivery of IT training must be as carefully considered as the delivery of any other sort of training. The methods chosen need to take into account the local environment, the existing level of knowledge of the staff involved, and the required outcomes.

The use of computer systems in delivering training goes beyond the development of IT skills. Developments such as virtual and managed learning environments as support for higher education courses demonstrate that the education sector has started to harness the potential of this means of delivery. Milligan identifies various types of training and staff development activities which could be delivered online. These include the sort of course which involves the participant working through notes at their own pace. Using an online environment enables elements such as animations or video clips to be included in the notes. Courses which involve people working closely together, for example in a mentoring relationship, could also be delivered in this way. Finally, this method can be appropriate when it is desirable to create a community of learners. E-mail lists and bulletin boards can be used to encourage discussion. Milligan notes that this last use 'requires a good tutor or facilitator to encourage high quality communication'.[52]

This final point again highlights the need to apply the same rigorous quality checks when selecting training which will be delivered using computers as those which are used when choosing more traditional forms of training. As part of the Training the Future project, consultants were commissioned and briefed in order to provide two guides for employers on assessing and purchasing/commissioning training materials. The resulting guides, together with the brief, are included in the appendices of *Staff in the New Library: Skill Needs and Learning Choices*.[53] The focus of the project was IT and related skills in the public library sector. Nonetheless, the three documents are excellent tools for ascertaining the training which is required and the appropriateness of methods which are being considered in a variety of contexts.

ON-THE-JOB TRAINING

On-the-job training (OJT), commonly known as 'sitting next to Nellie', is valuable as long as 'Nellie' is a good communicator and trainer and OJT is properly embedded in the training strategy of the organization. Without this structured approach, there is a danger that the training process will be jeopardized. In 1996, the Institute of Personnel and Development (IPD) undertook a study of OJT in four manufacturing companies. The companies were selected as being typical rather than best practice, and the study revealed that OJT 'appeared to have just evolved, and was not based on good practice and learning design principles'.[54]

In order to ensure that the training which is delivered via OJT is comparable in quality to that which is provided by other means, the staff acting as trainers need to be recognized as such, and given appropriate training themselves. This should be, at minimum, a one-day workshop, during which they write specific objectives for training and practising methods appropriate for attaining each of the objectives covered in this chapter. Finally, they should practise working out methods for evaluating the success of training, and ought to go back to their jobs with a much developed sense of responsibility for 'coaching' their staff on the job. The dividing line between training and supervision is rightly blurred, and skills associated with supervision are explored further in Chapter 8.

Following the background study involving the four manufacturing companies in 1996, the IPD conducted visits to 11 organizations which appeared to represent best practice in OJT. This work culminated in *The IPD Guide to On-the-job Training*.[55] This report seeks to promote best practice in OJT, and to provide assistance for the many employers who use this method. It is a useful reference point for anyone wishing to review the OJT which is delivered in their organization.

MONITORING AND EVALUATING TRAINING

In many areas of management, evaluation is not attempted in any systematic manner, not only because it is difficult, but also because managers prefer to 'do' rather than spend valuable time evaluating. But time spent on evaluation is time well spent, for how else can the effectiveness of what is 'done' be known?

At its crudest, evaluation is the comparison of stated objectives with achievements. As far as training is concerned, the achievements, especially in more complex areas such as interpersonal skills, cannot be measured easily or isolated from other influences so that it is difficult to be sure about the value of training. Evaluation is important if the quality of training is to be improved, and if it is to be made clear that it is the effect of training that matters most of all. In times of diminishing budgets, training needs to be good value, but even where cost is not an issue (if such a place exists!), training which delivers what it sets out to achieve should be identified and valued, whereas training which fails to meet the stated objectives should be redesigned, or in the case of external training, avoided. Otherwise, trainees will feel that they are participating in training for training's sake, and will quickly become jaded and disinterested in the process.

Evaluation should not be viewed as an 'optional extra'. The form from Essex Libraries (Figure 7.7) demonstrates a way in which trainees and line managers can be encouraged to think about evaluation before the training activity even begins. At the very least, staff participating in external or off-the-job training activities should be encouraged to feed back to other staff by circulating a short report, but for evaluation to be truly effective, the process needs to develop beyond this. It should cover all types of training activity, and should feed into the identifying needs stage and so into the planning stage of the training cycle shown in Figure 7.1.

There are several levels of evaluation which can be identified, each more difficult than the last, yet probably more important:

- **Completion** – there is a need to check that the training took place at all. This represents monitoring rather than evaluation *per se*, and can be noted by either the line manager or the trainee, or both. Many organizations now use personal development records or training logs as a means for staff to keep track of their training activities. Figure 7.15 reproduces the one in use at De Montfort University Library.

- **Reaction** – this considers the reactions of trainees to the training experience itself – what they thought about it, how they enjoyed it, what they would retain or leave out if it were offered in future.

230

**Division of Learning Development
Department of Library Services**

Personal Development Record

Name:

This form should be used to record all your development and training activities whether internal or external, formal or informal, including qualification courses. the activities may include: learning on the job self-study, coaching, professional meetings, conferences, external or in-house courses, projects, work-shadowing, academic or vocational qualifications, secondment. This list is not exhaustive!

Part A: Mandatory training activities e.g. Induction, Health & Safety and Qualification courses e.g. ILS NVQs, CLAIT, IBT II, Postgraduate courses

Date agreed	Signature of line manager	Title/Nature of activity	Date done	Key benefits & any further action

Part B: Other training and development activities

Date agreed	Signature of line manager	Brief description of development activity	Date done	Key benefits & any further action

Figure 7.15 Personal development record – De Montfort University Library

231

- **Learning** – the concern here is how well the trainees have learned the knowledge, skills and attitudes the trainers set out to teach them. Other learning may also have taken place, perhaps contrary to the desired objectives.

- **Job performance** – this checks how well trainees have 'internalized' the training and applied the learning to the job.

- **The library** – determining the effect of the training on the functioning of the library, and on its objectives. This focuses on good, or otherwise, that has resulted for both the department or unit and the library as a whole in terms, for example, of increased productivity, quality, atmosphere, morale.

In order to acquire a full picture of the effect of training, all the above should be measured. The means of evaluation will differ depending on which effect is being measured, and by whom. The first three can be measured during and at the end of the training, whilst the last two need a longer period before a true evaluation is possible. Trainees are dependent upon others who may not have been part of the actual training but whose co-operation and support is vital if organizational improvements are to be effected. Too often, trainees attend a course and come back full of enthusiasm, only to find they are unable to use their new knowledge and skills. In such situations, the training can prove counter-productive.

Figure 7.16 illustrates the points made in this section by showing how training in customer care might be evaluated.

The most popular form of evaluation is the written questionnaire completed at the end of training, preferably following the last session. Questionnaires given out at this time can either be returned immediately, or sent to the trainer later. Asking trainees to complete the questionnaire on the spot saves a great deal of time and ensures a good rate of return. This needs to be balanced against the benefit of allowing trainees time to reflect. Providing a means for questionnaires to be returned at a later date can result in more considered evaluation.

Williamson, in an excellent piece on the evaluation of training, states that the trainer may expect feedback on:

- The content of the programme. Was it the right level for the trainees? Was the timescale right?
- How good was the presentation? What was the quality of the speakers/ trainers?
- Were the domestic arrangements adequate?
- Did the course fulfill its own objectives and the personal objectives of those attending?[56]

Time	Level	Evaluator	Method
Mid-training	Reaction Learning	Trainer Trainees	Oral discussion among trainers and with trainees Observation Written tests
End of training	Completion Reaction Learning	Trainer Trainees	Written questionnaire to obtain trainees' opinions Oral discussion among trainers and with trainees Written tests Observation
Period after training	Job performance The library	Line manager Trainee	Observation and self- observation Coaching Analysis of complaints by users, other staff etc.

Figure 7.16 Example of training evaluation

Our own experience has been that a few questions will provide most of this information, and most participants will be happy to answer them, for example:

1. Did the course meet your expectations?   YES/NO
2. What were its strengths?
3. What were its weaknesses?
4. If the course were to be offered again, what changes would you recommend?
5. Any other comments?

It can also be useful to ask participants to rank certain aspects of the training, say from 1–4 (1 being the least favourable, 4 being the most).

STAFF DEVELOPMENT

The training discussed so far in this chapter should improve individual performance in the directions desired by the library manager. If it is done well, staff will also be developed personally, there will be a blending of the learned skills, knowledge and attitudes enabling individuals to make significant and

233

increasingly self-confident contributions to the library's performance, while feeling a sense of achievement and satisfaction. However, it is not the explicitly designed activities which alone develop staff as effective members of the organization. As was noted at the beginning of this chapter, CPD also applies to activities which are not geared to addressing specific training needs. Use of, and participation in, any of the methods shown in Figure 7.2 at 3 to 20 can provide the opportunity for staff development in the broader sense. Often, this aspect of CPD will be engaged in a serendipitous way, but the systematic approach to identifying, planning and delivering training outlined above can also be applied usefully to these less focused aspects of CPD.

A survey by Farmer and Campbell in 1997 of a small group of information professionals in the oil industry and the health sector revealed that: 'the three consistently important methods of professional updating are discussion with colleagues, external training events and reading the professional press'.[57] The results need to be treated with some caution, for as the authors themselves note, the fact that the respondents are an 'interested' sample may have bearing on the level of their CPD activity. The preparatory work for the survey revealed that employers do have qualms about supporting staff development. Initially, 175 information professionals were approached, and several of those who declined to take part 'appeared to be apprehensive about employers' reactions if they asked for time off to take part in research – or, indeed, CPD activities'.[58] The fact that two out of the three methods which are cited as most important do not have a cost at the point that they are used should go some way towards allaying the fears of employers that staff development is too expensive, but for some employers, the issue of the time spent on such activities remains a concern.

Griffiths and Pantry present a convincing argument for why information staff in the private sector should be given 'the same opportunities for continuing professional development (CPD) and training as other members of [the] business'.[59] However, for many in the special library sector, Webb's observation that 'while all types of libraries and information services undoubtedly benefit from the encouragement and support of staff training and development, managers in special libraries need to make a strong individual case for training in the absence of group or co-operative schemes',[60] will still ring true.

When staff development activities are scarce, there is an even greater need to maximize their effect. This can be achieved by encouraging staff to approach all their CPD in a structured way. Clearly, the benefits of this are not limited to staff who find themselves in organizations which may not be able to offer the same range of activities as those which are available in organizations where library staff represent a significant percentage of the workforce. The LA provides two tools which can help practitioners to adopt such an approach: *The Framework for Continuing Professional Development*,[61] and *The Toolkit for Turning Points*.[62] The latter is aimed at 'graduates who have worked in Library and Information Services (LIS) for some years (probably 2–4 years) and are at some "Turning Point" in their career'.[63] *The Framework for Continuing Professional Development* is directed towards all LA members. The use of schemes such as these helps staff to keep track of their development, and to plan their careers in a systematic way. For staff who work in an organization which encourages the use of training logs, it may not be necessary to make use of an alternative scheme. However, even in such a situation, use of these schemes can provide a healthy contrast to the (necessarily) organizational focus of in-house records.

Both the schemes available from the LA are based upon individuals taking responsibility for their own lifelong learning. Staff are invited to analyse their present jobs, future roles and personal priorities in order to identify their development needs and to work with employers in meeting those needs. Not only is it anticipated that services will improve, but also personal concerns, particularly career development, should benefit. Whilst both the schemes appear to be for *professional* staff, there is no reason why they should not be used by para-professionals at all grades who wish to provide some structure for their CPD or who are at a critical point in their working life.

The Framework for Continuing Professional Development encourages employers to create the climate and appropriate support systems for CPD as a positive contribution to meeting the objectives of the employing organization. Its guidelines for employers are shown in Figure 7.17. A partnership between the employer and the employee is a key element in the framework. In drawing up their plans, staff are encouraged to discuss their proposals with employers, to obtain their views, and to agree their role and support. A good organization will already be providing support information in the staff training and development policy statements referred to earlier in this chapter. Features of sound practice will include time off and expenses for attending professional activities, a staff library, a staff development programme with outside speakers, visits to other libraries, and a staff newsletter or journal. There should also be opportunities for comment on how the library is running as a whole, and the performance of the individual's own section. In Chapter 6, we have already discussed ways in which individual and group appraisal can meet many of these requirements.

The practice of visiting other organizations is often cited as a useful CPD activity. It is identified by the LA as one way in which Route A Chartership candidates can achieve professional awareness. This practice has developed into a more formal method of quality improvement referred to as *benchmarking*.

2. GUIDELINES FOR EMPLOYERS

The purpose of this guideline is to encourage employers to create the climate and appropriate support systems for continuous staff development as a positive contribution to meeting the objectives of the employing organisation.

ACTION	**Show commitment to continuing professional development.**
Good Practice	• Include a statement of CPD and a strategy for implementation in the relevant organisational documents. Communicate policy and plans to employees. • Specify the responsibilities of managers, staff and the relevant departments, for CPD activities. • Establish or utilise appropriate existing systems for career development to help match individual and organisational needs. • Promote continuing professional development and publicise results through annual reports, newsletters etc. • Provide encouragement for CPD and recognition of its benefits and achievements in the provision of effective library and information services.
ACTION	**Identify needs for continuous staff development.**
Good Practice	• Involve employees in identifying development needs of groups of staff and individuals. • Encourage use of a suitable CPD document. (See personal profile) • Commit resources to train managers to encourage, appraise, guide and develop staff. • Make available advice and information on CPD activities to all employees. • Establish plans for CPD to meet the employing organisation's operating requirements.
ACTION	**Implement continuing professional development plans.**
Good Practice	• Ensure that adequate resources (financial and human) are available for effective implementation. • Ensure that sufficient, relevant, cost effective CPD is carried out for each individual. As a guide (based on existing good practice) in each year, a range between 28-42 hours, (the equivalent of 4-6 average working days) of CPD activities is recommended. It should be noted that best practice already exceeds this figure. A proportion of this time will always be own-time learning. • Collaborate with providers and professional bodies in the provision of relevant CPD programmes.
ACTION	**Assess the benefits of continuous professional development in relation to the employing organisation's performance.**
Good Practice	• Evaluate, jointly with employees the results and benefits of CPD carried out against defined plans. • Monitor, review and revise, where necessary, the policies and plans for CPD in the light of experience of its operation.

Figure 7.17 The Library Associaton's guidelines for employers

236

Originally the preserve of the private sector, benchmarking has been recognized as a way to improve services whilst avoiding reinventing the wheel. Favret explores the use of benchmarking in the public library sector, and concludes that:

> it is set to grow in the public library sector, as evidenced by the fact that over 90 authorities have joined the CIPFA Libraries Benchmarking Club. This is to be welcomed as there is great potential for libraries to learn from each other. After all, we all must want to see continuous improvement in our services.[64]

Benchmarking involves these stages:

- identification of areas of own library where there is scope for improvement
- identification of libraries performing well in those areas
- preparation for visit(s) by a group of staff (the group needs to be clear about what it is looking for and how it is to proceed)
- investigation as to how new improved practices can be integrated into their own library
- negotiation for implementation.

Benchmarking is a valuable staff development activity, as it combines raising staff awareness and team working within a framework for measuring quality. In order for a benchmarking exercise to be successful, training in the associated skills will be necessary. Staff need to be aware of what they are measuring, and why. Following the quality route should have positive effects on staff development. When Newcastle University Library was preparing to apply for a Charter Mark, 'eight members of library staff from a variety of grades trained to become TQM [Total Quality Management] trainers'.[65] Among the benefits of TQM listed by Morrow is the effect on staff confidence:

> ... when they feel that the process in which they are working is not operating as well as they think it should TQM should encourage all staff to say so and have the confidence to know that they will be heard. This was of considerable value during the Charter Mark application process and is an important part of working towards continual improvement. [66]

A vital aspect of staff development is how to put into practice what has been learned. This can be particularly difficult in an inert library or in an environment which is positively hostile to new ideas or practice. Developing a culture in which all staff are able to voice opinions is a critical part of fostering staff development, and as Morrow identifies, encouraging this will have positive benefits for the service.

By supporting staff development beyond the types of training activities which directly and immediately benefit an organization, employers can work towards creating a climate in which staff relish learning, and once this has been achieved, adapting to the changes which are undoubtedly just around the corner will be all the easier. The Training the Future project identified the importance of developing a 'learning culture':

> A learning culture is one where learning is valued, library staff accept a measure of individual responsibility for their learning and the organization accepts its responsibility to enable and support the learner. In this culture the library becomes a 'learning organization' with the ambition for all its employees to become 'lifelong learners'.[67]

The shift towards lifelong learning has had enormous impact on the operations and strategies of library and information organizations, and on the roles of library staff. What must also be remembered is that in addition to supporting a culture of lifelong learning, library staff are entitled to expect that they should be able to participate in such a development: 'A learning organization works to create values, practices and procedures in which learning and working are synonymous throughout the organization.'[68] By moving towards this ideal, a library service can equip its staff with the means to contribute to the objectives of the service, and to evolve as those objectives evolve in response to the demands of the service's customers, the regional, and ultimately the national agendas.

8 Staff supervision and interpersonal skills training

STAFF SUPERVISION

Many library and information staff are involved in the supervision of other staff, though there are significant numbers who work alone and may receive help from other departments but have 'no line manager responsibility over them while they are working in the library'.[1] Similarly, homeworkers usually have no supervision responsibilities, but may present particular supervision responsibilities for managers,[2] and members of professional teams in public libraries, where supervision at service points has been handed over to para-professionals, may also have no supervision responsibilities. In the next stage of their careers, these professionals are likely to be required to supervise other staff, and they, like professionals in their first posts and para-professionals who supervise, need training if they are to perform effectively.

The most basic levels of supervision involve planning and allocating the workload so that all the jobs get done efficiently and on time. Logic and accuracy are required if staff are to feel that the tasks are shared out equally, and that there is sufficient time to do them properly. Follow-up is necessary to ensure that quality and quantity of work are being achieved, therefore the supervisor and staff must have some agreed standards for the work. Otherwise, there are likely to be mutually irritating exchanges between the supervisor and the staff, who have different expectations of what is required.

It follows from setting standards for the work that the supervisor must provide support and training so that staff may reach these standards. This is most often carried out by day-to-day on-the-job training by the supervisor, or by co-workers if the supervisor decides to delegate. Coaching is the most effective on-the-job training, and is a recognized management technique for encouraging staff to take more responsibility for their own jobs and their own learning. Coaching supervisors should try to avoid 'giving orders' and being prescriptive, and instead encourage initiative by giving broader guidance that leaves members of staff with a certain leeway to develop their own judgement and use their intelligence. The objective is to encourage staff to think more positively about their jobs, and to give them more practice in solving problems and working out answers for themselves. There are a number of difficulties with the coaching approach. It requires skill and sensitivity on the part of the supervisor, to avoid the equal dangers of giving too close supervision and not enough guidance. It demands from the subordinate a more active role than many are used to, or even want. The problem is theoretically explained by McGregor's Theory X and Theory Y. Staff who have been conditioned to a Theory X management style (close supervision, little delegation, authoritarian leadership, communication mainly down the hierarchy) may find it difficult to adapt to a Theory Y management style (expecting staff to set their own goals, being responsible for initiating projects, participating in decision-making, communication up and across as well as down the hierarchy). An example of this gap between Theory X and Theory Y assumptions in a university library centres on who is responsible for staff development and continuing education. Senior management assumes a Theory Y position:

> ... I think we probably have the attitude that, look, these are professional librarians. They are capable, ought to be capable, of being professional, and in that sense we have not structured anything – I suppose, haven't thought we ought to be structuring anything.[3]

Unfortunately, Konn goes on to comment that these attitudes of senior management were not known to lower-level staff, 'who still considered it the responsibility of senior management to give a positive lead in continuing education matters'. They were still maintaining a Theory X posture, in spite of management beliefs to the contrary, and neither side was aware of the attitudes of the other, which were quite conflicting.

The important question is how to communicate effectively. A first-line supervisor is expected to have adequate expertise and knowledge in the area of work supervised, but equally must be able to interact effectively with subordinates, senior management, and specialists such as training officers, or systems librarians. However, people are often raised to supervisory positions on the basis of previous work which does not involve staff supervision, and they can feel very inadequate and insecure. This is also a problem for librarians in their first professional posts, though many will have experienced role-plays and group work intended to develop relevant interpersonal skills on their professional courses. Later in this chapter, we suggest a framework for interpersonal skills training which could be used during professional education or as part of an in-service training programme. It covers the main problems for supervisory staff: leadership style, group skills, assertiveness training, Transactional Analysis, the management of stress, and time management.

Another problem area concerns the content of supervision. What exactly is involved in a supervisory role, beyond knowledge and expertise in the area of work (circulation, or acquisitions, or information services)? The following list provides a basic framework of supervisory activities:

1. planning and allocating work schedules, including provision for absences such as sickness and annual leave
2. helping staff to be effective in their work, by appraisal and training – formal or informal systems and structures
3. coaching staff on a day-to-day basis, to develop them in their work, and lead them to habits of taking more responsibility and initiative
4. checking that work is completed to agreed standards (quality and quantity), by agreed times, in regular consultation with individuals/teams
5. developing team work approaches in subordinates, by encouraging two or three to work together on specific activities (either for a fixed period, or permanently), to talk about their work, and to draw up reports on it where this is useful, for example in monitoring a new service
6. giving staff reasons and explanations for doing things in certain ways, and listening to their opinions about the best way to do things
7. treating staff fairly and consistently, so that they feel they can come to the supervisor with problems and ideas, whether work-related or personal
8. making a point of being aware of staff problems, without necessarily waiting for them to come to you explicitly
9. giving staff regular acknowledgement for work done
10. handling grievances and taking disciplinary action where necessary, knowing the legal requirements as well as the institution's own grievance procedures
11. having goals for the section or unit you are responsible for, and conveying these goals to your staff, as well as being clear about them yourself
12. communicating with senior management, to put your staff's viewpoint, and to channel the section or unit's ideas into the decision-making process.

In a survey of graduate trainees' experiences of on-the-job training carried out by Jones,[4] certain characteristics of 'good supervision' and 'poor supervision' emerged as significant for those on the receiving end. Rather more than half the supervisors explained why things were done in a particular way, as well as how to do them. However, 47 per cent were not in the habit of giving explanations, and trainees felt that this made their duties more difficult to grasp, and rather less interesting. More than half the supervisors did not check whether their juniors understood a task properly, so it was left to the juniors to speak out if they had any difficulties. This could be a problem when, in particular, they 'did not know enough to ask the right questions'. When awareness of difficulties was established between supervisor and trainee, supervisors were not always good at starting from the junior's viewpoint, as good teachers try to do. They tended simply to repeat instructions, rather than probing where the difficulty lay. Trainees would have preferred them to really listen and understand the problem, which usually looked different at their level.

Feedback on work performance was seen as very important to the motivation of staff. It seems there is a tendency in libraries to give more negative feedback (criticizing when something is not quite right) than positive feedback (acknowledging and giving credit for completed tasks or projects well done): 'There can be few situations more frustrating than that of the employee who makes a great effort to perform well in his job and finds his efforts totally unrecognized.'[5] The best kind of feedback was considered to be regular but informal sessions with the supervisor at the beginning and end of periods of work in different sections or on different duties. These brief but morale-boosting sessions should include some positive reviewing and summarizing of what the trainee had learned, what problems were experienced, and how these could be overcome. They should finish up with looking ahead to the next phase, and what was expected there.

The quality of day-to-day supervision, in the form of coaching, is important to trainees. They like to be given some guidelines on the standards of work expected, both quantity and quality, and apparently this is a vague area in many libraries. It was observed by trainees who had moved around a number of sections in the same library that output and expectations of performance vary considerably even within one library, depending on different supervisors and different work groups with varying degrees of motivation and informal 'group norms' for controlling output and socializing newcomers. When supervisors are not themselves clear about performance standards, this is quickly communicated to their staff, and an often amiable *laissez-faire* approach becomes the order of the day, ultimately to the detriment of service standards.

The communications skills of supervisors were graphically described in the survey, as were poor communications characteristics. In this respect, 'good supervisors' were 'approachable' and also accessible in the sense of making themselves available to talk to their trainees, rather than seeing that as an interruption to their real work. They were prepared to 'listen as well as instruct', were well informed about their work and able to communicate their expertise without the 'unnecessary use of complex jargon'. The word 'jargon' is used somewhat indiscriminately these days to include any kind of specialist terminology as well as the traditional meaning of 'insider language used to

242

impress or baffle outsiders'. What these trainees objected to was not the use of the appropriate terminology in explaining computers, say, or classification, but a sort of 'status chasing' used by some supervisors in erecting a verbal professional mystique. Preferred communication styles were informal, conveyed enthusiasm rather than cynicism, and were more outgoing and active than withdrawn or passive. Above all, 'instructional skills' were seen to be necessary in supervisors, because expertise and personal enthusiasm were to no avail if they could not be passed on by supervisors due to degrees of inarticulacy or incapacity to listen and appreciate the viewpoint of the learner.

An interesting aspect of conveying content, as opposed to style, was that trainees wanted their supervisors to cover problems and difficulties, and how to deal with them, rather than give them talks on an ideal situation (how library operations are supposed to be but rarely are in practice). In many cases, trainees had to turn to their peer group for this kind of advice on coping with the realities of library systems. However, this proved to be no bad thing, since peer group learning emerged in the survey as highly significant in training staff. This is in sympathy with current educational thinking, which argues that teaching someone else to do something is also beneficial for the teacher, who has to think things through in order to explain them to others. However, the supervisor must be careful to check that peer group learning is conveying helpful attitudes, and not the opposite. It has been known for new members of staff to be socialized by their co-workers into hostile attitudes to users, and sloppy routines which go unchecked by the supervisor, who keeps a low profile in the backroom until summoned by, say, user complaints when the situation has got out of hand.

A valuable variation on peer group learning occurs when the supervisor makes a habit of consulting with juniors, to elicit their ideas, or their responses to the supervisor's ideas. As one respondent put it:

I felt happy about the training I received because of the way it was done – i.e. participation and co-operation ... the feasibility of new procedures and equipment was discussed in 'brain-storming' sessions, which gave me a lot of experience/ confidence.

This indicates that a consultative style is possible even in supervising the most junior levels, and can be much appreciated, especially when, as is increasingly the case, juniors may be either graduate trainees or para-professionals working towards S/NVQs.

A final consideration is the encouragement and professional development of the supervisor's staff. Have they been given advice on available courses (part-time and distance learning approaches are available for library assistants, as well as for professional staff) and opportunities for progress? Has the

243

library's training officer (if there is one) or have individual supervisors (if there is no overall co-ordination of staff development) collected a file of prospectuses on courses?

It is probably worth commenting that while many of the above features of good supervision may be considered to be common sense, the survey indicated that such 'common sense' is not all that common among library supervisors. The trainees' rating of their supervisors' effectiveness is shown in Table 8.1.

Table 8.1 Trainees' rating of their supervisors' effectiveness

On the whole very effective	14%
Very effective in parts	20%
Moderately effective	23%
Poor in parts	26%
On the whole quite poor	17%

There seem to be two problems in developing librarians as supervisors. The first is that many staff are not aware of what supervision involves, and this has been covered above. The second problem is that some staff seem to think that supervision is an ability one is born with, or not, rather than a set of skills which may be acquired. The rest of this chapter sets out some approaches and strategies which have been used with student librarians and practising librarians to develop interpersonal skills. Librarians making use of these approaches should contribute to improving the unsatisfactory situation revealed in Levy's and Usherwood's survey of interpersonal skills training in library and information work.[6]

COPING WITH THE DIFFICULT MEMBER OF STAFF

There are regularly recurring problems in library and information work which may be grouped under the 'difficult staff member' heading, and which cause many moments of anxiety and feelings of inadequacy among supervisors, especially inexperienced ones. Watson's interviews with managers in their early careers in a variety of occupations suggested that people talk in three broad ways about the 'people problem': 'difficult cases' (giving bad news to employees, such as disciplining them or removing them from their jobs), 'awkward sods' (dealing with difficult individuals), and 'bloody human nature' (people in general – 'If it wasn't for the staff, the job would be a doddle.').[7]

The problem which occurs most frequently for supervisors is poor or variable work performance in terms of quantity or quality, or both. This may stem from personal life interfering temporarily or in the long term with work performance, and lowering staff motivation. The symptoms include lateness, absenteeism, unreliability, rudeness towards colleagues or the users, or irrational judgements leading to erratic and unpredictable work. At some point, the supervisor has to do something about it, though many put off the hour of confrontation, hoping it will right itself. In cases of temporary aberration due to domestic problems, love life and so on, this may happen, but postponing 'a little chat' with the problem member of staff often leads to an escalation, with complaints pouring in from readers and/or other staff. It should be noted that supervisors may experience problems from higher up as well as from their own subordinates. The 'difficult member of staff' may be the boss, who is constantly 'too busy' to talk to you about work problems, or refuses to delegate professional tasks (not trusting you 'as a recently qualified librarian' may be the excuse), or who makes inconsistent and irrational judgements and expects you to carry them out.

The vital phases for the supervisor are first to recognize the symptoms before they become aggravated, then to try and assign some possible causes and think about these before taking action, to give a 'counselling interview', and to plan future monitoring of the person's progress or otherwise. The literature identifies the most common causes as follows:

1. poor match between abilities/qualifications and the job tasks or degree of responsibility
2. motivational problems (see Chapter 2 for sources of job satisfaction among library staff)
3. work group problems – acceptance or rejection by the group, peer pressure to reject innovation, or to take industrial action, for example
4. managerial style or organization climate – clash between organic and mechanistic stances of different levels of staff
5. working conditions, such as space, heating, lighting, ergonomics of VDUs or other equipment
6. medical problems, which may be divided into physical and mental health problems, the latter often stemming from stress leading to 'fight or flight' symptoms such as 'picking arguments' with colleagues or readers, or drink problems or frequent sickness leave.[8]

The mechanistic approach to counselling difficult staff takes the rational, logical view that the supervisor is only concerned with the performance of the person involved, and should not get into deep and unproductive discussions about underlying causes, unless these are work-centred. This school of thought provides useful checklists for analysing the work-related background to problems, which may indeed lead to a solution in some cases, but may ignore the often complex 'whole-person' approach of genuine counselling. Stevens, for example, provides five steps to help problem analysis:

1. **Job analysis** – Is the person's job clearly defined, necessary to the library's goals, with responsibilities clearly set out?
2. **Recruitment skills** – Is the person right for the job, having the right capabilities, experience, qualifications?
3. **Training** – Has the person enough information, guidance and on-the-job coaching to be able to do the job?
4. **Appraisal of performance** – Do supervisor and staff member discuss regularly how the job is done, the problems and successes of the staff members?
5. **Incentives** – What are the rewards of the job for the member of staff, in terms of motivation needs – security, sociability, ego needs, self-actualization and so on? Are the needs of the staff member being met?[9]

The more organic approach to problem staff members advocates training supervisors in basic counselling skills – familiar in such professions as social work and clinical psychiatry, but increasingly being drawn on to help people in occupations other than the 'caring' professions. The most useful strategies which have been used in staff counselling, irrespective of the job content, centre on an understanding of 'styles of helping', and on a framework for conducting the necessary interview with the problem member. De Board identifies styles of supervisor behaviour which range along a continuum from problem-centred (basically, ignore the personal aspects which may underlie behaviour) to client or person-centred (basically, concentrate on the person as a whole).[10] Another continuum ranges from styles which 'exclude the client' (consisting almost entirely of telling or manipulating behaviour) and which 'include the client' (bringing them in to the discussion of what is to be done, and checking their understanding of the situation and of the supervisor's reactions and advice). By knowing of these possible choices of interview behaviour, the supervisors are at least more aware of what is happening during the 'counselling chat', and may avoid the trap of imposing their own *deus ex machina* solution without involving the other member of staff in arriving at an agreed solution.

It is essential to take an 'adult' role, rather than a 'threatening parent' role, if there is to be a two-way dialogue. In person-centred counselling, following the Rogersian model,[11] the counsellor is viewed as a 'facilitator and counselling as a process of authentically being with the client rather than something one does to or for the client'.[12]

Most counsellors, whatever their orientation, accept that Rogers' three core conditions must be present if counselling is to be effective, and we have found these to be valuable in our 'counselling' of individuals. First of all, there should be *unconditional positive regard*. Individuals should be accepted for what they are, and should be looked on favourably as worthy human beings, irrespective of their behaviour and the supervisor's own beliefs. This can be very difficult in a work situation, when, for example, a supervisor is angry with members of staff, but they will more readily feel free to express their own views and feelings if they feel warmth and regard is being communicated to them through, for example, tone of voice and body language. The second core condition, *empathy*, is concerned with understanding how someone else feels and thinks by entering into their world. It is not sympathy, and it is not identifying with the supervisor's own experiences, which may only serve to diminish what the other person has to say, though it can be helpful if used carefully. *Congruence* or *genuineness* is the third core condition, and occurs when supervisors are completely open to their own feelings, and are honest and true to themselves without front, mask or façade: 'Rogers is not advocating that the therapist should blurt out feelings at all times, but simply that the therapist should be aware of them and allow the whole situation to determine whether they are uttered or not, and if so, how.'[13]

Effective counselling requires a number of skills. Most important is the habit of *active listening*. This involves attention to 'all the signals given off by a person – not only sounds but using your sight to pick up the verbal signals'.[14] Active listening is most importantly concerned with hearing what is being said between sentences and without words – listening with the 'third ear'. Communication of active listening requires responses in the form of reflection, paraphrasing and clarifying, as well as being clearly attentive. Paraphrasing is summarizing in a few words what the speaker has said. It is often best for supervisors to use their own words, to avoid parroting. Supervisors should not be afraid of silences, although it is a common human response to try to fill them to avoid awkwardness. Silences can be beneficial, as they give an opportunity for reflection.

Applying the core conditions and listening actively should allow the problem to be understood by both persons, and enable them to work towards a solution. Rogers had a very optimistic view of people, believing strongly that people themselves know inside them what is best for them, and the role of the counsellor is seen as enabling the individual to take responsibility for their own actions and solutions to problems. Thus a desirable outcome of an interview with a staff member would be for the staff member, working with the supervisor, to arrive at a solution him or herself which is acceptable to both, rather than the supervisor having to impose a solution in an authoritarian manner.

Whilst person-centred counselling outside the workplace can last a long time before progress appears to be made, practical action is usually necessary in the work situation, and no counselling interview should end without specific actions, with time limits, being agreed and understood on both sides. It is important to keep a record of the agreed action, both to monitor future progress, and also (if disciplinary procedures become necessary, ultimately leading to the dismissal of the problem staff member) to have a record showing that opportunity was given for improvement, and fair warnings of what was required, within a specified period.

The final stage is ending the interview, which requires the supervisor to summarize briefly what has been discussed and what action has been agreed. It is important to fix another interview in a month's time, or within an agreed period, so that both sides have a realistic understanding that the matter is not going to be brushed under the carpet, but must be satisfactorily resolved, with any necessary support being forthcoming.

Margerison has advocated a helpful approach which he calls 'conversation control'.[15] He accepts that in organizations, there will be times when a supervisor needs to put forward proposals, though when in doubt, a problem-centred approach should be used. The key is to recognize when to use 'problem-centred' conversation, which focuses on asking questions and trying to diagnose the nature and causes of the problem, and when to use 'solution-centred' conversation, which focuses upon proposals and directions for implementing action: 'A weakness of those who do not have conversation control skills is that they offer solutions when they should assess problems and concentrate on problems when they should be putting forward solutions.' In problem-centred conversation, we enquire, diagnose and summarize, whereas solution-centred behaviour is concerned with giving proposals, directing and informing. Once we are sure about a problem and we have tested this with the other person through summarizing and reflecting back the problem and received information that we have got it right, then we can proceed to solutions.

Margerison offers the following guidelines:

1. Be problem-centred when you are not sure of the facts or the feelings.
2. Be problem-centred when a closer identification of the problem will help with the formulation of a solution.
3. Be solution-centred when you have the facts and the feelings, and have sufficient technical competence to make a choice.
4. Be solution-centred when you feel it is time to put forward a proposal.
5. When in doubt, be problem-centred.
6. Summarize regularly before you change topic or reach a decision.

LEADERSHIP

Useful background reading to this section is given in Chapter 2 on motivation and participative management styles. It is possible, for example, to use the Blake/Mouton grid or the Likert categories to identify one's own management style in terms of concern for people proportionate to concern for output, or along the authoritarian–consultative–participative continuum. In order to help in this self-analysis, the following statements may be used as a checklist of how you tend to act in typical leadership situations, such as decision-making, discussion meetings, conflict situations and general effort put into work, and how you feel about the emotions involved. To assess your score in terms of the Blake/Mouton analysis of possible managerial styles, follow the instructions at the end of this chapter.

DECISIONS

1. I place high value on maintaining good relations.
2. I place high value on making decisions that stick.
3. I place high value on getting sound, creative decisions that result in understanding and agreement.
4. I accept the decisions of others without strong feelings about whether I agree with them or not – I don't want to get too involved.
5. I search for workable, even though not perfect, decisions.

CONVICTIONS

6. I go along with opinions, attitudes and ideas of others, or avoid taking sides.
7. I listen for and seek out ideas, opinions and attitudes different from my own. I have clear convictions, but respond to sound ideas by changing my mind.
8. I stand up for my ideas, opinions, attitudes, even though it sometimes results in stepping on others' toes.
9. I prefer to accept opinions, attitudes and ideas of others, rather than to push my own.
10. When ideas, opinions, or attitudes different from my own appear, I initiate middle-ground positions.

CONFLICT

11. When conflict arises, I try to be fair but firm, and to achieve an equitable solution.
12. When conflict arises, I try to cut it off and keep my position.
13. I try to avoid generating conflict, but when it does appear, I try to soothe feelings and to keep people together.
14. When conflict arises, I try to identify reasons for it, and to resolve underlying causes.
15. When conflict arises, I try to remain neutral or stay out of it.

EMOTION

16. When things are not going right, I defend, resist or come back with counter-arguments.
17. By remaining neutral, I rarely get stirred up.
18. Under tension, I feel unsure which way to turn or shift to avoid further pressure.
19. Because of the disturbance tensions can produce, I react in a warm and friendly way.
20. When aroused, I contain myself even though my impatience is visible.

HUMOUR

21. My humour fits the situation and gives a sense of perspective: I keep a sense of humour even under pressure.
22. My humour aims at maintaining friendly relations, or when strains do arise, it shifts attention away from the serious side.
23. My humour is seen by others as rather pointless.
24. My humour is a bit hard-hitting.
25. My humour sells myself or a position I am taking up.

EFFORT

26. I rarely lead, but extend help to my staff.
27. I exert vigorous effort, and others join in.
28. I seek to maintain a good, steady pace.
29. I exert enough effort to get by.
30. I drive myself and my staff.

To relate these leadership characteristics back to Chapter 2, it is worth re-stating the basic leadership problem: how to reach a satisfactory compromise between concern for work performance and output, and concern for people's needs at work in terms of esteem, sociability, security and using their potential. Examples of how this conflict is dealt with by individual leaders (who may be charted at representative positions on the Blake/Mouton grid) are given below.

At one extreme, the 1,1 Blake/Mouton position (see Figure 2.4), is the manager who refuses either to lead or to delegate leadership to others. The approach is often frustrated or cynical, as a result of the manager failing to influence the organization, and withdrawing from it as far as is practicable. This kind of manager manages as little as possible, keeps at a safe, impersonal distance, and avoids any face-to-face confrontations. Decisions are rarely taken unless there is some kind of crisis, and they are usually based on precedent or regulations, rather than creative thinking or management techniques, for these kinds of 'managers' are often proud of their ignorance of management.

At the other extreme, the 9,9 Blake/Mouton position, is the manager who tries to involve the entire staff in participative structures and creative approaches, and encourages everybody to undertake positive planning, self-appraisal and innovative projects. It sounds wonderful in theory, but in practice many staff are not ready for creative responsibility, and feel unhappy and exposed, so the results may be disappointing in both performance and job satisfaction. However, when the right people are in post, or on a work team, the results can be inspired, with high output and infectious enthusiasm. There is harmonious integration of tasks and human needs.

The 1,9 managerial style of high concern for people and low concern for output means that a lot of effort goes into keeping up staff morale, and giving staff the delegated authority. Direction from the manager is not strong, and this can be a problem when staff look for initiatives from their boss, and are told the boss will support whatever initiatives they feel like putting forward. Another weakness of this style may be that because the manager likes to be seen as counsellor/confidant, it is difficult to confront staff with their inadequacies, mistakes or failures, therefore performance tends to take second place to a cosy togetherness.

The 9,1 managerial style, on the contrary, is based on the view that staff only perform well when they are given strong direction, clear instructions, and firm guidance and appraisal from above. Power and decision-making is retained by the manager, and speedy compliance and accountability, rather than creativity or planning their own work, is expected of staff. Performance standards may be reasonably good, but this style of management puts staff on the defensive, and tends to reward compliance rather than positive or innovatory thinking. There is a heavy atmosphere of control, which may provide security for the average worker, but may stifle the above-average.

The Blake/Mouton grid may be used to train staff to identify their present managerial style, and its implications for their subordinates and for the library as a whole. This self-awareness may then lead to the identification of preferable managerial styles, towards which staff may move gradually. There is the possibility that they may be given greater incentive to modify their style, if, as in some organizations, appraisal by more junior staff takes place, and managers are made aware of how they are seen by their staff.

There is a strong element of leadership in supervision of staff, but the general view is that supervisors tend to be internally focused, whereas leaders are seen as externally focused and boundary-scanning, watching the future and trying to create a vision. Good supervision will ensure that a task is completed efficiently and effectively, whilst leadership provides the vision that led to the task in the first place.

The Public Library Workforce Study highlighted the urgent need for leadership when less than a third of their respondents were confident that they had suitable staff to succeed to senior posts and when the challenges of, for example, Annual Library Plans, Government standards, and Best Value Reviews have to be faced.[16] As the environment becomes more turbulent and unpredictable, the need for new and different models of leadership has been recognized. The contrast between traditional or transactional models of leadership and the now often prescribed model of transformational leadership is frequently highlighted.

Transactional leadership has been described as a favour-for-favour type of exchange – a 'tit-for-tat relationship of jobs for votes, subsidies for campaign contributions or raises for more production'.[17] The contrast can clearly be seen in the six-factor leadership model developed by Bass, which was originally based on results obtained by surveying US Army field-grade officers who were asked to rate their superior officers.[18] The most passive factor was seen as *laissez-faire* leadership, similar to Blake's and Mouton's 1,1 position. Officers employing this style tend to react only after problems have become serious enough to take corrective action, and often avoid making any decision at all. The two transactional factors were *active management-by-exception*, which focused on monitoring task execution for any problems that may arise and correcting to maintain performance levels; and *contingent reward*, which clarified what was expected of followers and what they will receive if they meet expected levels of performance. Transactional factors are viewed as insufficient in 'building the trust and developing the motivation to achieve the full potential of one's workforce. Yet, coupled with individualized consideration, they may potentially provide the base for higher levels of transformational leadership to have positive impact on motivation and performance.'[19]

The three transformational factors in the Bass model were *charismatic-inspirational leadership*, which provides followers with a clear sense of purpose and identification with the leader's vision; *individualized consideration* focused on understanding the needs of each follower and developing their full potential, and *intellectual stimulation*, which gets followers to question tried methods of solving problems, and encourages questioning current methods.

Kouzes and Posner studied over 1500 managers to discover the positive practices in which their leaders engaged.[20] Their findings have been widely publicized, and provide valuable guidelines for those wishing to practise transformational leadership.

Most of us tend to admire leaders who have credibility, those who are:

- honest
- competent
- forward-looking
- inspiring.

These credible leaders tend to be committed to consistently implementing ten leadership practices:

1. Search out challenging opportunities to change, grow, innovate, and improve.
2. Experiment, take risks, and learn from the accompanying mistakes.
3. Envision an uplifting and ennobling future.
4. Enlist others in a common vision by appealing to their values, interests, hopes and dreams.
5. Foster collaboration by promoting co-operative goals and building trust.
6. Strengthen people by sharing information and power and increasing their discretion and visibility.
7. Set the example for others by behaving in ways that are consistent with your stated values.
8. Plan small wins that promote consistent progress and build commitment.
9. Recognize individual contributions to the success of every project.
10. Celebrate team accomplishments regularly.[21]

Frank, in reviewing a book on leadership, has summarized neatly the modern view of leadership:

> The new leadership model states that vision and mission are more important than the activities associated with planning and allocation of responsibilities. Controlling people and solving problems are significantly less important than motivating and inspiring people. The de-emphasis on control is dramatic. Change and innova-

tion are valued over routine and equilibrium. Power is retained and valued in earlier models of leadership. New leaders do not emphasise power, and assist others to become empowered. The new leadership creates commitment (as opposed to creating compliance).[22]

LIBRARIANS AND LEADERSHIP

In an interesting article on librarians' and psychologists' view of leadership, Quinn states that 'in comparison to more traditional evaluation methods like the use of assessment centers, the use of subordinates' ratings can actually be more accurate in predicting the future performance of administrators'.[23] This makes Hall's study all the more illuminating.[24] He asked librarians on a Post Experience MA course over a period of six years to think of good leaders they had known at work, and to write down the qualities they possessed. His list bears some resemblance to that of Kouzes and Posner, but gives greater emphasis to the way staff are treated, and is understandably more public service-orientated:

> Good Leaders are intelligent, self confident, enthusiastic and consistent in their behaviour. They work hard, have high professional competence, can command professional respect, are visible and lead by example.
> They know what is happening in their organisation and in their own department. They have initiative and foresight, are decisive, don't let situations drift, are good at planning, have good organisational skills and are calm in crises.
> They treat all staff with respect, are fair, approachable, have a good sense of humour, are open and straightforward, keep staff informed, explain decisions and admit mistakes. They delegate, trust staff, consult staff and are open to others' ideas and views.
> They are considerate, sympathetic, understanding of individuals' problems, concerned with the welfare of staff, tactful, sensitive to feelings of others and are people you can confide in. They take an interest in the work of staff, praise good work, are supportive, give helpful advice, criticise in a constructive way, foster initiative and encourage staff development and advancement.
> Finally they work for the good of the team, fight for the team, get resources for the team, are loyal to subordinates and defend individual staff.

Hall's findings confirm our own view that it is not simply the 'vision thing' that matters. In itself, it is 'not sufficient to be an effective leader. Attention to detail and follow-through – the elements of execution – are also very important.'[25] A library leader with vision alone can easily become isolated and a de-motivating influence to those at the 'grass roots'.

It is no longer possible, or desirable, for leaders to be able to perform or even understand the details of their own staff's jobs: 'the Age of Information has made the Big Boss into a dinosaur. Nobody can possibly know enough to run the whole show.'[26] Twenty years ago, many chief librarians were able to perform most, if not all, of the jobs performed by their staff. This is now rarely possible, and some older librarians have found it difficult to accept this change. Leadership is also episodic, in that different leaders will be needed in different situations: 'leading from the front has been the hallmark of twentieth century leadership. Empowering from behind will be the hallmark of the twenty-first century.'[27]

CONFLICT

Analysis of leadership style using the Blake/Mouton grid includes the management of conflict. Dr Helen Dyson has identified five main ways of responding to conflict, and this analysis has been used to help staff to understand their own responses and to think about how appropriate they are.[28] The categories of response can be shown on a grid similar to that of Blake/Mouton. Stated briefly:

- **Competition** is the response you make when you think you are right, when giving way means loss of face. It assumes that conflict is inevitable.
- **Collaboration** is the response you use to eliminate negative feelings, and requires good interpersonal skills. It assumes that conflict is resolvable.
- **Compromise** is an expedient or mutually acceptable solution that partially satisfies both parties but does not really solve the problem. It assumes that each can only gain at the other's expense.
- **Avoidance** assumes that conflict is avoidable, but in fact achieves the least of all responses.
- **Accommodation** means that you satisfy the other's needs and neglect your own.

We have used these categories successfully in training sessions. Participants are asked to analyse a case study, and to discuss why particular responses were chosen and whether they were appropriate. An important factor in conflict is the norms which exist in an organization: which are the most accepted or socially desirable strategies, and what the pressures are upon a person to take one approach rather than another.

LEADERSHIP DEVELOPMENT

Because leadership is so important, a lot of attention is being paid to the development of leaders. In Chapter 2, the practice of identifying staff who have the potential to become the senior managers of the future in the organization was noted. Once identified, it is logical to provide leadership training. Large organizations, as Reynolds observes,[29] mainly take a competency-based approach, in which they identify skills and practices relevant to their own situations and corporate strategies, and develop those competences in future leaders. Best-practice organizations, as identified in an investigation of 35 organizations in the USA, 'develop leaders internally because of powerful and distinct cultures, which are critical to continued success'.[30] Action learning is seen to be the most appropriate method, with the participants solving real-time business issues, and the leadership development programmes are continually assessed to ensure they are having the desired effect.

The executive performance and development scheme at HSBC bank is an example of good practice. The scheme begins in January with the manager's annual review, with two Executive Development Forums (EDFs) following in April and October. These examine leadership skills and management potential. The EDF acts as a succession-planning mechanism to fill key positions, matching the right people to the right job, and avoiding unnecessary external recruitment.[31] Employees are able to assess the scheme at the annual roadshow, backed up with feedback from an annual opinion survey.

Alongside internal succession planning, there exists the realization that in today's climate, employees cannot be insulated. People will change not only employers, but careers several times during their working life. A change of emphasis towards 'succession management' rather than 'succession planning' has therefore been advocated, with company people being blended with outsiders 'unencumbered by corporate history', and the balance coming from internally developed executives, who provide continuity for the organization and corporate memory.[32]

MENTORING

With its emphasis on empowerment and the development of potential, new models of leadership naturally stress the importance of training, and the special form of support for individuals known as 'mentoring': 'The term is derived from Greek mythology. Before setting out on an epic voyage Ulysses asks his friend Mentor to look after his son Telemachus. Mentor was not only to keep a paternal eye on Telemachus, but also to groom him for his eventual position as head of state. Mentor was acting as a role model and counsellor to Telemachus.'[33] At the heart of mentoring is professional and personal development through a 'one-to-one relationship between the mentor and the mentored ... the relationship may be formal and part of an organisation's planned approach to career development. More often informal mentoring relationships simply develop where mutual interest prompts people to work together'.[34]

Nankivell and Shoolbred have carried out research on mentoring in library and information work,[35] and produced valuable guidelines available online.[36] They identified six types of mentoring commonly found:

1. mentoring for management skills – to help me as a manager
2. mentoring for support and development – to help me cope and develop within my current post
3. mentoring for career development – to help me move on
4. mentoring for specific skills – to coach me
5. mentoring for new recruits – to help me get to know the organization
6. mentoring for professional contacts – to help me network and reduce my professional isolation.

This list could easily represent a library's training and development objectives, which will benefit both the individual and the organization. In the case of mentoring, it is hoped the objectives will be achieved through a process between two individuals.

In formal schemes, a mentor may be found for the mentee, and the whole scheme co-ordinated, perhaps by a Human Resources Officer. Although the mentee's line manager has an important development role to play, it is normal for the mentor to be someone else in the organization – even someone in another department, which is the case at Staffordshire University, where the scheme for female staff does not permit mentoring by someone in the same school or service.[37] Apart from the problems which can arise if the manager and managed do not get on well together, there is the need to respect confidences, and for the mentor and mentee to feel free to discuss their feelings openly. There are also people who require mentors, but they cannot be found within their own organizations. In this case, PTEG (the Personnel, Training and Education Group of the Library Association) can help. A particular need is for mentor support of newly qualified librarians seeking chartership and requiring help with their professional development reports.

For a mentoring relationship to be successful, 'the rapport between mentor and learner is crucial ... The pairing of mentor and learner in a formal scheme is a bit like matching individuals through a dating agency ... In an informal relationship there is no forced relationship. It either grows or dies.'[38] All parties involved have to be prepared to devote time to the process, both in the initial planning and setting up and in the time set aside for the mentor and mentee to meet on a regular basis. In many schemes there is recognition that training of both mentors and mentees is necessary. At Staffordshire University, a one-day training session is held for mentors who may volunteer or be suggested by others.[39] PTEG has set up a Supervisors' Liaison Network to provide support and advice to supervisors of Library Association Registration candidates,[40] and training sessions are regularly held at Library Association Headquarters.

INTERPERSONAL SKILLS

Excellent interpersonal skills are essential when supervising staff, and as we have seen, being able to communicate, listen and motivate is crucial to successful management. These skills are equally important in developing good working relationships with colleagues and senior staff. Further, the move towards more staff working in direct contact with the users of the library service means that everyone, whether they manage others or not, needs to develop good interpersonal skills.

Two trends have brought the need for staff to acquire these skills to the fore. First, the emphasis in libraries on customer care has led many organizations to reassess the ways in which services are delivered, and customer care training is now, rightly, commonplace within the library and information service sector. Second, staff at all levels are likely to find that they need to be able to support readers in the use of IT. There is general agreement that sound technical knowledge alone is insufficient – staff also need the skills to communicate effectively with readers. For example, in the higher education sector, Morgan expressed two wishes for the new millennium. The first is that more library staff should become actively involved in managing, and the second is that the right balance is achieved between IT-related skills and 'softer' interpersonal skills:

> The traditional 'people skills' – the touchy/feely stuff – will still be needed more than ever as individuals become locked into their PCs and lose contact with the real world. Concerns have been raised about people becoming rusty at communicating face to face with their fellow human beings. Are messages conveyed by body language, facial expressions and the subtleties of vocal cadence going to be lost forever in the electronic mail-strom! We will still have the need to persuade, influence, motivate, train, mentor, counsel and to generally add value to the student learning experience – and perhaps even explain the reasons for the technology breaking down, as it surely will at some points.[41]

The group of skills which are essential to fostering productive relationships are inter-related and often inter-dependent: for example, successfully diffusing a situation in which a reader may become agitated requires good communication skills and an ability to be assertive. These skills are also necessary when managing your own workload, as they enable you to express your achievements and ensure that you can resist being overwhelmed with tasks you cannot complete. Those skills which help you interact effectively with colleagues also stand you in good stead when dealing with users. Four key areas can be identified, and interpersonal skills training should seek to develop and hone these:

1. **communication** – both verbal and non-verbal
2. **self-management/self awareness** – for example, reaching an understanding of your own personality and how you interact with others
3. **team/group working** – both within formal teams that exist as part of the staff structure, and within groups which are formed to address particular issues
4. **assertiveness** – an essential skill when dealing with staff whom you manage, your boss, colleagues, and those who use your service.

GROUP WORK

Attending meetings is an inescapable fact of life in library work. Most staff are members of a team or work group which may have regular meetings to review progress, solve problems and plan ahead. In addition, staff may be nominated to, or volunteer for, membership of temporary working parties on specific problems or innovations. There may also be informal groups in libraries which organize mainly social events. Staff associations may also produce internal bulletins or news sheets – part entertainment, part useful communication. As well as the internal groupings and teams which generate meetings, librarians increasingly find themselves playing a more significant role in their communities, in order to remain in touch with user needs and to have their say in their parent organization when funding and future developments are in question. Public library staff may attend meetings with other agencies, such as Citizens' Advice Bureaux, or Women's Royal Voluntary Service workers, or the numerous other voluntary and statutory agencies which support the variously disenfranchised in their area. Similarly, in academic libraries staff are expected to attend course boards and faculty meetings to ensure that the library's contribution to teaching, learning and research is visible and relevant to changing needs of the academic community.

The significance of these developments is that staff may expect to attend meetings on a regular basis, and that many may need training in how to get the best out of meetings. This is important in view of the number of hours staff spend in meetings, and the inevitable question that arises: is there a sufficient return for all this time, or have the meetings proved to be a waste of time, due to unclear aims, poor selection of members, and inadequate briefing, preparation and group process skills? Morris observes:

> Meetings, like interruptions, are regarded as a major time waster by most managers, and ... meetings can become very expensive indeed.
> However, meetings are essential to communication within the workplace, they create a sense of belonging and commitment, and enable us to involve staff in decisions which affect them.[42]

Some people's initial reaction to group work training is that it is all a matter of personality, therefore it is impossible to change people's behaviour in work groups. Research findings show that personality is indeed a significant variable, but that workers can learn to improve their performance in groups and meetings, thus making a more effective contribution to team work in their organizations. The influences of personality are observed in people's predispositions towards certain personality styles.

There are various different classifications of personality. One helpful inventory identifies four main categories of personality style: the *Enthusiastic*, which displays a blend of feelings and action; the *Imaginative*, which shows feelings plus intuition; the *Practical*, which prefers a combination of doing and thinking, and the *Logical*, which is marked by intuiting and thinking.[43] The Enthusiastic personality, it is suggested, enjoys new situations, likes change and risk, can be impulsive, and is generally open to others' opinions and feelings, as well as having 'gut reactions'. The Imaginative personality, on the other hand, is more hesitant, working in fits and starts as inspiration strikes. Such people avoid conflict, like to share ideas but only with a few others, and are open to alternatives. The Practical personality likes to use reason and be in control of a situation, by using data, evidence, theories to solve problems and test out theories. The Logical personality takes a basically theoretical position, preferring conceptual models to pragmatic models, and is suspicious of the gut reaction and the emotional overtone, preferring analysis and cool planning based on written papers or notes.

It can be inferred that the Practical and the Logical personalities may clash with the Enthusiastic and Imaginative personalities, since they attach far less importance to analysis and reason and theoretical models, and far less importance to people networks, intuition and creativity when considering problems and trying to reach solutions. However, a more positive way of looking at the influence of personality is to accept that any work group may benefit from a mixture of personality styles which, taken together, are able to display a range of behaviours, from abstract thought to reflective observation, and from active experimentation to concrete experience. Psychologists are anxious to point out that there is no best or worst style, but that it is helpful to be aware of one's own style in order to become conscious of its advantages and disadvantages in specific situations. It may then be possible to experiment with modifying one's style to fit better with particular circumstances at work, where it has been shown to be something of a hindrance.

Having accepted that personality styles are one element in group behaviour, the next stage is to consider the kinds of behaviour which help or hinder group effectiveness. There are a number of behaviour classifications, including those of Belbin[44] and Bales. The Bales 'interaction analysis' has been widely used in group training in organizations, both in industry and the public service sector. It is the classification we have found most useful. Rackham and Morgan[45] give a detailed analysis of the approach, but Table 8.2 shows the basic outline of behaviours, and how profiles of behaviour for individuals in a group meeting may be drawn up. Each column (A, B, C and so on) is filled in for one group member. While observing a meeting, the number of their contributions in each behaviour category is recorded with a tick. At the end of the meeting, a behaviour profile is compiled in the form of a histogram, which has a column for each group member, displaying the percentage of different kinds of behaviour which made up their overall contribution. An example is given in Figure 8.1. The assumption is that people thus become more aware of their own behaviour, and may modify it accordingly, for the sake of more effective and positive outcomes in team work, and in meetings in particular.

There are a number of important limitations to this training approach, which have become evident to the authors after using it in extensive training sessions with practising librarians. These include the following:

1. The quality of the contributions is not indicated.
2. The observations are not necessarily linked to the objectives of the meeting, and it may not be clear whether these objectives have been understood or finally achieved.
3. Some of the categories of behaviour are not clearly divisible. This makes recording kinds of behaviour difficult, as one may shade into another.
4. The kinds of behaviour displayed may be partly determined by the nature of the group task, and partly by the context of a meeting (friendliness, cohesiveness of real-life work groups, presence or absence of high-status people and so on).
5. Observers need to be trained in how to record behaviour, otherwise they may be inconsistent in what they record. Some inexperienced observers record non-verbals (a support nod, or threatening scowl, for example), others do not. Some record lengthy contributions with only one or two ticks, others use a tick for every sentence or short paragraph spoken by an individual. This may lead to confusing results which are not recognizable to the participants as genuine profiles of their respective behaviours.

Table 8.2 Group interaction record (derived from Rackham and Morgan)

Behaviour Category	A	B	C	D	E
Proposing					
Building					
Disagreeing					
Bringing in					
Supporting					
Open					
Testing understanding					
Summarizing					
Seeking information					
Giving information					
Defending/ attacking					
Blocking					
Shutting out					

When the recording is done reasonably consistently, groups are normally able to identify the resulting histogram as a fairly accurate record of their meeting, given the limitations listed above.

To develop group skills from growing awareness of one's own group behaviour patterns, it is necessary to persuade group members to carry out interaction analysis over a series of meetings, and to use the results to make conscious

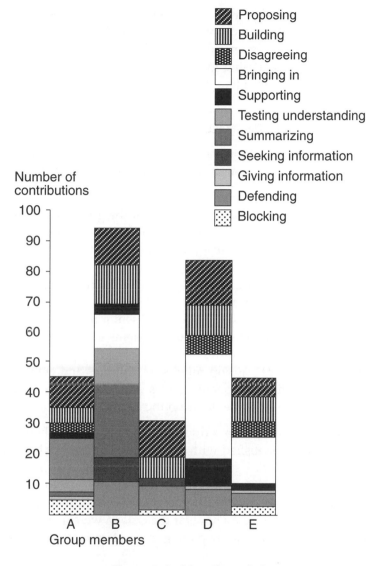

Figure 8.1 Interaction analysis

decisions about what kinds of behaviour would benefit the group. What could be tried out by members? More building, more constructive criticism? Less blocking, less difficulty stating? A willed attempt to provide more supportive behaviour, or to bring low contributors into the discussion?

The cumulative effects over a period of time can be considerable. The problem is that the strategy usually only works when a whole group is prepared to give it a try, preferably a group which meets regularly and is motivated to have more effective meetings. It is not so effective if only one or two group members learn the strategy and try to do something without involving the others significantly. However, in a fairly small group, the influence of one or two members who are practising group skills and who are trained to 'read' group behaviour may be considerable.

STRUCTURE AND DYNAMICS OF SMALL GROUPS

The components of group activity fall into three main spheres, which interact to provide the overall climate and degree of effectiveness of the group as a whole:

1. **The task and technology component** – what the group is supposed to be thinking and doing. Is there a clear set of objectives, agreed by group members, as to the problem to be discussed and the decisions or other outcomes to be arrived at?
2. **The group working arrangements** – formality or informality; voting on disagreements or arriving at a consensus through discussion; decision-making or merely consultative; chaired by a senior member of staff or peer group member; arrangements for putting items on the agenda, minute-taking, and circulation of minutes.
3. **The 'affective' element** – group members' attitudes and emotions, stemming partly from their personality styles and partly from their feelings about, or vested interest in the items on the agenda.

Criteria for more effective group work are listed below. Members of groups who feel frustrated or dissatisfied with their particular group's behaviours or outputs may use the criteria as a checklist for analysing what is wrong, and trying to improve matters. The group as a whole can learn to become more effective by having a short post-meeting analysis (with or without the help of a designated observer), to discuss how far the criteria were met, and how they may improve their next meeting by paying more attention to criteria not met this time round.

Here are some criteria for effective group meetings:

- The members agree on shared goals, have clear objectives, know what is expected to emerge from the meeting (recommendations or decisions, information-giving, agreed standards for some activity taking place on more than one site, such as stock editing or managing audio-visual materials).
- The members work at creating a climate of support and trust, so that there are no barriers to expression of ideas, and members are positively encouraged to contribute. The group develops and supports members.

264

- Communication is kept as open as possible, which involves members being prepared to disclose what they really think and feel, and to pay genuine attention to what others think and feel, during the meeting, rather than in the form of cliquey gossip before and after the meeting. Difficulties are brought into the open.
- Efficient procedures are adhered to for chairing, minutes, agenda.
- The members are appropriately qualified and prepared to contribute to the theme of the meeting. They have relevant expertise.
- There is evident leadership (whether formal, from the chair, or informal, from within the members), and thus a sense of direction.
- The group has positive ways of handling conflict, which often means encouraging constructive criticism, not making easy choices, modifying original ideas by incorporating other people's contributions; it also means moving the meeting on from negative conflict like personality clashes and *idées fixes* through the chair with the help of members.
- The group reviews its achievements, assessing progress at regular intervals through the meeting, rather than rambling inconsequentially. Time management is used to get through the tasks efficiently.
- The group pays attention to the three essential components of group activity: taking account of the nature of the task, the group's structure and formal working arrangements, and the personality, styles and attitudes of group members.
- The group recognizes its position in relation to other groups, and exercises positive influence on other groups rather than adopting defensive postures (building a bunker within the organization).
- The group is cohesive – that is, members use the word 'we', and develop some sense of belonging, achievement or even power, beyond what they experience as individual members of staff. Cohesive groups are most effective, and can be rich learning experiences, provided that they are not deflected to the ideological ends of the members rather than the agreed aims and objectives of the library.
- The group is rewarding to its members, both in terms of affiliative needs and task performance needs.

The problems which may arise in groups and prevent fulfilment of the above criteria are observable within any workplace meetings. Groups may be unclear about objectives, or confused about the exact purpose of a meeting. Different levels of staff may have conflicting objectives, whether overt or covert. The meeting may be seen as futile because it is not given enough power to be taken seriously in the decision-making hierarchy. There may be poor role differentiation, for example a lack of people with expert knowledge, leadership skills, or critical acumen, leading to poor-quality discussion and inconclusive 'conclusions'. Inter-group and intra-group conflict may restrict the meeting's effectiveness. Finally, there are tasks for which groups are inappropriate, and which are better done by an individual. These include taking operational, routine decisions, and implementing decisions. Creative ideas more often come from individuals than from groups, though groups may stimulate creativity and are useful in building and criticizing ideas. 'Brainstorming' is a well-known technique for stimulating creativity. It involves going round everyone in the group and asking them to list all the possible ideas or solutions to a problem that they can think of, irrespective of how practical or feasible they apparently are. When a comprehensive list has been assembled from everybody's spontaneous suggestions – and *only* then – criticism is applied to eliminate the wilder ideas, and to build up the possible.

Finally, it is important to note that groups need to go through certain stages before they become fully operational, or fully effective. Tuckman's theory of developmental stages identifies the necessary stages of Forming, Storming, Norming and Performing.[46]

During the *Forming* phase, group members suffer anxiety, are dependent on the leader (who may be equally anxious), and try to work out what is acceptable in the situation in which they find themselves. This involves mulling over the nature of the task, trying to agree on what they have to do, but also trying to infer acceptable approaches and methods of tackling the task which will fit in with everybody else's approaches.

The *Storming* stage is a rather turbulent one, where people begin to recognize that there are subgroups which may cause conflict and get in the way of agreement and swift solutions. There may be polarization of opinions, or even rebellion against the leader, all of which leads to resistance (often emotional) to getting on with the task.

The third stage, *Norming*, is essential before there can be concentration on the task. It involves developing some group cohesion, a sense of being a group and the need for mutual support. This enables group members to be more open about their views, and to see in practical terms how they can co-operate to produce a solution to the task. Acceptable modes of behaviour and ways of dealing with disagreement and conflict have been worked out.

In the final *Performing* stage, group members use these evolved behavioural norms to solve intra-group conflicts and work on solutions to the task. They are now able to get on with task-completion, since they have worked out ways of coping with interpersonal problems, and have also become clearer about possible methods of getting a solution to the task side of group work. They have found ways of coping with both the 'process' and the 'product'. Should new members enter the group at this stage, they will have certain problems adapting and learning the often unstated norms and nuances of vocabulary and styles and preferred strategies for solving problems. At first, they may try to satisfy their own perceived needs in joining the group, but there is nearly always a period of working out group norms, conforming to accepted patterns of behaviour, before the new member can become an effective and accepted contributor.

In practical, down-to-earth terms, meetings can only succeed when the following criteria are successfully met:

1. The meeting should have a clear purpose which is accepted by its members and by those to whom it reports. Has it the power to make decisions, or simply to give recommendations or advice? How representative is it of various staff levels and interests? In what ways can it authorize action to ensure that its deliberations are implemented?
2. The members should be selected carefully to include the necessary expertise and specialist knowledge of the topics the group will discuss. It should be noted that vertical meetings (members drawn from different levels of staff) will be less informal and possibly more inhibited than horizontal meetings (members drawn from the same level). On the other hand, it may contribute more to staff development if members need to learn to be open and express their genuine views (and the views of others whom they represent) in dialogue with more senior staff.
3. Members must be sufficiently informed in advance through explanatory agendas, with discussion papers attached, and encouraged to prepare adequately. Decisions made with inadequate information and ill-informed discussion are generally poor in quality. It is therefore necessary for the convener to ensure that time is given for, and members are informed of and invited to contribute, preparatory papers or lists of discussion points.

Meetings are expensive in terms of time and money, so it is important to keep the agenda to a realistic size which it is possible to cover in the time available. This is, of course, affected by the ability of the members to come informed and prepared, and not waste time trying to find out about matters during the meeting itself. The chairperson can help to complete the agenda effectively by starting with a clear statement of what is to be achieved, and noting background papers relevant to particular topics. At regular intervals, he or she may need to review progress and return wanderers to the point, as well as ensuring that points are understood. When agreement is reached on any issue, it is important to clarify what action will result, and to name an individual or group to undertake it. It is necessary for the chairperson to keep an accurate record of the outcomes, and to check these with the secretary or recorder before minutes of the meeting are finalized and circulated. Also, at the end of a meeting the chairperson should take any follow-up action promptly, by informing those concerned of what they are to do, or by negotiating or asking for advice or further information from people not at the meeting.

The job of the chairperson is made difficult in a variety of ways. The most common is perhaps that meetings can be seen by quite a high proportion of members as a waste of time, or as unrepresentative of staff views, because the same few people always seem to get their way, usually by monopolizing the discussion. Other problems are that important matters may be ignored, decisions taken may be unclear or inconsistent with previous decisions (in this or a related meeting), and it may not be clear who is responsible for acting on the decisions. The chairperson must be prepared to intervene to ensure that more tongue-tied members are heard, that compromises are negotiated when there is disagreement, and that the right questions are asked before hasty decisions are reached. The problem of reaching a consensus in the absence of formal voting – which is often seen as desirable – is another area where the chairperson needs a strategy. He or she must ensure that all opinions are heard, irrespective of their own partiality in favour of a particular solution. Through a series of supportive questions, the chair should achieve a balanced discussion between different views, even when the proponents of these may be rather inarticulate at putting their own case. It is too easy to write off 'light-weight' members and earn their hostility to any decisions taken. It is better to try to encourage others to build on what they say, to ensure that everyone is brought in and not ignored. Outbreaks of open hostility between members are another problem, which may be handled best by diversionary tactics before the meeting turns into a gladiatorial arena rather than a decision-making body engaged in rational discourse. The most commonly needed skill is probably the ability to restrain the over-talkative and draw in the embarrassed and shy, without antagonizing either type. To sum up, an effective meeting will result when the following conditions apply:

● a clear aim
● good organization
● maximum participation
● understandable communication
● generally accepted standards of behaviour
● good morale and mutual regard.[47]

ASSERTIVENESS TRAINING

Assertiveness training will be of benefit to library staff at all levels, who may have difficulty in negotiating with colleagues or users as a result of habits of either aggressiveness or non-assertion. Levy's and Usherwood's survey revealed strong support from library respondents on the desirability of assertiveness training as a basic foundation for academic and public librarians alike.[48]

Assertiveness means being honest and open with yourself and other people about what you think and feel and want to do, in any particular situation. Assertiveness implies self-confidence, being positive rather than negative, and being able to understand other people's point of view, so as to reach working compromises by negotiation. Non-assertiveness, on the other hand, implies failure to express your true thoughts and feelings. You tend to conceal your real reactions to other people's views, and your real needs at work are not made known. Responses to any situation tend to be passive rather than active, negative rather than positive. Another form of non-assertiveness is a hesitant or apologetic communication style, which has the unfortunate effect of causing little attention to be paid to views which may be quite sound and positive, though delivered in a negative manner. Aggressiveness, on the other hand, means expressing your own views, but at the expense of other people. You have no problem standing up for your own opinions and rights, but you are not prepared to give others the same rights you take for yourself.

The implications of these modes of communication in the workplace are considerable. Non-assertive persons are likely to be ignored, rather than getting the attention they hope for by not disagreeing and avoiding any kind of open conflict or argument. They are also likely to suffer a sense of frustration or futility as a result of failing to assert their own needs and real views. In avoiding conflict, such staff may then find themselves victims of other people's imposed views, plans and decisions, because they did not make their disagreement known or put forward alternatives. This can lead to unclear decisions, reluctantly done tasks, and simmering grievances never brought out into the open. The situation tends to be cumulative. Non-assertive people may be taken advantage of, taking on more work because they cannot say 'no'. They tend to be consulted less and less, because they never come out and say what they really think, or because their communications are mainly negative. They do not reveal any views or ideas of their own, and they do not disagree with other people's views. Eventually, nobody bothers to ask for their views.

Aggressive behaviour at work may be satisfying at the time, since it releases tension for the aggressor, gets the adrenalin flowing and gives a sense of 'I'm winning this game, anyway' or 'Now I've got the bastard.' However, clearly it is inappropriate for staff to display such behaviour in the workplace, and there will, of course, be consequences to such outbursts. The aggressor is likely to feel a certain amount of guilt afterwards, which puts them in a defensive posture, inappropriate for constructive decisions or solutions to a problem. This leaves the person at least temporarily isolated, so that the problem, unresolved, requires more time and effort when tempers have cooled. The effect on colleagues of aggressiveness can be either that they feel forced to retaliate in kind and there is a general increase in aggressiveness, or that they opt for non-assertion and leave more and more decisions to the aggressive boss. Many aggressive supervisors believe that this is the only way they can get results from their staff. In fact, in the long term they are likely to end up with a 'time-serving' staff leaving it all to the boss (since that's what he or she seems to want), or in the worst cases, with staff who channel a good deal of energy into chronic (if small-scale) conflicts, following the model of the aggressive boss. Difficult decisions may be delayed or avoided. Fewer initiatives may be taken, and implementing decisions may run into serious problems with a resentful staff.

Assertiveness training centres on a basic 'Bill of Rights', which covers the following principles:

- People have the right to have their views and opinions listened to, and be taken seriously.
- They have the right to say no, and have their reasons taken seriously.
- They have the right to criticize and be criticized, without manipulating or being manipulated.
- They have the right to ask for information and clarification.
- They have the right to receive the work/service/goods they were promised when they took up a job or purchased goods or services.

The most appropriate training for assertiveness is role-play, which can be used to give people practice in assertiveness strategies, as outlined below:

1. Decide what your true views are in any situation, before you go to a meeting or to a colleague's office to discuss a problem or project.
2. Make a few brief notes in advance which summarize your position and what you would like the outcome of the meeting to be. Decide on alternatives, or how far you can modify your position without giving up the most important points.
3. Listen properly to other people's points, and acknowledge their arguments, by such devices as reviewing what they have said or asking, 'Is this what you mean?', or linking their arguments to your own.
4. Make your own views known directly and honestly, even if others are adopting indirect or devious approaches. Show that you know they are being devious, preferably by a humorous acknowledgement of what they are up to. Repeat your views as often as is necessary to ensure a hearing.
5. If eventually your argument or solution is not accepted, try at least to

negotiate a modification of the winning argument so that it incorporates some of your views. This is the assertive way of losing, and is preferable to the aggressive (stalking out of a meeting, or attacking the other solution as viciously as possible) or the non-assertive mode (subsiding into passivity and the 'Poor me, I always lose' game).

Assertiveness training pays considerable attention to handling conflict and criticism. It is useful to check one's own typical behaviour against the following criteria.

Non-assertive ways of handling conflict include giving in to the other on most occasions, because of deference to the other's status or simply out of a long-term habit of trying to please in order to be liked. It is argued that women are more prone to this traditional kind of behaviour than men. Another approach is to give in to the other, to all appearances, but when their back is turned to gossip and express the opposite feelings and views to co-workers. A third possibility is that both parties to the argument behave in an insincere, accommodating way because they are both being non-assertive. The result is likely to be unhelpful vacillation rather than clear decisions, or if decisions are taken, they are unlikely to last long, because neither side supports them fully.

Assertive ways of handling conflict include stating your requirements openly and asking the other person to do the same early on in the negotiation. Assertiveness involves taking responsibility for your own position and actions, rather than trying to edge it off on to 'the organization' or 'this library section' (unless you are genuinely representing other staff, with their agreement). It is necessary to check that you have understood the view of the other by repeating their statements in your own words: 'Is this what you are saying …?' When you fully understand the other's view, you are then in a better position to find areas of agreement, however small. This is more realistic and positive than going all-out for a global solution (either yours or the other person's). When trying to reach an agreed outcome, it is more creative to spend time brainstorming a number of possible solutions than to cling obsessively to one's initial standpoint. It is even better if the other can also be encouraged to produce alternative strategies. The most helpful and productive negotiations are those in which both parties see the necessity of moving towards each other from their initial positions, but are clear on what they cannot give up because it is central to their thinking. By the end of a negotiation, both sides must be clear what has been agreed, and each should state their view of the outcome and say what action they have undertaken to carry out, within a time limit.

Assertive ways of handling criticism begin with an honest assessment, as far as is humanly possible, of how far the criticism is justified, and how far it is derived from your boss's emotional need to put someone down from time to time as a means of showing authority. If the criticism is entirely or mainly unjustified, concentrate on that as a main response. Give precise details of when you did complete the project, or send off the reply to an enquirer, or deliver your estimates. The point here is to establish the facts, rather than becoming embroiled in an emotional flurry on the boss's side, and resentment on yours. Practise saying, in the nicest possible way, 'No, it isn't like that ... it's like this ...' without being either aggressive or non-assertive in style, tone or non-verbals. If the boss is not listening the first time, go through it again until you have clarified your side of the story.

If, on the other hand, the criticism is only too true, or has an element of truth, acknowledge this rather than engaging in devious and evasive behaviour. The non-assertive response is to stay sullen and silent, or to make empty excuses or sweeping denials with little basis in reality. The assertive response is to explain the reasons for the shortcomings, which may well be understandable for a variety of reasons: temporary personal worries; lack of resources, in a climate of diminishing budgets, to carry out a job properly; demoralization at work, perhaps through failure to get a promotion, or through absence of any recognition of previous projects successfully completed. Practise being open about problems at work, rather than trying to deny or conceal them. In that way there is at least a possibility of getting others' ideas, or more resources, to help. End the interview by reaching a new agreement about completing the task or project, provided you get the necessary support. Make an undertaking of a positive kind.

If the criticism is a general 'put-down' rather than a specific complaint about your work, assert yourself by bringing this into the open. Express your feelings in response to this put-down: 'You've got this wrong, and what you seem to be doing is getting at me without any real justification. That makes me pretty fed up. What's behind this?' 'Put-downs' may usually be identified because they are rash generalizations and are not linked to any specific piece of work, and because there are strong emotional undertones, suggesting that it is the person who is being criticized, rather than the work. Dealing with aggressive criticism, especially if the person is worked up and in a rage, may involve going away and exercising your right to leave until things cool down. If you do stay and take it, defuse the situation by getting the person to listen to your view, and also to focus on the content rather than the emotions of their own view.

TRANSACTIONAL ANALYSIS

Transactional Analysis 'is intended to give you some comprehensible concepts so that you can improve yourself and help others to do the same. This process is not intended to be dangerous or impossible or to require the help of experts.'[49] Like assertiveness training, Transactional Analysis provides a method of analysing behaviour, especially confrontations between individuals, and enables individuals to adapt their behaviour to improve relationships. It has been used to improve personal relationships in a variety of work and domestic situations.

It is based upon the idea that each person has three ego states, which are separate and distinct sources of behaviour. The *parent* ego state comprises the attitudes and behaviour incorporated from external sources, primarily parents. It is often expressed towards others in prejudicial, critical and nurturing behaviour. Typical parental words are 'right', 'wrong', 'good', 'never', 'disgusting', 'shocking' and 'stupid'. Non-verbal clues include finger-wagging, arm-folding and head-shaking. The *child* ego state contains all the impulses which come naturally to an infant, such as joy, curiosity and enthusiasm. The assumption in Transactional Analysis is that the most appropriate ego state will be the *adult* one, which is oriented to current reality and the objective gathering of information. In other words, each person speaks and behaves in an adult manner. Ego states are usually depicted as in Figure 8.2.

```
    PERSON 1          PERSON 2
        P                 P
        A                 A
        C                 C
```

Figure 8.2 Depicting ego states in Transactional Analysis

Each transaction is shown by an arrow. Two adult-to-adult transactions are shown in Figure 8.3.

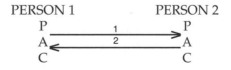

Figure 8.3 Adult-to-adult transactions

273

'*Crossed' transactions* occur when an unexpected response is made, stimulating an inappropriate ego state, and usually causing a good deal of ill-feeling (Figure 8.4). They should normally be avoided.

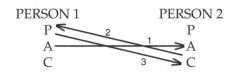

PERSON 1   PERSON 2

Figure 8.4 **Crossed transactions**

Person 1: 'Do you feel you have made any progress in liaising with departments this year?' (Adult to Adult)
Person 2: 'Do you think I am a miracle-worker?' (Child to Parent)
Person 1: 'I expect you to answer a question properly when I ask it.' (Parent
to Child)

Strokes are any forms of recognition, and can be verbal or non-verbal, positive or negative – a genuine smile would be a positive stroke, whereas a growl would be a negative one. A *game* is a series of complementary transactions between people which seem straightforward on the surface, but where there is an ulterior motive. Typical games in organizations are 'Harried', where a person plays at being very busy and overburdened and is self-righteous about it, and 'Wooden Leg', where a person always complains of a disadvantage which prevents achievement, yet may reject help because it only emphasizes the difficulty. The 'OK Corral' in Figure 8.5 shows four psychological *life positions*, each describing how one feels about oneself and about others. Although in certain circumstances other positions are tenable, it is generally assumed that position 1 is the most desirable.

I'm not OK			I'm OK
You're OK	3	1	You're OK
I'm not OK	4	2	I'm OK
You're not OK			You're not OK

Figure 8.5 **The 'OK Corral'**

MANAGING STRESS

There is growing evidence that workplace stress is on the increase. Handy has referred to research at Warwick University which 'revealed that British workers' stress levels had risen and job satisfaction plummeted'.[50] In the same issue of *The Times Magazine*, Walters reported that the Industrial Society has found that 74 per cent of employers thought 'that stress was "the number one up-and-coming health and safety issue over the next two years"'.[51] Yet, as Walters comments: 'only a third of employers monitor workplace stress'. This is despite the fact that since 1994 (see Chapter 1, pp.28–9) it has become even more important for managers to be aware of staff suffering from stress, as the courts may hold employers responsible.

Stress results from the way people feel about the pressures they perceive themselves to be under. One person may find it difficult to understand how another can be stressed by what appears to be no pressure at all. To understand stress, it is therefore necessary to realize that different people have different stress thresholds, and that all the sources of stress for one particular person are frequently not known by others.

Stress occurs 'when we feel that there are too many pressures or too few resources to deal with them'.[52] Looker and Gregson see stress as having three aspects:

1. **The Good** – excitement, stimulation, creativity, success, achievement, increased productivity
2. **The Bad** – boredom, frustration, distress, pressure, poor performance, decreased productivity, failure, headaches, indigestion, colds, unhappy and disharmonious relationships
3. **The Ugly** – ulcers, heart attacks, cancer, anxiety, depression, nervous breakdown, suicide.[53]

The results of stress are therefore not necessarily bad, and good managers will seek to take advantage of the good, while helping staff to reduce the bad and avoid the ugly sides of stress.

Surveys of stress among librarians have produced similar findings. Causes of stress discovered by Evans[54] and Bunge[55] are summarized in Figure 8.6. Work overload is a dominant factor, caused by increased student numbers in academic institutions and the demand made upon the library as the amount of formal teaching decreases and is replaced by student-centred learning. The working environment has become less pleasant through overcrowding and noise. The need for greater accountability has produced pressure for indicators of performance and the collection of management information not previously required. Although work with users is generally felt to improve

Evans

All staff	%	Professionals	%	Non-professionals	%
1 Work overload	58	1 Work overload	82	1 Money worries	83
2 Patrons	51	2 Patrons	61	2 Prospects	61
3 Money worries	45	3 Working environment	43	3 Patrons	39
4 Prospects	38	4 Poor administration	36	4 Work underload	22
5 Working environment	31	5 Pressure from management	25	5 Technological change	17
6 Poor administration	23	6 Prospects	18	6 Work overload	17
7 Technological change	18	7 Technological change	14	7 Satisfaction	13
8 Pressure from management	13	8 Money worries	14	8 Work environment	13
9 Work underload	11	9 Satisfaction	4	9 Poor administration	9
10 Satisfaction	8	10 Work underload	0	10 Personality conflicts	0
11 Personality conflicts	0	11 Personality conflicts	0	11 Pressure from management	0

Bunge

	%
1 Patrons	15.0
2 Workload	13.4
3 Supervisors and management	10.5
4 Schedule and work day	7.2
5 Lack of positive feedback	6.9
6 Other staff members	6.9
7 Lack of information and training	6.7
8 Feeling pulled and tugged	4.1
9 Technology and equipment	4.1
10 Physical facilities	4.1
11 Bureaucracy and red tape	3.6

Figure 8.6 Causes of stress in rank order

276

motivation (see Chapter 2), when demands from users become difficult to satisfy from limited resources, there is a build-up of pressure. 'Work underload' stands out in contrast, and can be seen as a response by library assistants to work which makes inadequate use of their abilities. Money worries are also a problem, particularly for library assistants. This evidence reinforces the points made in Chapter 2 about recruitment incentives in library and information work. The ideas presented in Chapter 2 have therefore become even more relevant if stagnation is not to set in. Change is a key contributor to workplace stress. Technological change continues apace, and for many staff the discrepancy between the potential of IT and the reality of slow computer networks, broken equipment and the sheer speed of change constitutes a major factor in the build-up of stress. Aside from changes in technology, the other elements identified in Chapter 1 as affecting the roles and function of library and information workers add to levels of change-related stress which may be experienced in the workplace.

One way of relieving stress is to provide more resources to enable staff to meet demands, but there are only limited possibilities in this area, and increasing resources for one activity is likely to be at the expense of another. Moreover, additional resources may not always be the solution: for example, if poor communication is giving rise to misunderstandings, this will probably result in increased stress. Ideas that have been put forward in other chapters on motivation, training, staff appraisal and selection of staff are all relevant to the relief of unnecessary stress. Maggie Forbes, Head of Counselling Services at the University of Huddersfield, ran a seminar for librarians in 1992 and provided a helpful list of ideas for coping positively with stress. The similarity between this list and the objectives of assertiveness training can be seen clearly:

1. Get to know your own limits. Respect them, and do not overstretch yourself.
2. Find out what works best for you in the way of stress moderation, such as talking to someone, practising relaxation, reorganizing your timetable.
3. If you are a worrier or prone to 'hurry-sickness', make sure you compensate in some way with quiet spaces in your life.
4. Organize and prioritize. Do not waste time and energy being in a muddle. Decide what is important to you, and leave the rest.
5. If you have a lot on, offload something. Be ready for it to hurt a bit. Admit you cannot do and have everything.
6. Stop trying to be perfect – no one would like you if you were anyway.
7. Accept the fact that other people will sometimes cause you stress.
8. Do not allow yourself to be a victim. Learn to ask for what you want; cope with rejection; say 'no', and stick to it.

9. Decide your goals, ones which are within your grasp and suit you rather than parents, a partner or 'society'.
10. Do not let other people do your thinking – you decide what matters to you.
11. Talk to someone – a partner, a friend, a counsellor.
12. Take exercise to provide an outlet for stress, and also to keep you in good shape for coping.
13. Have plenty of rest – sleep, breaks in the day, the week, the year.
14. Practise relaxation – whatever kind suits you best:
    - breathe deeply
    - self-hypnosis
    - meditation
    - visualization (using your imagination to produce pleasant images)
    - self-talk or affirmation (boost your own confidence, reduce your own fears).
15. Go easy on yourself – like yourself, forgive yourself, allow yourself to fail sometimes. You are human, not a machine – prize your humanity!

Visualization and affirmation are two methods recommended by Trickey as means to achieve 'a quick boost, a rapid adrenalin boost or just an element of calm to allow us to be more functional in the next task, work or social, we have to carry out'. He describes practical ways to practise using these 'so the response to the method becomes automatic [and] if you need them in a crisis they will be fully available to you'.[56]

There are plenty of tools which enable you to check whether you are suffering from stress. Looker and Gregson have produced a questionnaire with a scoring key (Figure 8.7),[57] and they also highlight the stress problems of workaholics or 'Type A' people (Figure 8.8).

As has been discussed, change is a common cause of stress. Hudson recommends some techniques for managers who are helping staff through change:

- Support each other through the transition process.
- Keep your sense of humour.
- Make sure there is plenty of communication.
- Use stress management techniques to take care of yourself.

Hudson observes:

> The ultimate goal is to create an atmosphere where the energy created by conflict and stress can be turned to a positive force.[58]

Type A Behaviour

For each question, tick the box that best represents your behaviour.

	Never	Almost never	Sometimes	Usually	Almost always	Always
Are you late for appointments?	☐	☐	☐	☐	☐	☐
Are you competitive in the games you play at home or at work?	☐	☐	☐	☐	☐	☐
In conversations, do you anticipate what others are going to say (head nod, interrupt, finish sentences for them)?	☐	☐	☐	☐	☐	☐
Do you have to do things in a hurry?	☐	☐	☐	☐	☐	☐
Do you get impatient in queues or traffic jams?	☐	☐	☐	☐	☐	☐
Do you try to do several things at once and think about what you are about to do next?	☐	☐	☐	☐	☐	☐
Do you feel you do most things quickly (eating, waking, talking, driving)?	☐	☐	☐	☐	☐	☐
Do you get easily irritated over trivia?	☐	☐	☐	☐	☐	☐
If you make a mistake, do you get angry with yourself?	☐	☐	☐	☐	☐	☐
Do you find fault with and criticize other people?	☐	☐	☐	☐	☐	☐
TOTAL						

(*From*: Terry Looker and Olga Gregson, *Managing Stress*, 1997, p.88 and p.198)

Figure 8.7 Stress assessment questionnaire

279

SCORE

5 ALWAYS   2 SOMETIMES
4 ALMOST ALWAYS   1 ALMOST NEVER
3 USUALLY   0 NEVER

Total your scores and multiply by 2.

EVALUATION

Type B	0–39	You are slightly and/or rarely impatient and aggravated. You create hardly any unnecessary stress for yourself, and your health is probably unaffected.
Mild Type A	40–59	You are fairly and/or occasionally impatient and aggravated. You create some unnecessary stress for yourself, and this may affect your health.
Moderate Type A	60–79	You are very and/or often impatient and aggravated. You generate much unnecessary stress for yourself, and this may affect your health.
Extreme Type A	80–100	You are extremely and/or usually impatient and aggravated. You generate TOO MUCH unnecessary stress for yourself, and this may affect your health.

Note: This is a self-ssessment of your Type A behaviour. It is only as accurate as you are honest in your answers. Furthermore, Type As are often blind to their own behaviour: for example, doing things fast. Type As may not think they are as fast as they actually are

Figure 8.7 concluded

Your attitude to work – Workaholism

	YES	NO
• Do you take work home most nights?	○	○
• Do you frequently think about work problems at home?	○	○
• Do you voluntarily work long hours?	○	○
• Do work problems affect your sleeping habits?	○	○
• Do your family and friends complain that you spend too little time with them?	○	○
• Do you find it difficult to relax and forget work?	○	○
• Do you find it difficult to say 'no' to work requests?	○	○
• Do you find it difficult to delegate?	○	○
• Is your self-esteem based largely on your work?	○	○
SCORE		

SCORING AND EVALUATION

If you answer 'yes' to one question, you may simply be dedicated to your work, However, there is a fine dividing line between dedication and obsessive devotion to work (workaholism) so be on your guard!
Score: 1

If you answer 'yes' to two questions, you are obsessive about your work and could easily succumb to workaholism. Beware!
Score: 2

Answering 'yes' to three questions indicates you have an obsessive and compulsive devotion to work. The higher the score, the more you are hooked into workaholism. You need to question your priorities for the sake of your marriage, social relationships, health and career; it may seem hard for you to believe you can be damaging the career that you are striving obsessively to enhance.
Score equals the number of 'yes' responses.

(*From*: Terry Looker and Olga Gregson, *Managing Stress*, 1997, p.88 and p.198)

Figure 8.8 Workaholic checklist

TIME MANAGEMENT

The now common expectation from parent organizations that libraries, along with all other sections, will deliver more services of a higher quality with less resources means there is a emphasis on developing more efficient ways of working, and there is a pressing need for staff to be more productive. Most of this book is devoted to making this possible, and if time is not used efficiently, productivity will suffer.

The first stage in managing time, as in many areas of management, is self-analysis. This can take two forms. The first is to analyse how your time is spent; this can be carried out over a week or so by keeping a log of your activities. It can either be an open log which records the time spent daily on each task, or it can be structured according to known activities of the job, such as planning, meetings, interruptions, telephone, correspondence, reading projects. The log is then analysed according to what you consider to be the key tasks, so that you can see whether you are concentrating upon important areas, and to identify where time is 'wasted'.

A second self-analysis will concentrate upon the sort of person you are. The self-analysis questionnaire already introduced in this chapter (pp.249–50) will have told you about your management style, and this will certainly affect your management of time. You need to decide what your role should be. For example, many managers now get out of their offices, talk to their staff about their work and have an open-door policy for staff to come and see them. This approach, termed Managing By Walking About (MBWA) in the 1970s, is a means of breaking down barriers and improving communications. Whilst it appears to be time-consuming and may be considered time-wasting by some analysts, it can result in excellent effects: 'Seeing and being seen is one of the most important aspects of motivating staff'.[59] Thus, the investment is usually worthwhile. You also need to know what works best for you: for example, the time of day when you work at your best, which is probably when you should concentrate on clearing backlogs of desk work, and how much sleep you need to keep you energetic each day.

All the literature on time management analyses *time-wasters* – those things which hinder us most in getting work completed on time – and there is a general consensus on the main causes. Gothberg has studied time management among librarians, and her findings are shown in Figure 8.9.[60]

Managing time is about dealing with these time-wasters, and the literature is awash with hints and tips for the manager (as summarized in Figure 8.10). Most of the solutions shown are interconnected and therefore affect each other, so once you have started to manage time systematically using a particular tip, many of the others are likely to come into play.

Special Libraries	State Libraries	Academic Libraries
1 Meetings (scheduled and unscheduled)	Meetings (scheduled and unscheduled)	Attempting too much and estimating time unrealistically
2 Telephone interruptions	Telephone interruptions	Cluttered desk and personal disorganization
3 Drop-in visitors	Attempting too much at once and estimating time unrealistically	Meetings (scheduled and unscheduled)
4 Inadequate, Inaccurate, or delayed information	Lack of self-discipline	Lack of, or unclear, communications or instructions
5 Attempting too much at once and estimating time unrealistically	Drop-in visitors	Crises (personal and/or staff)
6 Crises (personal and/or staff)	Inadequate, inaccurate or delayed information	Drop-in visitors
7 Inability to say no	Crises (personal and/or staff)	Inadequate, inaccurate, or delayed information
8 Indecision and procrastination	Inability to say no	Telephone interruptions
9 Lack of self-discipline	Cluttered desk and personal disorganization	Ineffective delegation and involvement in routine and detail
10 Leaving tasks unfinished	Lack of, or unclear, communications or instructions	Lack of self-discipline

From studies by Helen M. Gothberg.

Figure 8.9 Library time-wasters

283

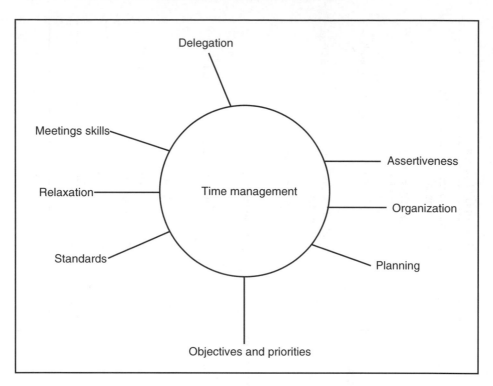

Figure 8.10 **Dealing with time-wasters**

A consideration of objectives and priorities is the most appropriate place to start. It is therefore necessary to list (writing things down is an important element in time management) our personal, professional and job objectives, and the steps by which we hope to achieve them. Documents such as *The Framework for Continuing Professional Development* and *The Toolkit for Turning Points* (see Chapter 7) can help with this, and regular appraisals will enable managers and staff to identify and focus on job objectives which reflect the aims and priorities of the organization for which they work.

These objectives and priorities can only be tackled practically each day by systematic planning. A daily list of tasks to be completed is a strong recommendation in all time management literature. One approach, recommended by Seiwert,[61] is LEADS:

- **L**ist activities
- **E**stimate time needed
- **A**llow time for unscheduled tasks
- **D**ecide on priorities
- **S**can scheduled tasks at end of each day.

It is unlikely that you will be able to achieve all your scheduled tasks in a single day. Wetmore suggests that planning more than you can accomplish can be a benefit:

> It allows you to take advantage of Parkinson's Law, which says, in part, that a project tends to take as long as the time allocated for it. If you give yourself only one thing to do, it will take all day to do it. If you give yourself three things to do, you will get them all done. If you give yourself 12 things to do, you may not get all 12 done, but you may accomplish nine.[62]

This needs to be balanced by remembering that it nearly always takes longer than anticipated to complete a task. Setting yourself challenging targets in terms of tasks to get through only works as an efficient means of managing time if you are also realistic about the effort which is involved.

Procrastination, the thief of time, must be conquered. Masterton recommends the following to assist with overcoming procrastination:

- **A little each day** – Tackle jobs which you find difficult and/or boring in small manageable chunks, rather than spending a day on them.
- **Unpleasant tasks** – Again, do at least one each day, and do it first, then your sense of achievement will carry you through the day.
- **Take a deep breath** – Just decide to do it in the same way that you would decide to jump off the diving board at the swimming pool – sometimes, there is no other way.
- **Give yourself a reward** – Choose to work on an interesting task after an unpleasant task, give yourself time off, or give yourself a treat.
- **Seek help** – If it really is difficult or if you feel unskilled in this area, someone else may be able to help you, and halve the problem.
- **Think positively** – Sometimes, thinking about unpleasant or difficult tasks in a positive way can make them much more manageable.[63]

Organize your day so that you have periods of 'quiet time' to clear backlogs of important work. There are certain times when you are least likely to be disturbed: early morning, lunchtimes and later in the evenings. Many managers stay late and arrive early to clear their work, and this will be a personal decision to make. If you have an answerphone or voicemail, use it as a means to protect time when you are at your desk but need to avoid interruptions. Alternatively, you may be able to ask colleagues to answer phone calls and take messages. At times, it may be best to move to another room out of communication to finish important work. Librarians can work in a far corner of a library. When receiving visitors, it is a good idea to stand up and remain standing if the visit is judged unimportant. Some people find it difficult to end conversations, and need to learn ways of concluding meetings. Standing up, thanking visitors and stressing the next stage should give clues to most peo-ple. Managers should also try to keep their desks uncluttered by clearing work quickly and learning to read quickly. E-mail has had a massive impact on how we manage our time. On one hand it provides a very quick and easy way to communicate with staff (although it should be remembered that it is not always the most appropriate means to use), on the other, there is an expectation that e-mail messages will be dealt with instantaneously. Whereas in the past taking two or three working days to reply to a letter was consid-ered acceptable, the widespread use of e-mail means that recipients often feel pressured to drop tasks and answer messages as soon as they arrive. This should be resisted. If you are already working on a demanding task, switch your e-mail off. Try checking it just twice a day, as you would with paper post.

The section on assertiveness in this chapter should be read carefully because the ability to say 'no' is an important factor in reducing work overload. Morris recommends learning 'to be ruthless with time, gracious with people'.[64] Many people believe they could manage their own time quite well if only the boss would stop imposing upon them. Some of the effects of this can be overcome by learning to negotiate workable compromises.

Delegation, discussed in Chapter 2, is a fundamental strategy in the saving of time. It is not 'allocating duties' or 'work scheduling'. It is about letting somebody else do something you would normally do. It demands giving away some of your authority to enforce action. It gives others freedom of action while you continue to 'carry the can'. It is risky and painful. It can seem unnatural to people who have succeeded so far by doing things well them-selves. Delegating will free managers to concentrate on more important issues, but it involves informing, training and supporting your staff. It represents a means for staff to develop new skills, but you will need to allow time for them to get up to speed. Remember this when deciding what to delegate, otherwise you could end up saying 'It would have been quicker to do it myself.'

Meetings are thought by many to be the greatest time-wasters, therefore read the section in this chapter on effective group meetings carefully.

Managers should find time to relax, both at work and at home. Most people can only concentrate for limited periods and need short relaxation breaks. It is a good idea to do something you enjoy each day to compensate for those activities which you dislike. Good time management will enable individuals and organizations to reach standards of excellence which are necessary if their aims and objectives are to be achieved.

Table 8.3 Managerial styles

Your selection	Managerial style
1	1,9
2	9,1
3	9,9
4	1,1
5	5,5
6	1,1
7	9,9
8	9,1
9	1,9
10	5,5
11	5,5
12	9,1
13	1,9
14	9,9
15	1,1

Your selection	Managerial style
16	9,1
17	1,1
18	5,5
19	1,9
20	9,9
21	9,9
22	1,9
23	1,1
24	9,1
25	5,5
26	1,9
27	9,9
28	5,5
29	1,1
30	9,1

An overview of the possible styles

CONCERN FOR PEOPLE — HIGH 9 / LOW 0

CONCERN FOR PRODUCTION — HIGH 9

1,9 Management
Thoughtful attention to needs of staff for satisfying relations with others leads to a comfortable tempo and lack of conflict

9,9 Management
Work objectives are achieved through committed people; interdependence through a common stake in organizational goals (integration of tasks and human needs)

5,5 Management
Adequate organizational performance is possible through balancing the need to get work done with the maintenance of morale at a satisfactory level

1,1 Management
Exertion of minimum effort to get required work done is just sufficient to sustain membership of the organization. Conflict with people inevitable

9,1 Management
Efficiency in operations of planning, directing and controlling work results from arranging conditions in such a way that human elements interfere to a minimum degree

ASSESSING ONE'S PERSONAL LEADERSHIP STYLE, USING THE BLAKE/ MOUTON GRID

Using the 30 statements on leadership given on pages 249–50, summarize your personal selection in Column II below by entering the numbers of statements 1–30 which you personally identify with. The related management style may be found in Table 8.3, coded in Blake/Mouton terms. For an interpretation of these, refer to the Blake/Mouton grid (Figure 2.4).

Table 8.4 Scorecard

I Element	II Your selection	III Managerial style
DECISIONS		
CONVICTIONS		
CONFLICT		
EMOTION		
HUMOUR		
EFFORT		

References

CHAPTER 1

1. Orna, Liz (1992), 'Information policy issues and challenges for organisations', *Aslib Information*, **20**(3), March, pp.107–10.
2. Investors in People, available online at <http://www.iipuk.co.uk/TheStandard/TheStandard.htm> (accessed on 17 June 2001).
3. Goulding, Anne et al. (2000), 'Investors in People in library and information services in the United Kingdom', *Library and Information Briefings*, **91**, February, p.5.
4. Goulding, Anne et al. (1999), *Investing in LIS People: The impact of the Investors in People Initiative on the Library and Information Sector*, British Library Research and Innovation Report 141, London: British Library Research and Innovation Centre, p.14.
5. Ward, Sandra (1999), 'Information professionals for the next millennium', *Journal of Information Science*, **25**(4), pp.239–47.
6. Jones, Browen et al. (1999), *Staff in the New Library: Skill Needs and Learning Choices*, British Library Research and Innovation Report 152, London: British Library Research and Innovation Centre, p.iv.
7. Abell, Angela (1999), 'Carrying change to the core', *Library Association Record*, **101**(10), pp.590–2.
8. For example: Abell, Angela (1999), 'New roles? New skills? New people?', *Library Association Record*, **99**(10), pp.538–9; Blizzard, Andy (1998), 'Changing times and challenging roles for school librarians', *School Librarian*, **46**(2), Summer, pp.66–7; Garrod, Penny and Sidgreaves, Ivan (1997), *Skills for New Information Professionals: The SKIP Project*, London: Library Information Technology Centre; Goulding, Anne et al. (1999), *Likely to Succeed: Attitudes and Aptitudes for an Effective Information Professional in the 21st century*, Library and Information Commission Report 8, London: Library and Information Commission; Jones, Browen et al. (1999), *op. cit.*
9. Joint Funding Councils' Library Review Group (1993), *Report*, Bristol: Higher Education Funding Council for England.
10. John Fielden Consultancy (1993), *Supporting Expansion: A Report on Human Resource Management in Academic Libraries, for the Joint Funding Councils' Libraries Review Group*, Bristol: Higher Education Funding Council for England.
11. Joint Funding Councils' Library Review Group (1993), *op. cit.*, p.12.
12. Hendry, J.D. (2000), 'Past neglect and future promise: The condition of UK public libraries now and over the last 20 years', *Library Review*, **49**(9), pp.442–7.
13. Library and Information Commission (1997), *New Library: The People's Network*, available online at <http://www.lic.gov.uk/publications/policyreports/newlibrary/index.html> (accessed on 16 July 2001).

14. Library and Information Commission (1998), *Building the New Library Network*, available online at <http://www.lic.gov.uk/publications/policyreports/building/index.html> (accessed on 16 July 2001), p.1.
15. Ibid., p.51
16. Abell, Angela and Chapman, Darron (2000), 'Even greater expectations', *Library Association Record*, **102**(10), pp.572–3.
17. Abell, Angela (1998), 'Skills for the 21st century', *Journal of Librarianship and Information Science*, **30**(4), December, pp.211–14.
18. Abell, Angela and Chapman, Darron (2000), *op. cit.*
19. TFPL (1999), *Skills for Knowledge Management: Building a Knowledge Economy*, London: TFPL, p.100.
20. 'KM goes rural' (2001), *Library Association Record*, **103**(8), p.453.
21. Available online at <http://www.lifelonglearning.co.uk/> (accessed on 25 July 2001).
22. Library and Information Commission (2000), *Empowering the Learning Community*, available online at <http://www.lic.gov.uk/publications/policyreports/empower/> (accessed on 25 July 2001).
23. O'Shea, Tim (2000), 'e-asy does it', *The Guardian*, 10 October, p.10.
24. Available online at <http://www.sconul.ac.uk/TFeUniversity.doc> (accessed on 31 January 2002).
25. *Modernising Government* (1999), Command paper 4310, London: Stationery Office, available online at <http://www.cabinet-office.gov.uk/moderngov/whtpaper/index.htm> (accessed on 24 July 2001).
26. Cabinet Office (2001), *Getting it Together: A Guide to Quality Schemes and the Delivery of Public Services*, London: Cabinet Office, available online at <http://www.cabinet-office.gov.uk/servicefirst/index/quality.htm> (accessed on 24 July 2001).
27. For example: Tucker, Mary (1995), 'Investor in People: The Gloucester experience', *Public Library Journal*, **10**(5), pp.127–8; Morrow, John (1996), 'Training for the Charter Mark', *Personnel, Training and Education*, **13**(1), April, pp.9–10.
28. Department of National Heritage (1997), *Reading the Future: A Review of Public Libraries in England*, London: DNH.
29. Favret, Leo (2000), 'Benchmarking, annual library plans and best value', *Library Management*, **21**(7), pp.340–8.
30. Thebridge, Stella and Nankivell, Clare (1999), *Working Together and Working Smarter: A Pragmatic Approach to Public Library Research. Themes from Two Study Schools for Public Librarians Held in October 1998 and April 1999 in Birmingham*, Birmingham: University of Central England in Birmingham, Centre for Information, Research and Training.
31. White, Peter (2000), 'Don't all scream at once', *Public Library Journal*, **15**(4) pp.108–10.
32. Department of Culture, Media and Sport (2001), *Comprehensive, Efficient and Modern Public Libraries: Standards and Assessment*, London: DCMS, available online at <http://www.culture.gov.uk/PDF/libraries_pls_assess.pdf> (accessed on 31 January 2002).
33. Ibid., p.3.
34. Ibid., p.14.
35. Goulding, Anne (2001), 'Setting the standard for comprehensive and efficient public library services', *Journal of Librarianship and Information Science*, **33**(2), June, pp.55–8.
36. *Learning to Succeed: A New Framework for Post-16 Learning* (1999), Command paper 4392, London: Stationery Office.
37. *Our Competitive Future: Building the Knowledge Driven Economy*, available online at <www.dti.gov.uk/comp/competitive/wh_int1.htm> (accessed on 26 July 2001).
38. *National Training Organisations: Strategic Guidance 2000–2001*, available online at <http://www.dfee.gov.uk/nto/guidance.pdf> (accessed on 25 July 2001).
39. *Modernising Government* (1999), *op. cit.*
40. *National Training Organisations: Strategic Guidance 2000–2001*, *op. cit.*

41. Corrall, Shelia and Pluse, John (2000), 'Vision for a skilled and learning workforce', *Personnel, Training and Education*, **17**(2), August, pp.3–5.
42. Lockton, Deborah J. (1999), *Employment Law*, 3rd edn, Basingstoke: Macmillan.
43. Chandler, Peter (2000), An A–Z of Employment Law, 3rd edn, London: Kogan Page.
44. Clarke, Alison (2001), *Women's Rights at Work: A Handbook of Employment Law*, London: Pluto.
45. Advisory, Conciliation and Arbitration Services (1977), *Disciplinary Practice and Procedures in Employment*, London: HMSO.
46. Lockton, Deborah J. (1999), *op. cit.*, p.193.
47. Chandler, Peter (2000), *op. cit.*, p.113.
48. Burns, T. and Stalker, G.M. (1961), *The Management of Innovation*, London: Tavistock.
49. Aitken, Olga (1992), 'Why firms must show a lack of discrimination', *Personnel Management*, August, pp.54–5.
50. Equal Opportunities Commission (1985), *Code of Practice: Equal Opportunity Policies, Procedures and Practices in Employment*, London: HMSO.
51. *The Law at Work* (2000), London: LRD Publications, p.64.
52. Clarke, Alison (2000), *op. cit.*, p.82
53. Ibid., p.83.
54. Chandler, Peter (2000), *op. cit.*, p.382.
55. Pannick, David (2000), 'Has Labour taken leave of its senses on parental breaks?', *The Times*, 6 June, p.9.

CHAPTER 2

1. Lofquist, L.H. and Davis, R.V. (1969), *Adjustment to Work*, New York: Appleton-Century-Crofts.
2. Levin, James M. and Kleiner, Brian H. (1992), 'How to reduce organizational turnover and absenteeism', *Work Study*, **41**(6), pp.6–9.
3. Rooks, Dana C. (1988), *Motivating To-day's Library Staff: A Management Guide*, New York: Oryx Press.
4. Gilbreth, F.B. (1912), *Primer of Scientific Management*, New York: Van Nostrand.
5. Taylor, F.W., 'The principles of scientific management', in Vroom, Victor H. and Deci, Edward L. (eds) (1970), *Management and Motivation*, London: Penguin, pp.295–301.
6. Ashworth, W. (1976), *Organizing Multi-site Libraries*, London: Library Association, p.1.
7. Roberts, Norman (1978), *Personnel in Libraries and Information Units*, London: British Library, p.24 (British Library R & D Report 5449).
8. Industrial Society (1985), *Introducing New Technology into the Office*, Leaflet PH/03, London: Industrial Society.
9. Parker, Sandra (1999), 'Changing places', *Library Association Record*, **101**(2), February, p.92.
10. Ritchie, Sheila (1984), *Training and Management Development in Librarianship*, Report to the British Library R & D Department, London: Ealing College of Higher Education, p.108.
11. Ibid.
12. Barlow, Richard (1989), *Team Librarianship: The Advent of Public Library Team Structures*, London: Clive Bingley, p.122.
13. Rooks, Dana C. (1988), *op. cit.*, pp.14–16.
14. Roethlisberger, F.J. and Dickson, W.J. (1939), *Management and the Worker*, Cambridge, Mass.: Harvard University Press.
15. Rose, Michael (1988), *Industrial Behaviour: Theoretical Development Since Taylor*, 2nd edn, London: Penguin, p.123.
16. Maslow, Abraham (1970), *Motivation and Personality*, New York: Harper & Row.
17. Trist, E.L. (1963), *Organizational Choice*, London: Tavistock Institute of Human Relations.

18. Sykes, Paul, 'Case study: Converged working at Liverpool John Moores University', in Hanson, Terry and Day, Joan (eds) (1998), *Managing the Electronic Library: A Practical Guide for Information Professionals*, London: Bowker-Saur, pp.63–78.
19. Bluck, Robert (1996), *Team Management*, London: Library Association Publishing (Library Training Guides).
20. Holbeche, Linda (1998), *Motivating People in Lean Organizations*, Oxford: Butterworth Heinemann, pp.18–19.
21. Rose, Michael (1988), *op. cit.*, p.201.
22. McGregor, Douglas (1960), *The Human Side of Enterprise*, New York: McGraw-Hill.
23. Likert, Rensis (1961), *New Patterns of Management*, New York: McGraw-Hill.
24. Stewart, Linda (1982), *What do UK Librarians Dislike About Their Jobs?*, Loughborough: CLAIM.
25. Ritchie, Sheila (1984), *op. cit.*
26. Barlow, Richard (1989), *op. cit.*, p.49.
27. Leicestershire County Libraries and Information Services (1977), *The Effective Use of Team Time: A Training Package*, Leicester: Leicestershire County Council Libraries and Information Services.
28. Blake, R.R. and Mouton, J.S. (1964), *The Managerial Grid*, Houston, Texas: Gulf Publishing Company.
29. Ibid., p.10.
30. Plate, K.M. and Stone, E.W. (1974), 'Factors affecting librarians' job satisfaction', *Library Quarterly*, **44**(2), April, pp.97–110.
31. Herzberg, Frederick, 'How do you motivate employees?', in Beach, Dale S. (ed.) (1971), *Managing People at Work: Readings in Personnel*, New York: Macmillan, p.241.
32. Holbeche, Linda (1998), *op. cit.*, p.21.
33. D'Elia, George P. (1979), 'The determinants of job satisfaction among beginning librarians', *Library Quarterly*, **49**(3), pp.283–302.
34. Dutton, B.G., 'Staff management and staff participation', in Shimmon, Ross, (ed.) (1976), *A Reader in Library Management*, London: Clive Bingley, pp.129–45.
35. Ibid.
36. Ashworth, W. (1976), *op. cit.*
37. John Fielden Consultancy (1993), *Supporting Expansion: A Report on Human Resource Management in Academic Libraries*, Bristol: Higher Education Funding Council for England, p.6.
38. Bluck, Robert (1994), 'Team management and academic libraries: A case study at the University of Northumbria', *British Journal of Academic Librarianship*, **9**(3), pp.224–42.
39. Tunley, Malcolm (1979), *Library Structures and Staffing Systems*, London: Library Association, p.25.
40. Jones, Ken (1984), *Conflict and Change in Library Organizations*, London: Library Association, p.146.
41. Ibid., p.147.
42. Vroom, Victor M. (1964), *Work and Motivation*, New York: Wiley.
43. Fiedler, Fred (1967), *Theory of Leadership Effectiveness*, New York: McGraw-Hill.
44. Schein, Edgar M. (1988), *Organisational Psychology*, 3rd edn, Englewood Cliffs, NJ: Prentice-Hall, p.94.
45. Ibid.
46. Plate, K.M. and Stone, E.W. (1974), *op. cit.*
47. Howard, K.W. (1989), 'A comprehensive expectancy motivation model: Implications for adult education and training', *Adult Education Quarterly*, **39**(4), Summer, pp.199–210.
48. Crowder, Mary and Pupynin, Kate (1993), *The Motivation to Train: A Review of the Literature and the Development of a Comprehensive Theoretical Model of Training Motivation*, London: Department of Employment.
49. Touraine, A. (1965), *Sociologie de l'action*, Paris: du Seuil.
50. D'Elia (1979), *op. cit.*

51. Russell, Norman (1984), 'The Job Satisfaction of Non-professional Staff', unpublished CNAA MPhil. thesis, Leeds Polytechnic.
52. Bundy, Alan (1988), 'Job satisfaction of subject librarians in British and Australian polytechnics', *Australian College Libraries*, **6**(1), March, pp.24–8.
53. Burgess, S. (1991), 'Job satisfaction of reference librarians and cataloguers', *Australian Academic and Research Libraries*, **23**, pp.73–80.
54. Marchant, Maurice P. (1970), *The Effects of the Decision Making Process and Related Organizational Factors on Alternative Measures of Performance in University Libraries: A Dissertation*, Ann Arbor, Mich.: University Microfilms.
55. Bengtson, Susan Dale and Shields, Dorothy (1985), 'A test of Marchant's predictive formulas involving job satisfaction', *Journal of Academic Librarianship*, **11**, May, pp.88–92.
56. Mirfakhrai, Mohammed (1991), 'Correlates of job satisfaction among academic librarians in the United States', *Journal of Library Administration*, **14**(1), pp.117–31.
57. Horenstein, Bonnie (1993), 'Job satisfaction of academic librarians: An examination of the relationships between satisfaction, faculty status, and participation, *College and Research Libraries*, **54**(3), May, pp.255–69.
58. Leckie, Gloria J. and Brett, Jim (1997), 'Job satisfaction of Canadian university librarians: A national survey', *College and Research Libraries*, **58**(1) January, pp.31–47.
59. van Reenan, Johann (1998), 'Librarians at work: Are we as satisfied as other workers?', *Information Outlook*, **2**(7), July, pp.23–8.
60. Russell, Norman (1984), *op. cit.*
61. Thapisa, A.P.N. (1991), 'The motivation syndrome: Job satisfaction through the pay nexus', *International Library Review*, **23**, pp.141–58.
62. Parmer, Coleen and East, Dennis (1993), 'Job satisfaction among support staff in twelve Ohio academic libraries', *College and Research Libraries*, **54**(1), January, pp.43–57.
63. Goulding, Anne (1995), 'I want to work with books and people: The job satisfaction of public library support staff', *Public Library Journal*, **10**(3), pp.71–4.
64. Banks, Julie (1991), 'Motivation and effective management of student assistants in academic libraries', *Journal of Library Administration*, **14**(1), pp.133–51.
65. Goulding, Anne (1995), *op. cit.*
66. Thapisa, A.P.N. (1991), *op. cit.*, p.153.
67. Miletich, Leo N. (1991), 'Pulling together: A 21st century management primer for the befuddled, benumbed and bewildered', *Journal of Library Administration*, **14**(1), pp.35–49.
68. American Library Association (1970), *Library Education and Manpower: A Statement of Policy*, Chicago: American Library Association.
69. Walton, Graham, Day, Joan and Edwards, Catherine (1996), 'Role changes for the academic librarian to support effectively the networked learner: Implications of the IMPEL project', *Education for Information*, **14**, pp.343–50.
70. Stewart, Linda (1982), *op. cit.*
71. Nankivell, Clare (c.1993), 'Class of '88', British Library Research and Development Department, unpublished.
72. van Reenan (1998), *op. cit.*
73. Stewart, Linda (1982), *op. cit.*, p.16.
74. Hirst, John (1996), 'Managing through people', *Personnel Training and Education*, **12**(3), January, pp.12–14.
75. Walton, Graham, Day, Joan and Edwards, Catherine (1996), *op. cit.*
76. Edwards, Catherine, Day, Joan, and Walton, Graham (1995), 'Impel project: The impact on people of electronic libraries', *Aslib Proceedings*, **47**(9), September, pp.203–8.
77. Konn, Tania and Roberts, Norman (1984), 'Academic librarians and continuing education', *Journal of Librarianship*, **16**(4), October, p.267.
78. Proctor, Richard, 'Fighting professional stagnation: Staff development in practice', in Hall, John (ed.) (1982), *Fighting Professional Stagnation*, Leeds: Leeds Polytechnic School of Librarianship, pp.53–73.

79. Ibid.
80. Dutton, B.G. (1976), *op. cit.*
81. Walley, Ed (c.1980), 'Public library purpose', unpublished paper, Leeds: Leeds Polytechnic School of Librarianship.
82. Muddiman, David (1999), 'Everyone on board?', *Public Library Journal*, **14**(4), pp.96–8.
83. Rogers, Carl (1961), *On Becoming a Person: A Therapist's View of Psychotherapy*, London: Constable.
84. Hofstede, Geert (1980*), Culture's Consequences: International Differences in Work Related Values*, London: Sage.
85. Rooks, Dana C. (1988), *op. cit.*, pp.4–6.
86. Vaughan, W.J. and Dunn, J.D. (1974), 'A study of job satisfaction in six university libraries', *College and Research Libraries*, **35**(3), May, pp.163–77.
87. O'Bryan, Bernard Burch III and Pick, Roger Alan (1995), 'Keeping information systems staff (happy)', *International Journal of Career Management*, **7**(2), pp.17–20.
88. Stewart, Linda (1982), *op. cit.*, p.15.
89. Konn, Tania and Roberts, Norman (1984), *op. cit.*
90. Bowey, Angela (1980), 'Perceptions and attitudes to change: A pilot study', *Personnel Review*, **9**(1), pp.35–42.

CHAPTER 3

1. Bramham, John (1994), *Human Resource Planning*, 2nd edn, London: Institute of Personnel and Development, p.155.
2. Library and Information Services Council (1984), *Basic Professional Education for Library and Information Work: A Discussion Paper*, London: Office of Arts and Libraries; Library and Information Services Council (1984), *Continuing Professional Education for Library and Information Work: A Discussion Paper*, London: Office of Arts and Libraries; Library and Information Services Council (1984), *Training for Library and Information Work: A Discussion Paper*, London: Office of Arts and Libraries.
3. Library Association, Futures Working Party (1985), *Final Report*, London: Library Association.
4. Ibid., p.3.
5. Taylor, Stephen (1998), *Employee Resourcing*, London: Institute of Personnel and Development, p.61.
6. Corrall, Sheila and Pluse, John (2000), 'Vision for a skilled and learning workforce', *Personnel Training and Education*, **17**(2), August, pp.3–5.
7. Oppenheim, Charles and Smithson, Daniel (1999), 'What is the hybrid library?', *Journal of Information Science*, **25**(2), pp.97–112.
8. Ibid.
9. Garrod, Penny (1999), 'Survival strategies in the learning age – hybrid staff and hybrid libraries', *Aslib Proceedings*, **51**(6), June, pp.187–94.
10. Pantry, Sheila (2000), 'Changing roles', *Impact*, **3**(9) October, pp.130–2.
11. Ibid.
12. Goulding, Anne, Bromham, Beth, Hannabuss, Stuart and Cramer, Duncan (1999), 'Supply and demand: The workforce needs of library and information services and personal qualities of new professionals', *Journal of Librarianship and Information Science,* **31**(4), December, pp.212–22.
13. Abell, Angela and Chapman, Darron (2000), 'Even greater expectations', *Library Association Record*, **102**(10), October, pp.572–3.
14. Kinnell, Margaret (1996), 'Management development for information professionals', *Aslib Proceedings*, **48**(9), September, pp.209–14.

15. Pluse, John (1999), 'Human resources: Time to take stock?' *Public Library Journal*, **14**(2), pp.40–1.
16. Usherwood, Bob et al. (2001), *Recruit, Retain and Lead: The Public Library Workforce Study*, Sheffield: Centre for the Public Library and Information in Society, University of Sheffield.
17. Goulding, Anne and Kerslake, Evelyn (1996), 'Flexible working in UK library and information services: Current practices and concerns', *Journal of Librarianship and Information Science*, **28**(4), December, pp.203–16.
18. Bramham, John (1994), *op. cit.*, p.63.
19. Shaughnessy, Thomas W. (1996), 'Lessons from restructuring the library', *Journal of Academic Librarianship*, **22**(4), July, pp.251–6.
20. Rider, Mary M. (1996), 'Developing new roles for paraprofessionals in cataloguing', *Journal of Academic Librarianship*, **22**(1), January, pp.26–32.
21. Ibid.
22. Stevenson, Janet (2000), 'Raising academic standards – an equal opportunities issue? The case for Information and Library Services NVQs', *Personnel Training and Education*, **17**(2), August, pp.11–16.
23. Corrall, Sheila (1998), 'Assistants as change agents', *Library Association Record*, **100**(11), November, pp.583–4.
24. Handy, Charles B. (1989), *The Age of Unreason*, London: Hutchinson.
25. Ibid., p.72.
26. Goulding, Anne and Kerslake, Evelyn (1996), *op. cit.*
27. Goulding, Anne and Kerslake, Evelyn (1997), 'Training the flexible library and information workforce: problems and practical solutions', *Information Services and Use*, **17**(4), pp.261–72.
28. Handy, Charles B. (1989), *op. cit.*, p.80.
29. Kenney, Donald J. and Painter, Francis O. (1995), 'Recruiting, hiring, and assessing student workers in academic libraries,' *Journal of Library Administration*, **21**(3/4), pp.29–45.
30. *Recruit, Retain and Lead: The Public Library Workforce Study, op. cit.*
31. Cookman, Noeleen and Streatfield, David (2001); 'Volunteers are en vogue', *Library Association Record*, **103**(2), February, p.100.
32. Hamilton, Val and Wells, Valerie (2000), 'Two for the price of one', *Library Association Record*, **102**(2), February, pp.90–1.
33. Bobay, Julie (1988), 'Job-sharing: A survey of the literature and a plan for academic libraries', *Journal of Library Administration*, **9**(2), pp.59–69.
34. Goulding, Anne and Kerslake, Evelyn (1996), *op. cit.*
35. Lett, Brenda (1993), 'Teleworking: An organic organizational model for the 21st century', *Library and Information News*, **17**(58), Winter, pp.15–16.
36. Ibid.
37. Lawes, Ann (1995), 'Managing people for whom one is not directly responsible', *Law Librarian*, **26**(3), September, pp.421–3.
38. Readman, John (2001), 'Rewriting contractor relationships', *Library Association Record*, **103**(1), January, pp.35–6.
39. Lawes, Ann (1995), *op. cit.*
40. Mayo, Andrew (1990), 'Linking manpower planning and management development', *Industrial and Commercial Training*, **22**(3).
41. *Recruit, Retain and Lead: The Public Library Workforce Study, op. cit.*
42. SCONUL (2000), *Annual Library Statistics 1998–99*, London: SCONUL.
43. Ennis, Kathy (ed.) (2000), *Guidelines for Learning Resource Services in Further and Higher Education: Performance and Resourcing*, 6th edn, London: Library Association.
44. '23 steps to pleasing the DCMS' (2000), *Library Association Record*, **102**(6), June, p.303.
45. 'Public library standards: More demands fall on staff' (2001), *Library Association Record*, **103**(3), March, p.131.
46. Bray, Felicity and Turner, Christopher (1991), *Monitoring the Library and Information Workforce*,

295

London, British Library Research and Development Department (British Library Research Paper 97).

47. Nankivell, Clare, 'Class of '88', British Library Research and Development Department, unpublished.

CHAPTER 4

1. Casteleyn, Mary (1996), *Job Descriptions for the Information Profession*, London: Aslib, Association for Information Management, p.6.
2. Casteleyn, Mary and Webb, Sylvia (1993), *Promoting Excellence: Personnel Management and Staff Development in Libraries*, London: Bowker-Saur, p.17.
3. John Fielden Consultancy (1993), *Supporting Expansion: A Report on Human Resource Management in Academic Libraries, for the Joint Funding Councils' Libraries Review Group*, Bristol: Higher Education Funding Council for England, p.26.
4. Ibid., p.45.
5. Ibid., p.26.
6. Equal Opportunities Commission (2000), *Job Evaluation Schemes Free of Sex Bias*, Manchester: Equal Opportunities Commission, available online at <http://www.eoc.org.uk/PDFS/GPjobev.pdf> (accessed on 26 July 2001).
7. Fowler, Alan (2000), *Writing Job Descriptions*, London: Institute of Personnel and Development, p.32.
8. Rodger, A. (1970), *The Seven-point Plan*, 3rd edn, London: National Institute of Industrial Psychology.
9. Fraser, J.M. (1978), *Employment Interviewing*, 5th edn, London: Macdonald and Evans.
10. Jago, Alison (1996), 'Selecting your team: How to find the right people', *Librarian Career Development*, **4**(3), pp.27–31.
11. Equal Opportunities Commission (2000), *Fair and Efficient Selection: Guidance on Equal Opportunities Policies in Recruitment and Selection Procedures*, Manchester: Equal Opportunities Commission, p.15.
12. Parry, Julie (1994), *Recruitment*, London: Library Association Publishing, p.10.

CHAPTER 5

1. Jago, Alison (1996), 'Selecting your team: How to find the right people', *Librarian Career Development*, **4**(3), pp.27–31.
2. Jordan, Peter J. (1986), *Succession at Senior Management Level in Libraries*, MPhil. thesis, University of Bradford.
3. Gould, G. Raymond (1990), 'Finding the right candidate: Part 2', *Records Management Journal*, **2**(1), pp.61–7.
4. Goulding, Anne et al. (1999), 'Supply and demand: The workforce needs of library and information services and personal qualities of new professionals', *Journal of Librarianship and Information Science*, **31**(4), pp.212–23.
5. Parry, Julie (1994), *Recruitment*, London: Library Association Publishing, p.11.
6. Institute of Personnel and Development (2000), *Recruitment*, IPD Survey Report 14, London: Institute of Personnel and Development, p.2.
7. lis-link is an e-mail discussion list managed by JISCmail. Further information is available online at <http://www.jiscmail.ac.uk/lists/LIS-LINK.html> (accessed on 26 July 2001).

8. Hill, Susan and Jago, Alison (1993), 'Recruitment and selection of staff', in Lawes, Ann (ed.), *Management Skills for the Information Manager*, Aldershot: Ashgate, pp.4–25.
9. Roberts, Gareth (1997), *Recruitment and Selection*, London: Institute of Personnel and Development, pp.38–9.
10. Helen Osborn, Borough Librarian of Newport, provided some interesting notes on research she has carried out, and we have used some of her findings.
11. Equal Opportunities Commission (2000), *Fair and Efficient Selection: Guidance on Equal Opportunities Policies in Recruitment and Selection Procedures*, Manchester: Equal Opportunities Commission, p.19.
12. Ibid., p.23.
13. Roberts, Gareth (1997), *op. cit.*, p.151.
14. Institute of Personnel and Development, *op. cit.*, p.13.
15. Parry, Judith (1994), *op. cit.*, p.22.
16. Roberts, Gareth (1997), *op. cit.*, p.181
17. Dewberry, C. (1998), 'The selection interview', in Gatewood, R.D. and Field, H.S. (eds), *Human Resource Selection*, 4th edn, London: Dryden Press, pp.479–522.
18. Commission for Racial Equality (1996), *Race Relations Code of Practice for the Elimination of Racial Discrimination and the Promotion of Equality of Opportunity in Employment*, London: Commission for Racial Equality, available online at <http://www.cre.gov.uk/publs/dl_empcp.html> (accessed on 26 July 2001).
19. Parry, Judith (1994), *op. cit.*, p.29.
20. Hill, Susan and Jago, Alison (1993), *op. cit.*, p.14.
21. Pluse, John (1998), 'Human resource management', in Prytherch, Ray (ed.), *Gower Handbook of Library and Information Management*, Aldershot: Gower, pp.231–48.
22. Fear, R.A. (1984), *The Evaluation Interview*, 4th edn, New York: McGraw-Hill.
23. Equal Opportunities Commission (2000), *op. cit.*, p.28.
24. Ibid.
25. Fear, R.A. (1984), *op. cit.*
26. Chaudhuri, Anita (2000), 'Beat the clock', *The Guardian*, 14 June, pp.6–7.
27. Stoakley, Roger (1990), 'The selection and appointment of professional staff', *Public Library Journal*, 5(5), pp.115–17.
28. Roberts, Gareth (1997), *op. cit.*, p.164.
29. Jones, Stephanie (1993), *Psychological Testing for Managers*, London: Piatkus, p.13.
30. Fletcher, Clive et al., (1997), *Psychological Testing: A Manager's Guide*, London: Institute of Personnel and Development, p.78.
31. British Psychological Society (1995), *Psychological Testing: A User's Guide*, available online at <http://www.bps.org.uk/documents/test_standards.pdf> (accessed on 26 July 2001), p.11.
32. Ibid.
33. Equal Opportunities Commission (2000), *op. cit.*
34. Goulding, Anne et al. (1999), *op. cit.*
35. Smith, Mike and George, Dave (1992), 'Selection methods', in Cooper, C.L. and Robertson, I.T. (eds), *International Review of Industrial and Organizational Psychology*, Volume 7, Chichester: John Wiley and Sons, pp.55–97.
36. Kline, P. (1973), 'Personality threats', *New Society*, 24(552), pp.241–2.
37. Jones, Stephanie (1993), *op. cit.*
38. Fletcher et al. (1997), *op. cit.*
39. Morgan, Steve (1995), 'A qualified "yes" to selection by assessment', *Library Manager*, 9 (July/August), p.15.
40. *Spring* v. *Guardian Assurance plc and others*, 1994 3 All ER 129–224, HL.
41. Howard, Gillian (1995), 'Troubled references', *The Times*, 21 February, p.31.
42. Gould (1990), *op. cit.*
43. Roberts, Gareth (1997), *op. cit.*

CHAPTER 6

1. Cooke, Rachel and Holman, Janet (1995), 'Developing people', in Carmel, Michael (ed.), *Health Care Librarianship and Information Work*, 2nd edn, London: Library Association Publishing, pp.218–31.
2. Aluri, Rao and Reichel, Mary (1995), 'Performance evaluation: A deadly disease?', *Journal of Academic Librarianship*, **20**(3), July, pp.145–55.
3. Edwards, Ronald G. (1998), 'Performance appraisal in academic libraries: Minor changes or major renovation?', *Library Review*, **47**(1), pp.14–19.
4. Randell, Gerry, Packard, Peter and Slater, John (1984), *Staff Appraisal: A First Step to Effective Leadership*, 3rd edn, London: Institute of Personnel Management.
5. Committee of Vice-Chancellors and Principals (1985), *Report of the Steering Committee for Efficiency Services in Universities*, London: Committee of Vice-Chancellors and Principals.
6. Committee of Vice-Chancellors and Principals (1987), *Twenty-third Report of Committee A*, London: Committee of Vice-Chancellors and Principals.
7. Green, Andrew (1993), 'A survey of staff appraisal in university libraries', *British Journal of Academic Librarianship*, **8**(3), pp.193–209.
8. Revill, Don (ed.) (1992), *Working Papers on Staff Development and Appraisal*, Brighton: Council of Polytechnic Librarians.
9. Stewart, Judith (1993), 'Performance management, staff appraisal', notes supplied with lecture given at Manchester Metropolitan University, April.
10. Knibbs, John and Swailes, Stephen (1992), 'Implementing performance review and career planning: Part two', *Management Decision*, **30**(2), pp.30–4.
11. Bentley, Trevor (1995), 'Being appraised', *Training Officer*, **31**(4), pp.110–12.
12. Brigden, David and Botton, Christopher (1999), 'Appraisal and staff development', *Training Journal*, April, pp.16–17.
13. Stewart, Judith (1993), *op. cit.*
14. Ruffley, S.C. (1991), *Staff Appraisal, Its Introduction and Role in an Academic Library*, MA thesis, Manchester Polytechnic.
15. Pollitt, Christopher (1988), 'Models of staff appraisal: Some political implications', *Higher Education Review*, **20**(2), Spring, pp.7–16.
16. Pennington, Gus and O'Neill, Mike (1988), 'Appraisal in higher education: Mapping the terrain', *Programmed Learning and Educational Technology*, **25**(2), May, pp.165–70.
17. Myland, Lesley (1999), 'Problems with appraisal', *Training Journal*, April, pp.18–20.
18. Green, Andrew (1993), *op. cit.*
19. Stewart, Judith (1993), *op. cit.*
20. Fletcher, Clive (1978), 'Management/subordinate communications and leadership style: A field study of their relationships to perceived outcome of appraisal interviews', *Personnel Review*, **7**(1), Winter, pp.59–62.
21. Aluri, Rao and Reichel, Mary (1995), *op. cit.*
22. O'Neilly, Jo (1995), 'When prejudice is not just skin deep', *People Management*, 23 February, pp.34–7.
23. Knibbs, John and Swailes, Stephen (1992), 'Implementing performance review and career planning: Part one', *Management Decision*, **30**(1), pp.49–53.
24. Stewart, Judith (1993), *op. cit.*
25. Aluri, Rao and Reichel, Mary (1995), *op. cit.*
26. Angiletta, Anthony M. (1991), 'On performance consultation with bibliographers: A non-rational and non-Machiavellian perspective', *Acquisitions Librarian*, (6), pp.123–30.
27. Brigden, David and Botton, Christopher (1999), *op. cit.*
28. Ibid.
29. Fletcher, Clive (1978), *op. cit.*
30. Platt, Kenneth J., *Effective Staff Appraisal*, Wokingham: Van Nostrand Reinhold, 1985, p.32.

31. Lanza, P. (1985), 'Team appraisals', *Personnel Journal*, **64**(3), pp.46–51.
32. Jordan, Peter (1992), 'Library performers: Groups and individuals', *British Journal of Academic Librarianship*, **7**(3), pp.177–85.
33. Randell, Gerry, Packard, Peter and Slater, John (1984), *op. cit.*
34. Jordan, Peter (1986), *Succession at Senior Management Level in Libraries*, MPhil. thesis, University of Bradford.
35. Fletcher, Clive (1978), *op. cit.*
36. Farmer, Jane C. (1992), 'Performance related pay for librarians: An overview', *Personnel Training and Education*, **9**(2), pp.53–7.
37. Green, Andrew (1993), *op. cit.*
38. Redman, Tom and Snape, Ed (1992), 'Upward and onward: Can staff appraise their managers?', *Personnel Review*, **21**(7), pp.32–46.
39. McDonagh, Brendan (1995), 'Appraising appraisals', *Law Librarian*, **26**(3), September, pp.423–5.
40. Aluri, Rao and Reichel, Mary (1995), *op. cit.*
41. Redman, Tom and Snape, Ed (1992), *op. cit.*
42. Rubin, Richard (1995), 'The development of a performance evaluation instrument for upward evaluation of supervisors by subordinates', *Library and Information Science Research*, **16**, pp.315–28.
43. Redman, Tom and Snape, Ed (1992), *op. cit.*
44. Green, Andrew (1993), *op. cit.*
45. Ruffley, Susan (1991), op. cit.
46. Bentley, Trevor (1995), 'Being appraised', *Training Officer*, **31**(4), May, pp.110–12.
47. Knibbs, John and Swailes, Stephen (1992), 'Implementing performance review and career planning: Part two', *Management Decision*, **30**(2), pp.30–4.
48. Bentley, Trevor (1995), *op. cit.*
49. American Library Association, Subcommittee on Personnel Organization and Procedure of the ALA Board on Personnel Administration (1952), *Personnel Organization and Procedure: A Manual for Use in Public Libraries*, Chicago: American Library Association, 1952.
50. McDonagh, Brendan (1995), *op. cit.*
51. Aluri, Rao and Reichel, Mary (1995), *op. cit.*
52. Revill, Don (1992), *op. cit.*
53. Hannabuss, Stuart (1991), 'Analysing appraisal interviews', *Scottish Libraries*, **30**, November/December, pp.13–15.
54. Brigden, David and Botton, Christopher (1999), *op. cit.*

CHAPTER 7

1. Goble, David S. (1997), 'Managing in a change environment: From coping to comfort', *Library Administration and Management*, **11**(3), Summer, pp.151–6.
2. Usherwood, Bob et al. (2001), *Recruit, Retain and Lead: The Public Library Workforce Study*, Sheffield: Centre for the Public Library and Information in Society, University of Sheffield.
3. John Fielden Consultancy (1993), *Supporting Expansion: A Report on Human Resource Management in Academic Libraries*, Bristol: Higher Education Funding Council for England.
4. Further Education Funding Council (1999), *Networking Lifelong Learning Making it Happen: An Implementation Plan*, available online at <http://194.66.249.219/documents/othercouncilpublications/index.html> (accessed on 8 May 2001).
5. Library and information Commission (1997), *New Library: The People's Network*, available online at <http://www.lic.gov.uk/publications/policyreports/newlibrary/index.html> (accessed on 16 July 2001).
6. Library and Information Commission (1998), *Building the New Library Network*, available online

at <http://www.lic.gov.uk/publications/policyreports/building/index.html> (accessed on 16 July 2001).

7. Goulding, Anne and Kerslake, Evelyn (1997), 'Training the flexible library and information workforce: Problems and practical solutions', *Information Services and Use*, **17**(4), pp.261–72.

8. Goulding, Anne and Kerslake, Evelyn (1996), *Developing the Flexible Library and Information Workforce: A Quality and Equal Opportunities Perspective*, British Library Research and Innovation Report 25, London: British Library Research and Innovation Centre.

9. Parry, Julie (1996), 'Continuing professional development', in Oldroyd, Margaret (ed.), *Staff Development in Academic Libraries: Present Practice and Future Challenges*, London: Library Association Publishing, pp.21–33.

10. Lobban, Margaret (1997), *Training Library Assistants*, London: Library Association Publishing, p.31.

11. John Fielden Consultancy (1993), *op. cit.*, p.38.

12. Curry, Sally and Watson, Margaret (1998), *Staff Development and Training*, IMPEL2 guide, Newcastle upon Tyne: University of Northumbria at Newcastle, available online at <http://is.unn.ac.uk/impel/stffdev.htm> (accessed on 8 May 2001).

13. Edwards, Ronald J. (1976), *In-service Training in British Libraries: Its Development and Present Practice*, London: Library Association, p.149.

14. John Fielden Consultancy (1993), *op. cit.*, p.37.

15. Smith, Peter (1974), *The Design of Learning Spaces*, London: Council for Educational Technology for the United Kingdom.

16. Investors in People, available online at <http://www.iipuk.co.uk/TheStandard/default.htm> (accessed on 8 May 2001).

17. Jacobs, Carol S. (1991), 'The use of the exit interview as a personnel tool and its applicability to libraries', *Journal of Library Administration*, **14**(4), pp.69–86.

18. Williamson, Michael (1993), *Training Needs Analysis*, London: Library Association Publishing, p.1.

19. Whetherly, June (1994), *Management of Training and Staff Development*, London: Library Association Publishing, p.10.

20. Williamson (1993), *op. cit.*, p.31.

21. Corrall, Sheila and Brewerton, Antony (1999), *The New Professional's Handbook: Your Guide to Information Services Management*, London: Library Association Publishing, p.173.

22. Usherwood, Bob et al. (2001), *Recruit, Retain and Lead: The Public Library Workforce Study*, Sheffield: Centre for Public Library and Information in Society, University of Sheffield.

23. Parry, Julie (1993), *Induction*, London: Library Association Publishing, p.1.

24. Webb, Sylvia P. (1993), 'Staff training and development', in Lawes, Ann (ed.), *Management Skills for the Information Manager*, Aldershot: Ashgate, pp.40–53.

25. Lobban, Margaret (1997), *op. cit.*, p.6.

26. Goulding, Anne and Kerslake, Evelyn (1996), 'Induction training for flexible information workers', *Personnel, Training and Education*, **13**(3), December, pp.9–12.

27. Arundale, Justin (1999), *Getting Your S/NVQ: A Guide for the Candidates in the Information and Library Sector*, 2nd edn, London: Library Association Publishing in association with the Information and Library Services Lead Body, p.15.

28. Oldroyd, Margaret (2000), 'Information and Library Services NVQs at De Monfort University', *SCONUL Newsletter*, **20** (Autumn), pp.24–6.

29. Herzog, Juliet (1996), *Implementing S/NVQs in the Information and Library Sector*, London: Library Association Publishing, p.27.

30. Arundale, Justin (1999), *op. cit.*, p.2.

31. Goulding, Anne and Kerslake, Evelyn (1997), *Training for Part-time and Temporary Workers*, London: Library Association Publishing.

32. Sykes, Phil (1996), 'Staff development for library assistants', in Oldroyd, Margaret (ed.), *Staff Development in Academic Libraries: Present Practice and Future Challenges*, London: Library Association Publishing, pp.81–93.

33. Wilson, Tom (1995), 'Are NVQs for robots?', *Library Association Record*, **97**(7), p.381.
34. Arundale, Justin (1999), *op. cit.*
35. Herzog, Juliet (1996), *op. cit.*
36. Dakers, Hazel (1997), 'NVQ's: Reflection upon the experience', *Personnel, Training and Education*, **14**(3), December, pp.11–13.
37. Stauch, Janet (2001), 'Information and Library Service NVQs – an opportunity lost?', *Personnel, Training and Education*, **18**(1), April, pp.4–5.
38. The Library Association (1997), *Associateship Regulations and Notes of Guidance*, London: Library Association.
39. Sharpe, Dave (2001), 'Boost your training power', *Library and Information Appointments*, **4**(10), 4 May, pp.225–7.
40. Curry, Sally and Watson, Margaret (1998), *op. cit.*
41. Paterson, Kathy and Munro, Julia (1998), 'The training hour at Reading University Library', *SCONUL Newsletter*, **14** (Autumn), pp.32–9.
42. Ibid.
43. Jones, Noragh (1985), *The Use of Simulation in the Teaching of Library Management*, PhD thesis, University of Bradford.
44. Jones, Noragh and Jordan, Peter (1988), *Case Studies in Library Management*, London: Clive Bingley.
45. *Can We Please Have That the Right Way Round?* (1977), London: Video Arts, VHS videocassette.
46. Brewerton, Antony (2001), 'Mastering presentation skills', *SCONUL Newsletter*, **22** (Spring), pp.24–8.
47. Biddiscome, Richard (1997), *Training for IT*, London: Library Association Publishing, p.35.
48. Ibid.
49. Garrod, Penny and Sidgreaves, Ivan (1997), *Skills for New Information Professionals: The SKIP Project*, London: Library Information Technology Centre, p.31.
50. Jones, Browen et al. (1999), *Staff in the New Library: Skill Needs and Learning Choices*, British Library Research and Innovation Report 152, London: British Library Research and Innovation Centre, p.55.
51. Sharpe, Dave (2001), *op. cit.*
52. Milligan, Colin (2001), from a talk given on 14 March 2001 at University College London to the M25 Consortium of HE Libraries – Staff Development Group. Notes available online at <http://www.icbl.hw.ac.uk/jtap-573/140301text.html> (accessed on 5 May 2001).
53. Jones, Browen et al. (1999), *op. cit.*, pp.199–225.
54. Cannell, Mike (1997), 'Practice makes perfect', *People Management*, **3**(5), March, pp.26–33.
55. Institute of Personnel and Development (1997), *The IPD Guide to On-the-job Training*, London: Institute of Personnel and Development.
56. Williamson, Michael G. (1986), 'The evaluation of training', in Prytherch, Ray (ed.), *Handbook of Library Training Practice*, Aldershot: Gower, pp.226–62.
57. Farmer, Jane and Campbell, Fiona (1997), 'Information Professional, CPD and transferable skills', *Library Management*, **18**(3), pp.129–34.
58. Ibid.
59. Griffiths, Peter and Pantry, Shelia (2000), 'Develop your information staff', *Business Information Review*, **17**(2), June, pp.103–10.
60. Webb, Sylvia P. (1993), *op. cit.*
61. The Library Association (1992), *The Framework for Continuing Professional Development*, London: Library Association.
62. Centre for Research in Library and Information Management (1998), *The Toolkit for Turning Points*, London: Centre for Research in Library and Information Management and Library Association.
63. Ibid., p.1.

64. Favret, Leo (2000), 'Benchmarking, annual library plans and best value', *Library Management*, **21**(7) pp.340–8.
65. Morrow, John (1996), 'Training for the Charter Mark', *Personnel, Training and Education*, **13**(1), April, pp.9–10.
66. Ibid.
67. Jones, Browen et al. (1999), *op. cit.*, p.63.
68. Rowley, Jennifer (1997), 'The library as a learning organization', *Library Management*, **18**(2), pp.88–91.

CHAPTER 8

1. Sanders, Kate (1999), 'You're on your own …', *Library Association Record*, **101**(4), April, p.229.
2. Cano, V. and Hatar, C. (1999), 'Teleworking: conceptual and implementation problems', *Vine*, **109**, February, pp.27–34.
3. Konn, Tania and Roberts, Norman (1984), 'Academic librarians and continuing education', *Journal of Librarianship*, **16**(4), October, pp.262–80.
4. Jones, Noragh (1986), 'On the job training: The trainees' view', *Training and Education*, **3**(1), pp.12–19.
5. Russell, Norman (1989), 'Library supervisors could do better', *Library Work*, **3**, January, pp.6–9.
6. Levy, Philippa and Usherwood, Bob (1992), *People Skills: Interpersonal Skills Training for Library and Information Work*, London: British Library (Library and Information Report 88).
7. Watson, Tony and Harris, Pauline (1999), *The Emergent Manager*, London: Sage.
8. See, for example, Stewart, Valerie and Stewart, Andrew (1982), *Managing the Poor Performer*, Aldershot: Gower.
9. Stevens, R.E. (ed.) (1978), *Supervision of Employees in Libraries*, Urbana, Illinois: University of Illinois Graduate School of Library Science.
10. De Board, R. (1982), *Counselling People at Work*, Aldershot: Gower.
11. Rogers, Carl R. (1961), *On Becoming a Person: A Therapist's View of Psychotherapy*, London: Constable.
12. Woolfe, Ray, 'Counselling in Britain: Present position and future prospects', in Palmer, Stephen and McMahon, Gladeana (eds), *Handbook of Counselling* (1997), London: Routledge.
13. Rowan, John (1983), *The Reality Game*, London: Routledge and Kegan Paul.
14. Frankland, Alan and Sanders, Peter (1995), *Next Steps in Counselling*, Manchester: PCCS Books.
15. Margerison, Charles (1988), 'Interpersonal skills – some new approaches', *Journal of European Industrial training*, **12**(6), pp.12–16.
16. Usherwood, Bob et al. (2001), *Recruit, Retain and Lead: The Public Library Workforce Study*, Sheffield: Centre for the Public Library and Information in Society, University of Sheffield.
17. Anderson, Terry D. (1998), *Transforming Leadership: Equipping Yourself and Coaching Others to Build the Leadership Organisation*, 2nd edn, Boca Raton, Fla., St. Lucie Press, p.50.
18. Bass, Bernard M. (1985), *Leadership and Performance Beyond Expectations*, New York: Free Press.
19. Avolio, Bruce J., Bass, Bernard M. and Jung, Dong I. (1999), 'Re-examining the components of transformational and transactional leadership using the multifactor leadership questionnaire', *Journal of Occupational and Organizational Psychology*, **72,** pp.441–62.
20. Kouzes, J. and Posner, B. (1987), *The Leadership Challenge: How to Get Extraordinary Things Done in Organizations*, San Francisco: Jossey-Bass.
21. Anderson, Terry D. (1998), *op. cit.*, p.51.

22. Frank, Donald G. (2000), review of Bryman, Alan, *Charisma and Leadership in Organizations*, *Journal of Academic Librarianship*, **26**(5), September, pp.366–7.
23. Quinn, Brian (1999), 'Librarians' and psychologists' view of leadership: Converging and diverging perspectives', *Library Administration and Management*, **13**(3), Summer, pp.147–57.
24. Hall, John (1993), 'Librarians and leadership', *Personnel Training and Education*, **10**(3), December, pp.10–11.
25. Quinn, Brian (1999), *op. cit.*
26. Bagshaw, Mike and Bagshaw, Caroline (1999), 'Leadership in the twenty-first century', *Industrial and Commercial Training*, **31**(6), pp.236–9.
27. Ibid.
28. Based on handout prepared by Helen Dyson and used on continuing education course organized by the Library Association.
29. Reynolds, Larry (2000), 'What is leadership?', *Training Journal*, November, pp.24–7.
30. Fulmer, Robert M. and Wagner, Stacey (1999), 'Leadership: Lessons from the best', *Training and Development*, March, pp.29–32.
31. Schofield, Graham (2000), 'Effective leadership', *Personnel To-day*, 28 March, p.14.
32. Bridgland, Angela (1999), 'To fill, or how to fill – that is the question: Succession planning and leadership development in academic libraries', *Australian Academic and Research Library*, **30**(1), March, pp.20–9.
33. Berry, Claire (1998), 'Mentoring – putting theory into practice', *Personnel Training and Education*, **15**(2), August, pp.3–9.
34. Corrall, Sheila (1993), 'Mentoring: The role of PTEG in promoting continuous development', *Personnel Training and Education*, **10**(3), December, pp.6–7.
35. Nankivell, Clare and Shoolbred, Michael (1996), 'Mentoring research: The story continues', *Personnel Training and Education*, **13**(3), December, p.5.
36. PTEG Mentoring Guidelines, available online at <http://www.la-hq.uk/groups/pteg/mentoring.html> (accessed on 24 June 2001).
37. Atkinson, Maureen (1995), 'Staffordshire University mentoring scheme', *Personnel Training and Education*, **11**(3), June, pp.7–8.
38. Berry, Claire (1998), *op. cit.*
39. Atkinson, Maureen (1995), *op. cit.*
40. Burton, Sheron (1998), 'Support for supervisors of registration candidates', *Personnel Training and Education*, **15**(1), April, p.13.
41. Morgan, Steve (2001), 'Change in university libraries: Don't forget the people', *Library Management*, **22**(1/2), pp.58–60.
42. Morris, Beryl (1993), 'Time management', in Lawes, Ann (ed.), *Management Skills for the Information Manager*, Aldershot: Ashgate, pp.157–78.
43. Leeds University Counselling and Career Development Unit (c.1985), 'Personality style inventory' (handout).
44. Belbin, Raymond Meredith (1981), *Management Teams: Why They Succeed or Fail*, London: Heinemann.
45. Rackham, Neal and Morgan, Terry (1977), *Behaviour Analysis in Training*, London: McGraw-Hill.
46. Tuckman, B.W. (1965), 'Developmental sequence in small groups', *Psychological Bulletin*, **63**, pp.384–99.
47. Thorne, Marie L. and Fritchie, Rennie (1985), *Interpersonal Skills for Women Managers*, Bristol Polytechnic/Manpower Services Commission.
48. Levy, Philippa and Usherwood, Bob (1992), *People Skills: Interpersonal Skills Training for Library and Information Work*, Library and Information Research Report 88, London: British Library Research and Development Department.
49. Honey, Peter (1997), *Improve Your People Skills*, London: Institute of Personnel and Development, p.151.
50. Handy, Charles (2001), 'The workers' revolution', *The Times Magazine*, 28 April, pp.12–16.

51. Walters, Guy (2001), 'Work to rules', *The Times Magazine*, 28 April, pp.21–22 and 23.
52. Hodges, J.E. (1990), 'Stress in the library', *Library Association Record*, **92**(10), October, p.751.
53. Looker, Terry and Gregson, Olga (1997), *Managing Stress*, London: Hodder and Stoughton, p.4.
54. Evans, Jacky (1991), *Manchester Polytechnic Library: A Report Discussing the Management and Control of Stress Within the Organisation and Its People*, BA Information and Library Management project at Manchester Polytechnic.
55. Bunge, C. (1987), 'Stress in the library', *Library Journal*, **112**(15), 15 September, pp.47–51.
56. Trickey, Keith (2001), 'Trickey's column', *Personnel, Training and Education*, **18**(1), April, pp.1–4.
57. Looker, Terry and Gregson, Olga (1997), *op. cit.*
58. Hudson, Mary Pelzer (1999), 'Conflict and stress in times of change', *Library Management*, **20**(1), pp.35–8.
59. Morris, Beryl (1993), 'Motivation of staff', in Lawes, Ann, (ed.), *Management Skills for the Information Manager*, Aldershot: Ashgate, pp.26–39.
60. Gothberg, Helen M. (1988), 'Time management in academic libraries', *College and Research Libraries*, **49**(2), March, pp.131–40; Gothberg, Helen M. (1991), 'Time management in special libraries', *Special Libraries*, Spring, pp.119–30; Gothberg, Helen M. (1991), 'Time management in state libraries', *Special Libraries*, Fall, pp.257–66.
61. Seiwert, Lothar J. (1989), *Managing Your Time*, London: Kogan Page. p.28.
62. Wetmore, Donald (2000), 'The juggling act', *Training and Development*, **54**(9), September, pp.67–8.
63. Masterton, Ailsa (1997), *Getting Results with Time Management*, London: Library Association Publishing, pp.54–5.
64. Morris, Beryl (1996), *First Steps in Management*, London: Library Association Publishing, p.77.

Index

ability tests 149–50
action theory 59
advertising 130–35
Advisory, Conciliation and Arbitration Service (ACAS) 15
aggressiveness 269
American Library Association 175
annual leave 27
annual library plans 2
application forms 135–7
appraisal 157–82, 194–5
Arizona, University of 83
assertiveness training 268–72
assessment centres 152

Barnet, London Borough of 111–13
Bath, University of 188–190
benchmarking 235, 237
Best Value 3,10–11
biodata 137–8
Birkbeck College 177–8
Birmingham University Integrated Library Development and Electronic Resource (BUILDER) 81
Blake-Mouton Grid 49–51
Bolton Metropolitan Borough 167, 191
brainstorming 266
Brent, London Borough of 91
British Library of Political and Economic Science at LSE 174–5, 213–14
British Library Research and Development Department 81
British Library Research and Innovation Centre 82
British Psychological Society 150
Building the New Library Network 6–7, 184

case studies 147, 224–5
Cattell's Sixteen Personality Factor 151
Central School of Speech and Drama 148, 150
change 5–6
chairpersons 268
chartership (Library Association) 213, 235
Civil Service 171
coaching 239
communication
    job satisfaction 66–8
    organization analysis 35
    participative management 53, 55
    staff appraisal 164
    supervision 240, 242–3
complex systems 58
computer-based training 227–9
Computer Literacy and Information Technology (CLAIT) 228
conflict management 255, 271
congruence 247
continuing professional development (CPD) 185, 233–8 *see also* lifelong learning
contract of employment 14
contract workers 91–2
conversation control 248
counselling 245–8
criticism handling 271–2
curriculum vitae 137

data protection 20
Data Protection Act (1998) 20, 149, 152
Dayton-Montgomery County Library 172
De Montfort University 162, 230–31
delegation *see* participative management

difficult staff 244–8
disability discrimination 22–3
Disability Discrimination Act (1995) 22–3, 122
Disability Rights Commission 122
disciplinary procedures 15–16
discrimination 20–23
    interviews 145–6
    tests 150
discussion groups 222–4
dismissal of staff 16–17, 24–5
distance learning 9

education, changes in 8–9
Electronic Libraries Programme (e Lib) 6, 81
empathy 247
employment tribunals 13–14
Employment Relations Act (1999) 28
Employment Rights Act (1996) 15,17, 18, 24, 26
Employment Rights Act (1999) 24
Equal Opportunities Commission 21, 22, 105, 123, 136, 145, 150
Equal Pay Act (1970) 20, 105
Essex Libraries 137, 195–7, 205–8, 230
European Computer Driving Licence (ECDL) 228
evaluation
    training 230–33
exit interviews 195, 198
expectancy theory 59

feedback 242
Fielden Report 6, 102, 103, 183, 185, 187–90, 216
flexibility
    location 84
    skills 83–4
    staffing structures 85
    work patterns 84–6
Follett Report 6, 56
Framework for Continuing Professional Development (Library Association) 235, 284
Fraser's five-point plan 121–6
Futures Working Party (Library Association) 80

Getting it Together 9–10
gays 23
Gilbreth, F.B. 33
group appraisal 167–8

group selection 147–8
group skills 225, 259–68

HSBC bank 256
headhunting 132–3
health and safety 25–9
Health and Safety at Work Act (1974) 25–6
Hertfordshire, University of 102–3
Herzberg, Frederick 51–3
Hofstede, Geert 73–4
homeworking 91
hours of work 26–8
human relations theories 39–40
Human Rights Act (1998) 23
hybrid libraries 9, 81

ICI Information Unit 54, 71
ICL 94
Impact on People of Electronic Libraries (IMPEL) 65, 68, 185, 215
induction training 204–10
in-house training 213
Information Services Training Organisation (IsNTO) 12, 80–81
Information technology 81–2
    stress 277
    training 184, 228, 258
Institute of Information Scientists 5
interaction analysis 261–4
interpersonal skills 258–64
interviews
    appraisal 178–82
    formal (staff selection) 139–47
    informal (staff selection) 138–9
Investors in People 3–4,10, 194

Jarratt Report 158
job analyses 100–104
job descriptions 100–101, 106–17
job design 104
job enrichment 70
job evaluation 104–6
job rotation 68–9, 212
job satisfaction 33, 51–3, 60–64
job sharing 90
job specifications 117–19

knowledge management 7

leadership 249–56
lectures 218–22
legislation 13–29

lesbians 23
Library Association 80, 97, 213, 235–7, 258
Library and Information Services Council (LISC) 80
Lifelong learning 8, 185, 235 see also continuing professional development
Likert, Rensis 47–9
listening 146–7, 247

McGregor, Douglas 45–7
management
    by objectives 3
    cycle 2–5, 13
    definitions 2
    styles 47, 49–51, 164–5, 192, 249–52
Manchester Metropolitan University 23, 87, 167
Maslow, Abraham 41–5
maternity rights 24–5
Mayo, Elton 39–40
mechanistic management 34–5, 165
meetings skills 259–68
Modernising Government 9, 11
motivation 31–78

Napier University 180
National Grid for Learning 8
New Library: the Peoples Network 6–7, 184
National Training Organisations (NTOs) 11
National Vocational Qualifications 84, 203, 210–12
New Opportunities Fund 184, 215, 228
Newcastle, University of 237
non-professional staff 62–4, 102 see also para-professional staff
Northumbria, University of 56, 163

on-the-job training 229
organic/organismic management 55, 165, 192

para-professional staff 83–4, 102
parental leave 25
participative management 47–9, 53–7, 76–8
part-time staff 17, 86–91, 209
peer appraisal 172
peer group learning 243
performance review 157, 166–8
person specifications 117–26

personality 260
personality tests 150–52
Personnel, Training and Education Group (Library Association) 257, 258
post-separation surveys 198
potential reviews 94, 157, 168–70
presentations 148
procrastination 285
promotion of staff 131, 168–70
Public Library Workforce Study 82, 87, 94, 183, 203, 252

quality management 9–1, 237

race discrimination 20–23
Race Relations Act (1976) 20–22
Reading, University of 107–9, 216–18
Reading the Future 10
recruitment agencies 132
recruitment of staff 127–56
redundancy 18–19, 24
references 20, 152–4
Rehabilitation of Offenders Act (1974) 136
rest breaks 27
retirement 19
reward reviews 157, 170–71
risk assessments 25, 26
Rogers, Carl 72, 246–8
role-play 226–7,270
Rorschach Ink Blot Test 151
Royal Society of Medicine 114, 139, 140–42

scientific management 33–8
search consultants 132–3
selection of staff 127–56
self appraisal 162, 173
sex discrimination 20–23, 123, 136
Sex Discrimination Act (1975) 20, 136
Sex Discrimination Act (1986) 20
sexual harassment 21–2
sexual orientation 23
Sheffield, City of 118–19, 120
Sheffield Hallam University 159, 160
shortlisting 135
Shropshire Information and Community Services 68
sick leave 17–18, 32
Skills for knowledge management: building a knowledge economy 8
social exclusion 72

Society of College, National and University Libraries (SCONUL) 9, 203
staff appraisal *see* appraisal
staff development 185–94 *see also* continuing professional development
Staffordshire University 257
standards
  of performance 10–11
  of provision 97
stress 28–9, 275–81
student workers 87
subordinate/upward appraisal 172
supervision 239–44
Sutton, London Borough of 159

talks 218–22
Taylor, F.W. 33
teams 42–3, 48–9, 56–7, 70
technological change 6–9
temporary staff 86–7, 209
testimonials 154
tests
  staff selection 149–52
theory X 45–6, 77, 165, 240
theory Y 46–7, 77, 240
theory Z 73
time management 282–6
time off work 27–8
Trade Union and Labour Relations (Consolidation) Act (1992) 18, 28
Trade Union Reform and Employment Rights Act (1993) 16, 106
training 183–238

accommodation 190
equipment 190
evaluation 230–33
identifying needs 194, 198
leadership 255–6
methods 218–29
monitoring 230–33
policies 187–94
staff appraisal 161–2, 167
training groups 187
training hours 215–218
training officers 186–7
Training the Future project 229, 238
trait-rating 175
transactional analysis 273–5
transactional leadership 252
Transbinary Group on Librarianship and Information Studies 80
transformational leadership 252
Tuckman's theory 266
Twenty-third Report of Committee 'A' 158

unconditional positive regard 247
University College London 199–202
University for Industry 8

volunteers 87–90

wastage 94–6
work study 33
Working Time Regulations(1998) 26–7
Wrexham County Borough 176
written instructions 222